D0442091

DISCARD

BEFORE THE LIGHTS GO OUT

TS
601A
.A4
1949
2 pt

TJ
807.9
.46
K64
2012

BEFORE THE LIGHTS GO OUT

Conquering the Energy Crisis before It Conquers Us

Maggie Koerth-Baker

WILEY

John Wiley & Sons, Inc.

Copyright © 2012 by Maggie Koerth-Baker. All rights reserved.

Published by John Wiley & Sons, Inc., Hoboken, New Jersey
Published simultaneously in Canada

No part of this publication may be reproduced, stored in a retrieval system, or transmitted in any form or by any means, electronic, mechanical, photocopying, recording, scanning, or otherwise, except as permitted under Section 107 or 108 of the 1976 United States Copyright Act, without either the prior written permission of the Publisher, or authorization through payment of the appropriate per-copy fee to the Copyright Clearance Center, 222 Rosewood Drive, Danvers, MA 01923, (978) 750-8400, fax (978) 646-8600, or on the web at www.copyright.com. Requests to the Publisher for permission should be addressed to the Permissions Department, John Wiley & Sons, Inc., 111 River Street, Hoboken, NJ 07030, (201) 748-6011, fax (201) 748-6008, or online at http://www.wiley.com/go/permissions.

Limit of Liability/Disclaimer of Warranty: While the publisher and the author have used their best efforts in preparing this book, they make no representations or warranties with respect to the accuracy or completeness of the contents of this book and specifically disclaim any implied warranties of merchantability or fitness for a particular purpose. No warranty may be created or extended by sales representatives or written sales materials. The advice and strategies contained herein may not be suitable for your situation. You should consult with a professional where appropriate. Neither the publisher nor the author shall be liable for any loss of profit or any other commercial damages, including but not limited to special, incidental, consequential, or other damages.

For general information about our other products and services, please contact our Customer Care Department within the United States at (800) 762-2974, outside the United States at (317) 572-3993 or fax (317) 572-4002.

Wiley also publishes its books in a variety of electronic formats. Some content that appears in print may not be available in electronic books. For more information about Wiley products, visit our web site at www.wiley.com.

Library of Congress Cataloging-in-Publication Data:
Koerth-Baker, Maggie, date.
  Before the lights go out : conquering the energy crisis before it conquers us / Maggie Koerth-Baker.
      p. cm.
    Includes index.
   ISBN 978-0-470-87625-1 (cloth); ISBN 978-1-118-17557-6 (ebk);
ISBN 978-1-118-17558-3 (ebk); ISBN 978-1-118-17559-0 (ebk)
   1.   Renewable energy sources—United States. 2.   Energy development—United States. 3.   Energy consumption—United States. 4.   Energy conservation—United States. 5.   Energy policy–United States.   I. Title.
   TJ807.9.U6K64 2012
   333.790973—dc23
                                                                    2011043334

Printed in the United States of America

10 9 8 7 6 5 4 3 2 1

For Grammy

Contents

ACKNOWLEDGMENTS

Nobody writes a book all on their own. I started working on the proposal for what eventually became *Before the Lights Go Out* in 2008. That seed of an idea would never have grown without help.

First and foremost, I want to thank my husband, Christopher Baker, who first encouraged me to write a book about energy. His insight and suggestions helped shape my perspective. His emotional support has been invaluable. His pumpkin pancakes are amazing.

Mark Frauenfelder, David Pescovitz, Xeni Jardin, Cory Doctorow, and Rob Beschizza at BoingBoing are amazing people and even more amazing people to work for. I am very grateful to them for their encouragement, their ideas, and their flexibility as I worked on this project. I would be significantly less sane right now without the Happy Mutants.

Seth Fishman, my agent, helped me take some half-formed ideas and shape them into a story. Thank you for believing in this idea, reading my drafts, and helping me navigate the strange new world of publishing.

Eric Nelson, my editor at Wiley, pushed me to write a book that was far better than what I would have written on my own. Thank you for asking the right questions, telling me when my words didn't quite work, and helping me put the pieces in the right order.

I am indebted to the many, many people who have talked shop on energy, climate, and infrastructure with me over the last few years. Those conversations are the mortar that binds this book together. That gratitude extends to more people than I could possibly count, but there are a few I'd like to thank in particular. Eli Kintisch, Alexis Madrigal, David Biello, and Christopher Mims have helped turn my Twitter stream into a virtual think tank full of insanely smart colleagues. I am grateful for the ideas they offered and for their willingness to read some of this book in its early stages. Someday, I will get them all in one room, and we will take over the world. Prasad Vaidya, David Eijadi, and Alicia Ward at the Weidt Group got my research started off right, and helped put me in contact with some valuable sources. William Moomaw at Tufts was gracious enough to let me drag him into hour-long interviews several times early in my research, and in doing so helped shape my perspective in this book. Skip Laitner, Karen Turner, Steven Sorrell, Harry Saunders, and Blake Alcott have spoken with me multiple times and answered innumerable e-mail questions about the rebound effect. I hope that I have managed to take all the information that they shared with me and do justice to that nuanced and complicated issue. Gavin Schmidt and RealClimate helped me explain risk and uncertainty. Michael Noble at Fresh Energy and John Foley at the University of Minnesota's Institute on the Environment offered some great ideas and pointed me in the right direction.

Thanks is also due to the Pacific Northwest National Laboratory, Argonne National Laboratory, Oak Ridge National Laboratory, Sandia National Laboratory, the National Renewable Energy Laboratory, the American Council for an Energy Efficient Economy, and the Electric Power Research Institute, all of which were invaluable resources in the creation of this book.

Also thanks to some wonderful people who gave me a lot to think about after the book was finished: David Isenberg, Tom Evslin, Stephen Kamman, Jim Baller, and Bill St. Arnaud. There were far more people whom I interviewed for this book than could ever be mentioned in the main text. Thank you all for your contributions and insights. I never did an interview for this book that didn't teach me something important.

I also need to thank my friends and journalism colleagues who let me bounce ideas off of them, read chapters of this book, and generally helped me ensure that I was writing for everybody and not just energy wonks. Esther Porter, in particular, was a wonderful editor. Maryn McKenna, Dennis Cass, and John Pavlus read some of my earliest drafts, and their advice kept me from making some seriously terrible mistakes. Maryn and Dennis also need to be thanked for giving me an impromptu master class in how to write and organize a book. Tim Carmody and Matt Novak are New Optimists who helped set the tone for my writing here.

When I realized that the work on this book wasn't going to end when I turned in the final draft, the following people helped me figure out some great ideas for marketing: Rebecca Skloot, Joel Fitch, Carrie Downing, Lars Ostrom, Esther Porter, Christopher Baker (again), Jennifer Harmening, and Jessica Deutsch. Extra special thanks to Kristin Verby, who designed several sample covers for this book that really helped me communicate my ideas to the designers at Wiley.

While researching this book I did a fair amount of traveling, and I am grateful to the friends (and strangers) who opened their homes to me: Donovan Atkinson and Ryan Garceau; Astrid and Chris Hayden; Kim Tholen and Nicholas Bohac; Amanda Kim Stairrett (who was also invaluable in helping me navigate the Department of Defense and gave me some great insight into the culture of the military); John Schlueter and Emily Hagen; and Heather Christian and Couchsurfing.org.

I also need to thank my friends and family, who have been a support network for me over the past couple of years. You provided advice, you cheered me up and distracted me when I needed it, and you kept Baker company when I was physically and/or mentally gone, and many of you offered ideas or questions that ended up shaping the book. Thank you all.

Many thanks to BoingBoing readers whose comments over the years have helped me improve my writing and helped me find the ideas and issues that really need explaining.

Finally, no one should write anything without thanking their copy editors. Production editor Lisa Burstiner and her team do the Lord's work.

....

CHOICE AND CHANGE

Pretty much everything will come to him who hustles while he waits. I believe that restlessness is discontent, and discontent is merely the first necessity of progress.

—THOMAS EDISON

If we can take the buggaboo out of, "your world is finished," and put instead of that, "the world is begun," we have a marvelous place to live and a marvelous future ahead of us.

—CHARLES KETTERING

Climate change is a lie." The man leaned back in his chair and folded his arms over his chest. "Climate change is a lie," he said again. "It's just something made up by environmentalists to scare us."

I heard this story a few years after it actually happened, from Eileen Horn, one of the environmentalists who watched this man's speech from the other side of a two-way mirror. At the time, Horn and her colleagues were about to launch a new nonprofit organization called the Climate and Energy Project (CEP), an environmental activism group based in the state of Kansas. The man was a participant in one of a series of focus groups that the CEP had put together in Wichita. The idea behind the focus groups: don't be stupid. Too often, Horn told me, environmental activism started with what the activists *thought* the public believed. Focus groups were a nice way to get around the sloppy art of assumptions. Instead, the Climate and Energy Project could get a bunch of Kansans together in a room, lob some ideas at them, and watch how they respond. What did the intended audience already know, and what did they not know? What did the people of Kansas think about the future of energy?

It was a nice plan, but it wasn't too enlightening at first. The participants talked about where they got their news—NPR and CNN on one side, Fox News and a handful of radio talk shows on the other. Opinions on climate change split right along the lines of favorite news sources. You will probably not be shocked to learn that the man who declared climate change a lie fell squarely on the Fox News side. Whether or not you disagree with him, his position was fairly predictable. You and I have met any number of people with the same background and ideas.

Yet Horn remembered that man, specifically, because he changed her outlook on the world. In a way, he changed her life. Not because of his position on climate change, but because of what she learned about him—and other people like him—as the focus group continued.

"No matter how the conversation started, whether they believed in climate change or not, the discussion always, eventually, turned to energy solutions," she told me. "And when it did, it turned out that this guy drove a hybrid car and had changed all his lightbulbs out to CFLs."

Now *that* is surprising information. It surprised Horn, too. Like many people who might describe themselves as "green," Horn thought of climate change as an idea you had to accept before you'd be willing to care about energy change. Before the focus group, she saw climate and energy as a couple of nested boxes. Open the alternative energy box, and you'd find a box full of climate change fears inside. She was wrong.

"We came away with multiple examples where people who didn't believe in climate change were taking action anyway for other reasons," Horn said. "A lot of it was energy security and also conservation, which is just an ethic that we have in the Midwest. Prudence came up a lot, with people saying, 'Well, even if we aren't sure, maybe we should take action just in case.' One thing that was said in all groups was, 'We need another Apollo project,' this fiercely nationalistic response where even if we don't believe in global warming, we still want to lead the world in fuel-efficient vehicles. We want to be number one."

That lesson—that you don't have to care about climate change to care about energy—was enough to alter the way the Climate and Energy Project did business. Instead of kicking off their campaign by trying to lead a bunch of very stubborn horses to the lake, they just skipped right ahead to the part where everybody gets a glass of water.

I like this story, a lot. I'm a Midwesterner myself—raised in various parts of Kansas and now living in Minneapolis, Minnesota. The Climate and Energy Project's focus groups gracefully documented the more widespread nature of behavior I'd already noticed popping up, in isolated examples, within my own family. Politicians may have manipulated climate change into becoming a straw man for partisan slap fights, but that wasn't the case for the concept of taking action on *energy* change. You can see this dichotomy reflected in polls, too. Between 2006 and 2010, American concern about climate change fell.[1] During the same years, however, U.S. interest in alternative energy and sustainable lifestyle choices remained strong.

Today, somewhere on the order of 60 percent of us believe that climate change is a serious threat supported by evidence. Yet depending on the poll and the specific questions being asked, between 70 percent and 90 percent of us support increasing funding for alternative energy and mass transit, raising fuel efficiency standards for cars, instituting tougher energy efficiency standards in other areas of our lives, and requiring utility companies to get more of their energy from renewable sources. Even a majority of self-described Republicans support alternative energy and energy-change policies that you might suspect they'd be against.[2] Sometimes, you can even find low belief in climate change and high support for alternative energy in the *exact same poll*.[3] In addition, since the year 2000, large majorities of Americans have made personal choices that reflect energy-conscious values: 90 percent of us have recycled in the last year, 85 percent of us reduced our household energy use in some way, and 81 percent replaced standard lightbulbs with compact fluorescents.[4]

When I told my family that I was writing a book about the future of energy in the United States, I got pretty much the same response from everyone, whether liberal or conservative. They were curious. They were excited. They had ideas they wanted to contribute and questions they wanted to ask. The United States has an energy problem. Americans may not agree on the cause or the solutions, but we can all tell that something needs to change.

I was born in 1981. In the years I've been alive, the United States has made some big changes to the way we use energy. Specifically, we've become more efficient, able to get more—more work, more conveniences, more money—out of the same amount of energy. Back when I was born, we had to consume more than 12,000 British thermal units (BTUs) of energy to produce $1 of gross domestic product. Today, each dollar costs us only about 7,500 BTUs. Yet at the same time that energy efficiency increased, reliance on fossil fuels has barely budged. In 1980, coal, oil, and gas made up 89 percent of the energy we used. In 2010, those fuels accounted for 83 percent of our energy use. Americans used only a little less energy per person in 2009 than we did in 1981 (and in 2007, we used more). Overall, our total energy use has gone up.[5] Basically, our energy efficiency has made us wealthier, but it hasn't done much to solve our energy problems.

Americans may not agree on the reasons for conservation, but most of us support the idea of using less fossil fuel. Actually doing that, though, takes more than just superficial support. We need to break with more than a century of steadily increasing dependence.

Today, we use 25 percent more energy in a year than we did when I was a baby.[6] We're currently on a course to use 28 percent more energy a year in 2030 than we do now.[7] If that comes to pass, we'll need more of everything: more coal, more nuclear, more oil, more gas, more wind, more solar, and a whole lot more money to pay for it all. "Staying the course" will not be as simple as it sounds. Meanwhile, making a change—tacking toward a world where we use less energy overall and getting it from different places than we do today—is unlikely to be any easier or cheaper. Nuclear energy is incredibly expensive and unpopular. Clean coal, as we'll see, isn't yet a reality and will cost a lot of money. Wind and solar are "free" but will require huge investments and the creation of new technologies. More oil at ever-higher prices? Some of it from countries that hate us? You already know the problem with that.

Where we stand with energy today is a little like finding yourself deep in debt on a low-paying job. At that point, change is inevitable. The future won't be like the present, because the present isn't working. Neither are there any simple, pain-free ways to crawl out of that hole. How do you solve a problem like that? You make hard choices, and you do what you have to do.

Today in the United States, our choice isn't between the energy system we have and what somebody, somewhere says we *ought* to be doing. Rather, the choice we are left with is whether or not we want some control over what happens next. That's not happy talk. We probably won't get everything right. We might not love the future we plan. Yet we'll probably like it a lot more than the future that will happen to us if we simply do nothing.

We aren't bereft of options. During the next twenty years, we have the ability to cut about twenty quadrillion BTUs' worth of fossil fuels from our annual energy budget, by wasting less and investing in alternatives. I'll tell you more about that number and what it really means as you read on. For now, though, you should know three facts: this goal is achievable and necessary, and meeting it will force us to make some difficult decisions. Nobody gets everything he or she wants. The changes embedded in that goal are huge, but the result won't be a utopia. If we do manage to cut twenty quadrillion BTUs of fossil fuels in twenty years, we'll still have to deal with some of the effects of climate change. We'll still put oil into our gas tanks and coal into our power plants. Energy will not be cheap, but we *will* be in a much better situation than if we didn't meet the goal.

You can already tell this isn't a book about quick fixes that promise no downsides. We can't just sit around, hoping to win the lottery. This is not about bold, one-off experiments that nobody ever tries again. Those are interesting and important, but they aren't the same as solutions. Nor is this book about small-scale, feel-good changes that lack a wider impact. You might be able to save $8 a day by giving up smoking, but that's not going to solve your budget problems if all of your other expenses keep increasing.

Instead, this book is about the inconvenient complications, unforeseen side effects, and less-than-perfect solutions that are always a part of taking a huge, looming problem and making it smaller. This is a book about what we'll have to deal with and the changes that will have to happen, because we really have no other choice.

This isn't about planting a tree, buying a hybrid car, and proving that you're a good person. That's not how energy crises get fixed. Economics and a century of social incentives got us a country full of gas-guzzling cars, long commutes, inefficient houses, and coal-fired power plants out in the middle of nowhere. Economics and incentives will change our world. The change will happen, one way or the other. The only question is this: Are the changes we're granting incentives to the same as the changes that we want?

There are two questions I hear all the time, from friends, family, and readers at BoingBoing.net, the blog where I'm the science editor.[8] First, people want to know, "Why should I care about energy? Why can't we just keep doing exactly what we're doing?" Later, after they've decided they *do* care, they ask, "Now what? How do we change?"

Those are tangly questions with multiple right answers. Neither can be solved with true or false, A or B. But I think the second question—Now what?—is infinitely more confusing. Compared to the list of reasons to worry about the future of energy, the list of options available for *shaping* that future isn't nearly so concise.

Choosing from those options is not as simple as filling in the bubbles on a multiple choice exam. The future of energy is more like an essay question.

Scientists say the way we make, use, and think about energy will have to be very different from today's status quo, especially if we want to maintain the comfortable, connected, and convenient lives we Americans now enjoy. You need to understand that while reading this book. What I'm talking about here isn't a small tweak or a simple swapping of one source of energy for another. In fact, if I've done my job right, by the time you read the last page it should be clear to you why a *simple* solution doesn't exist. But here's the problem: the more complex the solution is, the harder it is for people to wrap their heads around it.

Imagine for a minute that you could travel back in time to the early nineteenth century. On arrival, you step out of your traveling contraption, grab some random people off the street, and start to tell them about the way you use energy in your daily life. Now, how do you think they'll respond? Remember, these are people whose energy use centers around either fuels they burn directly in their own homes or the physical strength of large, domesticated animals. Explaining a computer to them would have to start with explaining electricity—which would, in turn, have to start with explaining how modern Americans can burn coal in one place and use the energy hundreds or thousands of miles away.

Very quickly, describing one simple part of daily life would snowball into an interlinked explanation of dozens of complicated concepts, policy decisions, and technologies—none of which can build up to the computer-as-we-know-it without all of the others. Your new friends could look at their own lives, and they might understand your snapshot of the future well enough, but everything in between—the details of how to get here from there—would probably confuse the hell out of them. It's certainly possible to turn the nineteenth century into the twenty-first. It did happen, after all, and from our end, the path from the past to the present looks deceptively straight and clear. But it's harder (a lot harder) to plan that journey out from the perspective of Mr. and Ms. 1815.

This is, essentially, what's going on today with energy. You and I can observe the world as it is, and we can imagine a better world, but we can't predict the future. The path that will take us to the future is a big, gray blur. No time traveler is going to show up with an atlas. We're stuck mapping out this trail as we go along. So, now what?

This book assumes *that's* your question. I don't know exactly what the future of energy holds. I'm not a mystic. In fact, even though I've spent almost two years researching this topic, I'm not even really an expert—I leave that title to scientists and others who dedicate their entire lives to the study of energy. I have *talked* to a lot of experts, though. I've read their research, and I've come away with some big ideas, key concepts that the experts already know, but that you might not. Put together, these big ideas can bring some clarity and color to how you imagine that foggy path between today and tomorrow. They'll help you make sense of the options and, I hope, help you start finding ideas that you and your fellow Americans can agree on.

I want to convince you that it is possible to change the way we make energy—and the way we use it—with technology that already exists. I also want you to know what *isn't* possible, because what we want to do and what we can do are not always the same. I want you to see how changes are already starting to happen, all around the country, and I want you to understand what those first successes and first failures are telling us about the future.

Personally, I care about this stuff because I want to mitigate the impact of climate change and because I'm concerned about the risks our society is taking by being so utterly dependent on fossil fuels. I'll explain briefly why I think this way, because, of course, how I answer the question "Why do I care?" influences how I'll answer the question "What next?" The emphasis is on the latter, however, not on the former. Even if you and I vehemently disagree on the whys, there are many other reasons we might still end up at some of the same what nows. Essentially, this book takes the approach that the Climate and Energy Project took, after the group realized that even dyed-in-wool climate change deniers still wanted to change the way we use energy: skip the arguments and go straight to the action.

CHAPTER ONE

MAKING APPLE PIE FROM SCRATCH

If you want to understand what's wrong with energy in the United States today and how it might work better tomorrow, you need to start with the electric grid—that network of wires that ties electric generators to consumers and consumers to one another. Today, the electric grid stretches from coast to coast, linking subdivisions in Alabama with grocery stores in British Columbia. Here, there, and everywhere in between, our daily lives are dependent on this grid, from the moment the digital alarm clock buzzes us awake at dawn. But reliable, always available electricity service—the ability to flip on a light, anytime, anywhere, and know it will work—doesn't just happen.

A simple experiment can help explain the basics of generating electricity. Take a bar magnet and slide it quickly in and out of a coil of copper wire. Every time you do this, you'll produce a small electric current (and a large potential for immature jokes). The physical tango of a conductive metal moving through a magnetic field produces electricity. The interaction of magnets and metal doesn't actually "generate" something out of nothing. Instead, the magnetic field simply forces electrons to move. You know how an atom is set up—a central nucleus surrounded by a cloud of electrons. In conductive metals, the electrons aren't tied down to any one atom. Rather, they mingle, forming something akin to a river of electrons in which atomic nuclei float like buoys. The magnetic field makes the electron "river" flow along, from one buoy to another. What we call "electric service" is simply the movement of electrons around a closed loop of wire. On one end is the generator; at the other is your house.

That's the simplified version. In reality, the grid is vast and mighty. Yet it had a humble birth. In 1882, the first two permanent central electric plants in the world—within a month of each other—began to push electrons around some very short loops of wire.

These first experiments in grid building were very different from what we know today. None of the customers were farther than a short walk away from the power plants. Neither proto-grid operated during the day. At the time, there wasn't much you could *do* with electricity besides turn on light bulbs, so electric service started at sunset. Both systems were still little more than working prototypes, buggy and prone to mishap. However, the first plant, which opened on September 4, had a slight advantage over the second. Installed in a warehouse in what is now New York City's financial district, it was built and run by Thomas Alva Edison. The project was his baby, the result of countless hours of work. Earlier that same year, Edison and his hand-picked team had set up a temporary centralized electrical system in London, part of a larger Edison exhibit at London's Crystal Palace.[1] They were literally the only people in the world with practical experience in controlling a grid. What's more, they'd invented or improved nearly every part—from the coal-powered generators right on down to the very lightbulbs.

Twenty-six days later, the second permanent centralized electric system—and the first hydroelectric power plant in the world—began operations. It was in Appleton, Wisconsin. Yes, seriously. London, New York, Appleton, and the story gets a bit weirder from there. See, the Appleton system was only a licensee—the brainchild of a group of local businessmen who bought a couple of Edison generators and built a power plant around them. They had no experience with controlling electricity. In fact, the nearest electrical engineers of any quality were two hundred miles away, in Chicago. If Thomas Edison's New York system was an epic triumph of biblical proportions, then Appleton was more like *Waiting for Guffman*.

And yet it worked. Mostly. I could tell you about the successes of Edison, but there's no risk there. You, me, the nineteenth-century civic leaders of New York City—we all trust the Menlo Park boys a little too much. If you really want to understand how hard it was to build a functioning grid, you can't follow the exploits of the team of geniuses who could simply invent their way out of any problem. If you think the American public was optimistic about the electric grid or that it was an instant business success, then you need to see what was happening outside the confines of the Edison Electric Company. Appleton gives you a more rough-and-tumble view of history, unpolished by all of the mythology surrounding a great historical figure. To make sense of what's happening to our electric infrastructure today, you have to start in Wisconsin.

Appleton sits on the Fox River, a little south and west of Green Bay, part of a chain of small cities that ring Lake Winnebago. Back in 1882, that waterfront location wasn't only about great views or good fishing. The river and the lake themselves were vital parts of the infrastructure. In a time before reliably passable highways, water was the interstate. When energy meant hauling coal or felling trees, the Fox River was a cheap and easy power source that could run entire factories. The water made products. The water shipped those products, and Appleton got rich.

Or, at least, *some* people in Appleton got rich: H. J. Rogers, for instance. Rogers was a man of industry and action—a Gilded Era capitalist, with a fabulous, fluffy mustache to prove it. The *Appleton Post* and the *Appleton Chronicle* considered his dinner parties legitimate news. When his family took a jaunt to Chicago, it made both papers. So it wasn't terribly surprising when the local media printed a short announcement that Rogers had taken a fishing trip in July 1882, along with a salesman who was working for the Western Edison Light Company. The papers printed a longer article when he came back from that vacation, a proud Edison Electric licensee. Take it as hubris. Take it as evidence of why you should never go fishing with salesmen. But, despite owning the city's gas light company and without ever having so much as seen an electric light himself, Rogers decided that he was going to electrify Appleton, starting with his own house. Ever enthusiastic, the papers crowed about the coming success—and then promptly stopped discussing the plans surrounding Rogers's new venture for the rest of the summer.

You have to read between the lines to get at the local public sentiment. For instance, whenever the *Post* and the *Chronicle* made any mention of electric light after July 1882, it came with the solemn assurance that such lights were *perfectly* safe. Decades later, the *Wisconsin Magazine of History* would report that the lack of news during the summer of 1882 led to rumors that Rogers wasn't planning on building an electric system at all but had simply bought the rights in order to keep his gas company's monopoly on artificial light.[2] Meanwhile, even the personal letters of A. L. Smith, one of Rogers's business partners in Appleton's new electric lighting utility, imply that not everyone was entirely convinced that this "electric light" thing would pan out. A few months after Rogers and Smith *did* manage to get their system up and running, Smith wrote to his sister and asked, about her husband, "What does Walter think now about Edison?"[3]

There were good reasons to be skeptical. Gas lights, for instance, had been around since the 1790s and had proved to be somewhat flawed. The gas was delivered via wooden pipes, built like long, skinny links of pickle barrel. That design held liquid okay, but it tended to leak gas. When you added gas light to your home, you were making a trade—convenience in exchange for a weird, oppressive stench.[4]

Electric lights offered a tidier option, but dozens of researchers had been fiddling with the incandescent lamp for eighty years, and nobody had been able to translate that into real commercial success. Worse, Thomas Edison had sold some decentralized electric systems to rich first-adopters, and the results of those experiments weren't totally comforting. In the spring of 1882, Edison wired W. H. Vanderbilt's New York City mansion for electric light, powered by a generator installed in the Vanderbilts' basement. The wires had very little insulation. The wallpaper in the Vanderbilts' parlor was actual cloth, interwoven with bits of metallic tinsel. When Edison switched on the lights for the first time, the wall went up like a match. In the end, the house was saved but not the electrical system. Understandably freaked out, Mrs. Vanderbilt ordered it removed.[5]

It's a little mind-blowing to think about how much the way we use energy changed in a century and a half—and, at the same time, how *little* it changed. On the night of the Vanderbilts' parlor fire, Americans consumed about 5 quadrillion BTUs (British thermal units) of energy per year—not counting the energy from the sweat of their own brows or the muscles of their livestock. At this point, burning wood was still our number-one energy source. Back then, Americans used energy for heat, for light, and to turn water into the steam that powered trains and factories.[6]

Today, we consume a lot more energy than that, and we use it to accomplish different tasks. The most recent complete data is from 2009, when we used 94.6 quadrillion BTUs. Because of the "quadrillion" and the somewhat abstract unit of measurement, this number might not mean a lot to you. Let me put it another way: in 2009, Americans used enough energy to completely boil away the Great Salt Lake twice over.[7] Most of that energy use went into making electricity. We used 38.3 quadrillion BTUs—a full 41 percent of our total energy consumption—for that purpose. Of that, most (48 percent) came from coal, with a little help from nuclear power (22 percent) and natural gas (18 percent). Renewables, mainly hydroelectric power, accounted for 11 percent of electricity generation.[8] All of this would have left the Vanderbilts boggled.

Ditto for our second largest energy expenditure: transportation. In 2009, we used 27 quadrillion BTUs—or 29 percent of the total—on transportation. Mostly, we're talking about petroleum here, the gasoline for cars, the jet fuel that makes planes fly, and the diesel that moves semitrucks from coast to coast.

In contrast, the last two sectors of energy use would have been much more familiar to nineteenth-century Americans. Industry used 18.8 quadrillion BTUs—20 percent of the total. That sector burns natural gas or coal on-site at factories for heat or to make electricity that never enters the national grid. The industrial sector also used a lot of petroleum but not for transportation. Instead, industries turn petroleum into everyday chemicals and products. Finally, residential and commercial buildings consumed 10.6 quadrillion BTUs—11 percent of our national total—in the process of making buildings, food, and water warmer. Most of that was natural gas, which heats up your oven, keeps your morning shower cozy, and powers the radiators that make Wisconsin winters bearable.

Obviously, a lot has changed since the 1880s, but some key details remain the same. For instance, nineteenth-century Americans would have understood our reliance on fossil fuels. By 1885, coal had overtaken wood as America's main energy source. Since then, fossil fuels have ruled. No other energy source even comes close.

Yet even though a lot more Americans use electricity today than they did in 1882, most of us don't understand it any better than the Vanderbilts or the citizens of Appleton did back then. Case in point: most of the energy we put into electricity is wasted. We burn it and never get a benefit. Of the 38.3 quadrillion BTUs that go into electricity production, 66 percent never becomes usable electricity. Instead, it falls victim to conversion losses—turning into heat that warms up the air around a power plant, rather than actually producing electricity. Only 12.8 quadrillion BTUs make it to us through the grid.

Finally, electricity was and is primarily something we use in buildings. Back then, it was only for lightbulbs. Today, the uses of electricity have multiplied. Out of that 12.8 quadrillion BTUs' worth of electricity, 72 percent is used by houses, apartments, offices, stores—the places we live and work. That's the lights and the air conditioners, the electric heaters and the stoves. It's appliances, computers, cell phones, and all manner of plug-in gadgets. In 1882, few people imagined how much American lives would one day depend on the electric grid, but they could identify with the difficulties involved in keeping that grid up and running.

On September 23, 1882, the Appleton newspapers announced that the first of two electric generators had arrived. This generator had a squat, bulbous metal base that sprouted three pairs of tall copper cylinders, which were topped off with another thick block of metal. Metal prongs stuck out of the top, and wires connected to those prongs tied the generator to the power lines. The Edison K Dynamo is a complicated-looking piece of machinery, but how it works is really really fairly simple.[9] Electricity generation in 1882 and, for the most part, still today is based on the phenomenon I mentioned earlier—the movement of conductive metal through a magnetic field.[10] So the issue of where electricity should come from, one of the most contentious questions covered in this book, really boils down to, "How should we make that metal move?"

Today, we have a lot of different options. In 1882, there were only two. You could move the metal using steam produced by burning coal, or you could use the power of water. In Appleton, Rogers chose the latter, building the world's first hydroelectric power plant. It was installed at a riverfront paper mill, which was also owned by Rogers. There, the Fox River turned a water wheel that moved a system of gears, which spun a cylinder of conductive metal between the six tall magnets. That got the river of electrons flowing, and wires carried that river throughout the paper mill and to the power plant's only residential customer: Rogers himself. Or, at least, that was what was supposed to happen. On September 27, Rogers turned the generator on, but the lights at his house did nothing. A second attempt, on the morning of September 30, also failed. It wasn't until after dark—by which point, a sizable crowd had gathered near Rogers's hilltop mansion—that the electrical system worked as promised. Even at the birth of electrified life in America, how energy got from here to there was just as important as how it was made in the first place.

The success, however, was not unequivocal. "Two and a half months after [the salesman] had first talked to Rogers about it, the first hydroelectric central station in the world was in business," wrote Forrest McDonald in *Let There Be Light*, his 1957 book on the history of electric utilities in Wisconsin. "But this speed was accomplished partly by the omission of several of the safety and reliability features of the complete Edison system and partly by the use of makeshift equipment."[11]

There are several important lessons that you need to learn about the way energy works in the United States. This is the first: our current energy infrastructure isn't the same as an *ideal* energy infrastructure. These systems that we stake our lives and livelihoods on every day weren't designed so much as they evolved, the sum of lots of little decisions made to meet immediate needs or solve short-term problems. There are inefficiencies. There are kludgey temporary fixes that became long-term staples. If it looks as if we're making it up as we go, it's because, in a lot of ways, we're making it up as we go. The result serves our current needs—most of the time—but you shouldn't be surprised that the energy infrastructure will require a serious overhaul before it can meet the needs of future generations.

Appleton is a great example of how this happened. The infrastructure was built quickly and built to be cheap. Whether it could do the best job possible didn't factor into the equation. Even the very location of the generator turned out to be a bad decision. To save time and money, Rogers initially opted to have the generator be powered by the same water wheel that ran the pulp beaters on his paper mill. It was the mill's activity, however, not the electrical system, that determined how fast the wheel needed to turn. This meant, on a busy day at the factory, that the wheel would be set to go at top speed, with little regard for what the generator wanted to do—and that meant trouble.

Think back to our river of electrons. It can't simply flow from place to place randomly. It's not a wild force of nature that we can sit back and watch. We're not talking about some mountain stream or even the dammed and barricaded Mississippi. In reality, the electric grid has more in common with the lazy river at a water park. Imagine the grid as a channel of water running in a loop. This lazy river has to be just the right depth, an analogy that corresponds to what electrical engineers call *voltage*. It also has to move at a constant speed—what the engineers call *hertz*. Rogers didn't take either of those issues into account. To maintain the right balance of hertz and voltage, you have to produce just about exactly as much electricity as is being used at any given point in time. There's not much wiggle room. The water that's being dumped into the channel has to equal the amount of water being pumped out of it. Basically, Rogers's system left the spigots on at full force but without nearly enough drains. So the water backed up, the channel flooded and, in the Rogerses' home, electric lightbulbs burned out—bulbs that cost the equivalent of $35 a pop. Inadvertently, Rogers had stumbled onto an important rule about electricity, one that you'll soon find we're struggling with even to this day: having too much electricity is just as big a problem as having too little. Within two months, Rogers had arranged to move the generator to its own building, powered by its own water wheel.

I've peeked inside a replica of this power plant, constructed on the original site in the 1930s.[12] Really just a shack, it was smaller than my bedroom back home. At one end of the rectangular room, enthroned up on a little dais, sat the generator. At the other end was a chair, next to a bare electric lightbulb that dangled from the ceiling. Even after Rogers was forced to put the power plant in its own building, he still didn't learn his lesson about making the river run smoothly.

For years, that lightbulb was the closest thing Appleton had to a voltmeter. Staring at it was the only way anyone could tell whether the electron river was too deep, too shallow, or just about right. Edison had invented a meter to monitor the system more accurately, but Rogers and company didn't buy it. Instead, whoever was on duty simply watched the bulb, looking for signs that it was glowing a little too brightly or a little too dimly.[13]

The missteps didn't end at the generator itself. Today, electric wires are coated in thick layers of insulating plastic. In Appleton, if a wire was insulated at all, it was usually just wrapped in a thin coat of paper or silk. In that state, it was pretty easy for anything—a twig, a squirrel—to dam the electron river and short out the wire. When that happened, the entire grid had to be shut down. A. C. Langstadt, one of the early controllers who started working in Appleton after the system had picked up a few more customers, remembered regularly having to stop work, turn off the generator, and spend an hour—or even a full day—going from house to house looking for the shorted wire.

There wasn't even a good way to know how much electricity was being used. Again, Edison had invented an electric meter, but it would be years before that technology came to Appleton.[14] In the meantime, customers were simply charged a flat rate, per lightbulb, no matter how long they left the bulbs turned on. The generators didn't run at all during the day. The grid was activated in the evening and shut down again at daybreak. Because the price was the same, though, many customers simply left the lights on all night as a status symbol—their houses glowing long after everyone had gone to bed.

This brings me to the second fact you need to learn about energy in America today: we waste a lot of it. When you think about using less energy, you probably think about conservation, doing without something you want. This assumes, however, that we get something valuable out of all of the energy we use right now, and that's simply not true. Remember how much energy we burn through at power plants and how little electricity we get out of it? The same is true in our homes, our offices, and our cars. If we cut out the waste, we could use a lot less energy and still benefit from what energy does for us. That's called efficiency. Yet as in Appleton many years ago, we don't have a lot of good incentives out there today that lead us to be more efficient. In fact, the opposite is often true, particularly because getting efficiency right can be more complicated than it looks at first.

Without incentives, efficiency simply won't happen—and if efficiency doesn't happen, then we have a problem. In fact, a lack of efficiency also turned out to be a big problem for Rogers and his business partners. Back then, electricity was pretty cheap to make, but these men spent far more money building the infrastructure to run the grid than they made back from their customers. It wasn't just because of the poorly thought-out pricing scheme, either. Think of all of the ways you use electricity every day—all of the appliances and the gadgets that are plugged in 24/7. None of that existed in the early days. For decades, electricity was simply a tool to produce light and nothing more. Even after meters were installed, customers couldn't possibly use enough electricity for investors to make a return. In 1884, Rogers wrote of his accounts always being overdrawn. Within a few years, he de-invested from the utility and left Appleton entirely.

The utility company didn't fare much better. After the first three years, investors had plopped down the equivalent of more than $500,000 and found that they owned a business worth far less. They never got any dividends. By 1896, the Appleton utility was bankrupt—and it wasn't alone. Across the country, most of the companies that built the first grids failed. Edison made plenty of money from his patents, but very few people got rich off electricity itself. Today, we see electricity as a story of success, but that's with the benefit of long-term hindsight and big-picture thinking about what turned out to be good for you and me. For people such as H. J. Rogers, electricity was nothing but a dreadful, belly-up failure.

In that flop, you'll find two more lessons about energy in the United States. Energy is always about economics. When change happens—and when change *doesn't* happen—there are probably dollar signs behind it, and that's okay. As we pay attention to the symptoms of climate change, we can't ignore our wallets. Oil may be a limited resource, but so is money. Rogers made some big mistakes when he tried to build an energy system at the lowest possible cost, and we're facing our own consequences from that same sort of mentality today. Yet that doesn't mean the correct response is to spend as much as possible. We have to put some thought into this and get the changes we need at a price we can afford. Which brings me to another important lesson: "A price we can afford" is still going to be pretty damn high. We don't want to simply throw money at a problem without considering whether it's being spent wisely or whether we could get the same results for less cash. At the same time, however, we do have to accept that energy change will not be cheap. The biggest costs are always in infrastructure, which is why even "free" energy from the wind and the sun won't actually be free. The wires, the generators, the rights-of-way for transmission, and the controllers to make sure everything works—it all costs a lot of money. Even on the relatively small scale that Appleton was dealing with, infrastructure turned out to be far more expensive than most nineteenth-century businessmen would have realized.

"You had to put this enormous infrastructure in place before you could make a penny," says Gregory Summers, an associate professor of history at the University of Wisconsin-Steven's Point. "And it broke down all the time. Companies failed all the time. Utilities, railroads, lots of nineteenth-century businesses had this issue with fixed costs."

Summers studies the history of industrialization, technology, and environmental politics. He says the dawn of twentieth-century living—the increase in convenience and comfort that was dependent on the construction of new, massive infrastructures for transportation and energy—represented a major shift in how businesses operated. Right up until the end of the 1800s, the relatively cheap cost of operations—making the widget—was the main problem companies worried about. "If there was a recession, you'd just shut down the factory and reopen later," Summers says. "Now, think about something like an airline today. If it temporarily shuts down, it would keep on losing billions every day, because it would keep losing money on the infrastructure. [People in the nineteenth century] weren't accustomed to running a business where the biggest expense was fixed costs, rather than operating costs."

That sort of blew my mind, but, then, I've only known a world where infrastructure already exists. For all I knew when I was a little kid, electricity poles grew with the trees. But the truth is that Americans today are using a system that took a century to build. Some of the investments in that system were public and some were private. Either way, building that infrastructure cost a lot of money. As late as the 1930s, Summers told me, electricity was still something of a luxury—expensive and available only in urban markets where the costs could be spread among a large number of customers, without the utility having to build an equally large grid.

Rural America didn't get electricity until the government stepped in and was able to spread the cost of constructing an infrastructure across the entire country. For infrastructures where that kind of national investment didn't happen, it took a very long time to catch all Americans up to the same level of modernization. Case in point, the telephone. My maternal grandparents lived on a farm about fifty-five miles northwest of Kansas City, Kansas. In the mid-1980s, they were still stuck using a party-line system. Essentially, multiple households shared the same phone line. I can remember my grandma having me pick up her phone to check whether the line was in use before she could make a call.

Today, electricity is relatively cheap, because the basic infrastructure already exists. Utility companies build new power plants here and replace a stretch of wire there, but that's really maintenance of the grid—not creation of it. It's been thirty years since anyone made major investments in the network of wires that feeds electricity around the country. One big reason the people who own coal-fired power plants are so keen on keeping those plants up and running is that their investments were paid off long ago. They only have to worry about covering the cost of operation, and they pass those savings on to you. In some ways, with electricity, we've almost come back around to a point where—like H. J. Rogers and his business partners in Appleton—we have a hard time figuring out how to run a business that has to build its own infrastructure.

This is important stuff to think about. The national grid was pieced together from a quilt of little grids, such as the one in Appleton, which were themselves built partly on know-how and partly on after-the-fact engineering. The grid is like a river, but it's also like an old house that's been heavily remodeled and expanded, at different times and by different owners. In its current form, the grid can't handle lots of electricity coming from sources as variable as wind and solar. To make renewable energy work, in the long run, we'll have to upgrade, and that will get expensive. Yet you have to put those costs in perspective. For one thing, there are some pretty big chunks of the grid that will need replacing in the near-term future, anyway. Take transmission lines—the wires that carry electricity over the long distances between cities and states—and distribution networks, the wires that move electricity around your town. Neither of these systems has had much work done since the late 1970s, especially transmission lines.

At this point, the complexity and cost of changing America's energy systems sounds pretty daunting. Maybe it even sounds like something to avoid. Unfortunately, that's not really possible. For all of the problems associated with changing the way we use energy, doing nothing is likely to be worse. Despite its flaws, our infrastructure is something we can't live without.

CHAPTER TWO

....

ONE IN A QUADRILLION

Our world is built on shared systems, and those systems shape how much energy we use and where that energy comes from. The U.S. electric infrastructure—an old, haphazardly built network of wires and centralized, mostly fossil-fuel-dependent power plants— wakes me up in the morning. When my husband drives to work, he uses city roads, county highways, and a national interstate—systems that make it possible for cars to navigate a metro area that's been designed with car travel in mind. To do my job, I use the Internet—a tool that is itself a shared system and uses energy drawn from other shared systems, in order to facilitate even *more* shared systems. We eat food that's grown, processed, and packaged through an agricultural system that is simultaneously partly local and partly international and all of it powered by energy use that we never even see.

None of this is really a bad thing. Shared systems are nothing to lament. We belong to a society that pools its resources and connects individuals in a web of benefits and responsibilities. Because of that, we have services such as public education and a health-care system that's based on more than what one guy in your hometown thinks about the human body. Because of systems, we have heat, light, and power that are available on demand to the vast majority of Americans. Our systems have been good to us, in many ways.

I'm harping on this point a lot, but I think it's important. Too often, the narrative of how we solve America's energy problems is framed around the idea of abandoning shared systems, rather than changing them. For instance, consider Earth Hour—an annual event that tries to raise awareness of energy issues by convincing people to shut off the lights in their houses, businesses, and public buildings for one hour on one specific night. It's a public and popular way to express support for changing the way the world uses energy—more than a hundred countries participate every year, and thousands of famous landmarks, from Vegas to Giza, go dark for the occasion. Yet I'm not really a fan, and Earth Hour isn't something that we celebrate at my house. Why? Because I think it sends the wrong message.

The official goals of Earth Hour aren't bad. The World Wildlife Fund, which organizes the event, explains what Earth Hour is and isn't right on the main website. Earth Hour isn't specifically about saving energy. It's only one hour, one day a year. Whatever energy is saved by the event would be so small as not to matter at all. In fact, because of that, the World Wildlife Fund doesn't even keep track of the impact Earth Hour has on energy consumption and emissions. Nor is Earth Hour supposed to be about rejecting modern technology. The World Wildlife Fund specifically tells participants that they're asked to shut off only *nonessential* lighting.

That makes sense. As someone who understands the importance of energy efficiency, I think it's valuable to remind people that we all use a lot more energy than we'd really have to use to get the services we want from it. Yet I don't think that's the message people get from Earth Hour. When I hear people talk about it, when I see the media cover it, I don't see a discussion about energy efficiency. Instead, the people participating in Earth Hour, the people observing it, and the people critiquing it seem to think that Earth Hour is the opposite of what the World Wildlife Fund says it is.[1]

I have three big problems with Earth Hour and the message it sends. First, some people are going to be very easily disillusioned when they find out that Earth Hour doesn't actually do anything to combat climate change. In fact, in places where lots of people participate, there might even be a small, temporary uptick in emissions. When fossil fuel power plants are forced to rapidly increase or decrease the amount of electricity they produce, they also produce more emissions, just as your car burns more gasoline if you're rapidly accelerating and decelerating than if you maintain a constant speed. So, when everybody turns the lights back on at the end of Earth Hour, it means that some coal and natural gas power plants will have to quickly work extra hard to meet that sudden increase in demand. In order to do that, they produce more emissions than they otherwise would have. Just as turning your lights off for an hour won't save the planet, this short-term increase in the emissions output of a few power plants won't seal our fate, either. Yet there is a real risk that discovering this fact will convince some people to mistrust *any* effort to get them to change their energy-use behavior.

My second problem with Earth Hour: it inspires a reactionary push-back from people who think the event is a rejection of modern life, an attempt to show people how much better they had it in Appleton before that first power plant. It sets up a straw-man target that is easily attacked. Instead of discussing actual issues, groups such as the Ayn Rand Institute can point to Earth Hour and say, "See, environmentalists just want to reject comfort, convenience, and safety and force you to live in the nineteenth century."[2] We don't have to go back in time to counteract climate change and prepare for peak oil, but an energy event that encourages people to spend an hour in the dark certainly gives that impression.

Finally, although Earth Hour can make energy change seem too hard, it can simultaneously also make it seem too easy. Some people see Earth Hour and think that they're being asked to abandon everything that makes their lives nice. Other people see it and come away thinking that all they have to do is shut off some lights sometime, and everything will be fixed. It's easy to throw a party once a year and hang out with your friends in the dark, but real change is difficult. It doesn't end at home, either. Too much easy-to-do, feel-good awareness building can easily blind people to the hard work that's ahead of us.

Whether the promoters of events such as Earth Hour intend to or not, they send the message that energy change is about voluntary individual choices and choosing *not* to use our shared systems. Yet if you look at what the experts say—in the plans where scientists and analysts map out how we can actually make the biggest energy changes in the least amount of time—you'll find that their message is exactly the opposite.

• • •

In May 2011, the Intergovernmental Panel on Climate Change (IPCC) released a report aimed at detailing the global potential of existing renewable energy technologies and explaining what has to be done to make those technologies work the way we want them to. As with its reports on climate change, the IPCC didn't conduct new scientific research for this report. Instead, it looked at the body of research that scientists all over the world had produced, then it summarized all of *those* studies. Reading the IPCC report, you get the big picture on what science says about where renewable energy stands, what challenges we face in using it, and the best ways to deploy more of it quickly.

The report also compared the results of computer models. These programs can be used to help estimate the likely effects of climate change; they can also help us predict how much renewable energy the world might use and by when. When researchers model renewable energy deployment, they run many different scenarios, using various models. All of those scenarios are affected by different variables, such as government policy, environmental regulations, growth in energy demand, and budgetary bottom lines. The 2011 IPCC report compared 164 scenarios, which had been run using 16 models.[3]

The good news: researchers found that it's possible to change the way we generate energy. The bad news is that the majority of scenarios also show this change happening much slower than we might like.

In 2008, all of the countries in the world got 12.9 percent of their energy from renewable sources, sans nuclear energy.[4] By 2030, more than half of the scenarios showed the world getting around 17 percent of its energy from those sources. That is a significant increase, especially because of the details. In 2008, most of the renewable energy on this planet was used by people in developing countries, who directly burned biomass for heat, light, and cooking fires— essentially using energy the way Americans used it before 1885. Technically, this kind of energy is renewable, but there are some serious side effects, including deforestation and lung problems caused by living in houses that are constantly filled with the smoke of burning wood. By 2030, the models predict that this sort of bioenergy use will decrease and that there will be a big increase in the sort of renewable energy we're excited about today in the United States—a shift that represents cleaner, healthier lives for the people in developing countries, as well as more sustainable lives for us. This change isn't piddling, but, overall, it's not as big a change as we really need. People thought everyone would own a flying car by 2030. In reality, we all probably won't even be driving *electric* cars by then.

According to these models, in 2050—when I am sixty-nine years old—only 27 percent of the world's energy will be renewable. Now, you can't take this as the final word on the future of energy. The models are only meant to show what is likely under certain circumstances. (It's also important to remember that these are numbers for the entire world. In order to get this relatively small increase on a global scale, countries such as the United States will have to achieve much larger increases in our reliance on renewable energy.) These models don't provide a crystal ball, and some of the modeling tells a different story. The scenarios that came out on the high end predicted a world powered by 43 percent renewable energy in 2030 and 77 percent in 2050.

This report, combined with other, previous reports from the IPCC, tells us a few important things about the future of energy. First, there's no killer app for renewable energy, the IPPC says. Some forms of renewable energy will be more prominent in specific places, but, globally, nothing stands out as a clear winner. Our low-carbon energy future will feature wind, solar, bioenergy, and hydro working together, alongside other sources such as geothermal and ocean power. Even within those categories, we'll use more than one technology. When the IPCC talks about solar, it means photovoltaic panels, the big black tiles you may immediately think of in connection with solar power. Yet the IPCC is also talking about solar hot water, a very simple technology where pipes on your roof preheat the water for your showers and cleaning, so that your gas or electric hot water heater doesn't have to work as hard. "Solar" also means passive ways of lighting and warming a building with the sun. (It's worth noting that the way the IPCC breaks up categories here is a little weird. Most of the time, when people talk about solar power, they mean only solar photovoltaics or concentrating solar collectors. All of the other technologies I mention here usually get lumped under "energy efficiency.")

What's more, these renewable sources will have to be used as part of a larger, comprehensive energy strategy. The May 2011 IPCC report looks only at renewable energy generation sources, and it tells us that generation alone can't account for the changes we need in the amount of time we have. Climate change is already happening. Oil production is likely to peak by 2030. (I'll talk about both of these things a little more in chapter 6.) To make deep cuts in the production of emissions and our dependence on fossil fuels, we'll have to use more than *just* renewable energy. We'll need to cut our energy demand through efficiency. We'll need to regulate and then develop systems that use fossil fuels such as coal and natural gas in cleaner ways, because they'll be around for a while. We'll need to take nuclear energy seriously. All of that is important and it all has to happen simultaneously. That starts with policy.

What's the difference between the scenarios that show the Earth using 17 percent renewable energy in twenty years and the ones that predict a 43 percent renewable-powered planet in the same time frame? It's all in the variables. How fast we can roll out renewable energy depends on a lot of factors, the IPCC report says. It depends on changes to the electric grid, which would allow wind and solar to be better integrated into our energy mix. It depends on research and the regulation of biofuels, to ensure that we aren't damaging the land as we try to use it. It also depends on ongoing scientific research, to produce cheaper versions of certain renewable technologies, to build better batteries that will help the grid work, and to develop versions of renewable technologies—such as ocean power—that can be used in a large-scale, commercial way.

Yet it's more than only the technology policies. In scenarios with the highest and fastest rates of renewable development, governments all over the world agree to commit to keeping greenhouse gas concentrations in the atmosphere under 440 parts per million. Given that the planet's atmosphere is currently hovering around 390 ppm and rising all the time, that's a very stringent goal.[5] If we could agree to it, though, and follow through on the agreement, it would mean big increases in renewable energy and would leave us in a much, much better place, where climate change was mitigated and our energy supply was more diverse. It depends on social policies, too. Public education matters, the IPCC says. People who don't understand energy are doomed to repeat the same mistakes. Carbon prices matter, because they help average people see what different energy choices are really going to cost them, in the long term. Urban planning matters, because that has a big impact on how (or even whether) individuals can choose to be more energy efficient in their daily lives. Incentives also matter, because that's how you encourage more people to plan energy systems for the future, rather than ones that just make ends meet right now.

The more of these policy changes that happen, in more countries, the faster we can leave fossil fuels behind. The less our policies change, the less prepared we will be. It's that simple. This is a point I'll come back to later, because it's kind of a big deal. When I was little, I remember reading books about "what you can do to save the planet." The truth is, it's not the planet that needs saving. It's our way of life. More important, I'm not going to save anything, and neither are you. Not alone. The way we use energy is determined by the systems we share. The only way to change our energy use is to change the systems, and policy is the thing that can most easily and most quickly change systems. But what is it going to cost us?

Today, in general, renewable energy is more expensive than its fossil fuel counterparts. Specifics, though, are hard to sort out, and there's a good reason for that. Although I can tell you about relative costs—x is more expensive than y—the specific price tags on energy development and energy production are all tied to variable factors, such as location. The cost of solar electricity in Southern California is not the same as the cost of solar electricity in Minnesota.

There have, however, been some good estimates made about the scale of investment we'd need in order to create real, comprehensive energy changes. If you read these reports, you'll learn that energy change is going to be pricy, especially when we're talking about upfront costs. Yet you'll also learn that it's not *as* expensive as you might have guessed. More important, it's likely to be cheaper to change the way we use energy now than it would be to suffer through the consequences of inaction later on.

The IPCC looks at climate and energy from a global perspective. Depending on the specific policies used and the speed at which change happens, the IPCC estimates that the investments in energy change would reduce the growth of the *global* gross domestic product by somewhere from .06 percent to .12 percent per year between now and 2030. In other words, if we take this stuff seriously, the cost to us, as a planet, will be high but not all *that* high. The world will still get richer every year; it'll just happen a little more slowly. Even if we adopt the most stringent goals for carbon emissions reduction, the IPCC estimates that in 2030, Earth will be only 3 percent less wealthy than it would have been if we'd done nothing.[6] Even that doesn't reflect the full picture, though, because doing nothing isn't actually an option.

The money we spend on energy change will help us avoid costs associated with climate change and peaking fossil fuels. For instance, we know that as atmospheric concentrations of greenhouse gases and global temperatures have increased, the Midwestern U.S. has become a lot wetter. Precipitation in the plains region has increased by 5 percent, mostly in the form of more frequent large storms.[7] In fact, throughout the Midwest, heavy downpours occur twice as often as they did a century ago.[8] That equates to more dollars spent—money to repair and improve drainage systems, to upgrade water treatment facilities, and to clean up after flooding. On October 4, 1998, 5.6 inches of rain fell in a single day in Merriam, Kansas. Flash floods followed, and the city ended up spending more than $5 million to buy and demolish thirty-three houses that were damaged beyond repair. The next year, the county government spent more than $9 million remapping flood-prone areas, and another half million went to the countywide expansion of a flood warning system.[9] That's only one storm, in one town.

When the economic consequences of the wide-ranging 2011 floods finally shake out, we'll likely be looking at a bill for hundreds of millions of dollars. We can't say that any specific storm was a direct consequence of climate change, but the trend toward more big storms is in line with what we'd expect from climate change. A 2011 report found that the effects of climate change could cost the global transportation, construction, and manufacturing indus-tries alone $8 trillion by 2030. That's before you even take into account the impact on other industries or on governments.[10] Invest in reducing greenhouse gas emissions now, and you can avoid some of that spending later.

So far, we've been talking about the global outlook, but we can also zoom in and see what a system-driven energy change would mean for the United States, specifically. McKinsey and Company is a management consulting firm that specializes in helping CEOs and other business executives prepare for the future. In order to do that, the firm does a lot of independent research on various issues that are likely to affect businesses in decades to come. The economic impact of energy change is one of the situations they've studied. In 2008, McKinsey and Company released a report on how the world and certain specific countries can reduce the risks of climate change while sustaining economic growth. This report pulls no punches when it comes to assessing how difficult the job will be. To maintain economic growth while reducing our greenhouse gas emissions, we'll have to find ways to do a lot more with less carbon—something McKinsey analysts called "carbon productivity." In fact, the increase in carbon productivity that we need to achieve is similar to the increase in labor productivity—doing a lot more for less physical work—that we saw during the Industrial Revolution.

But here's the real problem: "While the extent of economic transformation implied is similar to the Industrial Revolution, the 'carbon revolution' must be achieved in one-third the time, if we are to maintain current levels of economic growth while keeping CO_2 levels below 550 parts per million by volume, a level that many experts believe is the maximum that can be allowed without significant risks to the climate."[11]

The McKinsey analysts think that as hard as it would be, the world could pull this off, and they don't expect it to have any more of a global economic impact than the IPCC does. Like the IPCC, McKinsey analysts believe this kind of change has to be driven by governments, multinational businesses, and other organizations that can directly affect the way lots and lots of individual people use energy.

If we had a carbon revolution, what would it look like? There are many different possibilities. I'm going to look at the predictions made by IGSM, a computer model created by researchers at MIT.[12] This model has been used to predict what could happen between 2012 and 2030 if Americans dedicated themselves to the idea of keeping global emissions below 550 ppm.[13] There's more than one way to reach this goal, and IGSM isn't likely to be 100 percent correct. It's only an example to show you how things could work out.[14]

To predict the future, IGSM runs various scenarios, allowing it to compare what would happen if we kept on using energy the way we do today and what would happen if we tried to change. If we do nothing, IGSM expects our energy use to keep on going up. In 2009, we used 94.6 quadrillion BTUs. By 2030, IGSM thinks we'll probably use 128 quadrillion BTUs. So, if we want to hit that 550 ppm target, the first thing IGSM says we have to do is reduce energy consumption. If we take action, IGSM predicts that we will use 21 quadrillion fewer BTUs by 2030 than we would have otherwise—this would be 107, instead of 128, quadrillion BTUs.

That's the equivalent of the energy produced by 336 coal-fired power plants. Of course, we won't achieve that energy-use reduction merely by shutting down 336 power plants. Energy is more complicated than that. Instead, it will come from reductions in energy consumption—people simply using less—and increases in energy efficiency, people doing the same work for less energy. You could probably guess that. But here's the thing: we won't get a 21 quadrillion BTU cut in our energy use in eighteen years by relying on everyone to do his or her small part on a voluntary basis.

Take cars, for instance. In 2009, the average American car got 22.6 miles to the gallon, and the average driver drove 13,500 miles in a year. That means we burn through about 931 trillion BTUs per year in our cars.[15] If we raised the average fuel efficiency of all cars to match the average fuel efficiency of a new 2010 car—33.7 mpg—we'd use only 625 trillion BTUs. That's a savings of 306 trillion BTUs per year. If we were to start in 2012, we could save more than half a quadrillion BTUs by 2030, just on this one thing alone. The savings go up if we can also reduce the number of cars on the road, decrease the number of miles traveled in a year, and/or get more people to share cars. None of that is likely to happen on its own, though, as individual volunteerism. Average fuel efficiency barely budged in the last decade, and it's gained only 2 mpg since 1990. This should give you an idea of how increases in efficiency can add up over time; why they have to happen on a national scale, not on an individual one; and why we'll need to increase efficiency a lot—in many different parts of our lives—if we're going to save 21 quadrillion BTUs by 2030.

The reduction in energy consumption is only one part of the changes predicted by the IGSM model. If we take action, IGSM assumes that by 2030 we'll be using more natural gas than we otherwise would have—and a lot less coal. In fact, alongside the reduction in energy consumption, the reduction in coal use is the biggest change IGSM expects in the next two decades. Today, thanks to those pesky conversion losses, we burn more than 21 quadrillion BTUs of coal to produce more than 8 quadrillion BTUs of usable electricity. If we choose to reduce our demand for electricity and increase the amount of natural gas we use, IGSM thinks we can cut our total coal consumption for electricity down to a little more than 13 quadrillion BTUs by 2030.

Those are the big changes. Here's the rest. In 2010, IGSM estimates that we got 43 percent of our energy from oil, 21 percent from coal, 25 percent from natural gas, 5 percent from nuclear power, 3 percent from renewables, and less than 1 percent from commercial biomass.[16] By 2030, if we take action, IGSM expects the amount of renewables we use to increase from 3 quadrillion BTUs to 5 quadrillion BTUs. Commercial biomass would grow under this scenario, too, from fewer than a quadrillion BTUs to more than 3 quadrillion. This is a small increase, and it's one of the biggest ways that IGSM differs from other predictions about how our energy systems might change by 2030. Other models, including the one used by McKinsey and Company, predict much larger increases in our reliance on renewable energy generation—and much larger increases are possible, in a practical sense. This just shows you how complicated planning for the future really is. It isn't only about setting a goal; we also have to decide how we'll reach the goal.

For fossil fuels, IGSM shows some increases and some decreases. I already told you that the model predicts we'll use a lot less coal, going from 21 quadrillion BTUs, or 21 percent of our total energy use in 2010 to 14 quadrillion BTUs, or 13 percent of the total by 2030. Meanwhile, however, it predicts that our use of oil and natural gas will increase, with oil consumption going from 43 quadrillion BTUs (43 percent of the total) in 2010 to 50 quadrillion BTUs (47 percent) in 2030. Natural gas is predicted to rise from 25 quadrillion BTUs (25 percent of the total) to 31 quadrillion BTUs (29 percent).

Nuclear power, on the other hand, would decrease under the IGSM scenario. In 2010, IGSM estimated that we used 5 quadrillion BTUs' worth of nuclear energy. In 2030, it predicts that we'll use 4 quadrillion BTUs.

This may not be the exact set of changes you'd pick, but there's room for alterations. For instance, are you worried about the long-term impact of nuclear power? You could put a little more invest-ment into cleaner coal, natural gas, and renewables, and see if we can't pick up the 4 quadrillion BTUs' difference through those tech-nologies. In addition, all of this assumes no major breakthroughs will be made in energy technology. There's not likely to be *any* cleaner coal on the grid until 2020, according to McKinsey. IGSM doesn't predict any until after 2030, and the costs of integrating all of these different sources of energy aren't likely to drop steeply. It is possible, though, that if we made some big investments in scientific research, those technological jumps might move a little faster.

What we can't do, according to McKinsey, IGSM, and the IPCC, is throw out either nuclear power or conventional coal altogether. Not if we want to have enough electricity to meet demand. That's another important lesson about energy. These systems are compli-cated, so there's no way that all of us are going to get everything we want. Your ideal world might be one without any nuclear reactors or any coal-fired power plants. We can cut back on those things, but we can't eliminate them. Not completely. Not yet. If you're imagining a future entirely free of both fossil fuel pollution and nuclear waste, you probably won't see that in your lifetime.

Back in 2008, McKinsey and Company estimated that a plan to change the way the United States uses energy by 2030 would cost just north of $1 trillion.[17] That's a lot of money. To put it in context, in 2007, some economists estimated that we had spent around $1 trillion on the war in Iraq, up to that point in time.[18] In the case of the war, however, we spent $1 trillion in fewer than five years.

What the McKinsey Report is talking about is something a lot easier to finance—$1 trillion over a little more than twenty years, 2008 to 2030.[19] That works out to around $50 billion a year. What else can you buy for $50 billion? In 2008, the *Washington Post* reported that state governments spend that much money every year on jails and prisons.[20] That same year, the federal government spent a little more than $50 billion on nuclear weapons and related programs, according to a report by the Carnegie Endowment.[21] So, we're still talking about a lot of money, but it's not an unprecedented amount of money to spend yearly on a single important goal.

The McKinsey Report also points out that it's completely reasonable to expect that the actual job of reducing greenhouse gas emissions could cost less than we think. In fact, historic precedent suggests that when government policies encourage businesses to work in a different way, those businesses come up with new technologies and new approaches that allow them to meet mandates for less money than anyone could possibly have guessed. In fact, that's exactly what happened when the U.S. government placed hard limits on the emissions of chlorofluorocarbons, the chemical responsible for the depletion of the ozone layer, and on sulfur dioxide, the chemical that causes acid rain. In 1988, when we agreed to cut chlorofluorocarbons by 50 percent, analysts thought the change would cost the United States $20 billion over ten years. Instead, within two years, those estimates had shrunk to $2.7 billion.

We tackled sulfur dioxide with a cap-and-trade system, which forced the companies that created the pollution to either find cleaner ways to do their business or pay the companies that *did* go clean for the right to pollute. When that went into effect in 1995, the McKinsey Report says, estimates for the cost ranged from $3 billion to $25 billion. By 2007, it was clear that sulfur dioxide cap-and-trade was going to cost, at the maximum, only $1.4 billion.[22] If governments make change mandatory, businesses find ways to make change cheap.

The basic point to all of this is that big changes to our energy systems won't come easily, but they are *possible*—if, and only if, policy makers are capable of taking smart action: focusing on the cheapest ways to hit our goals and setting up structures that allow us to use flawed technologies, such as biofuels, nuclear power, and cleaner coal, without turning a blind eye to where those technologies could go bad. Within that basic outline, there are reasons to be hopeful. Yet there are also reasons to fret.

I have to admit that when I think about all of the coordination, education, and nonpartisan (not merely bipartisan) decision making that needs to happen, I get the urge to go back to bed and hide under the covers. During the last two years, I've seen a lot of evidence that has led me to believe we have the technology to save ourselves. If we can be smart about strategy, we've also got the money. Instead, when I *do* get pessimistic, it's not because solutions are out of reach. It's because the coordination and planning necessary to make those solutions work, in the time frame we need them to work in, are completely unprecedented.

From Appleton to today, the energy systems we now enjoy took more than a century to evolve. Frankly, in a perfect world, I'd be happy to just sit back and let the future of energy happen at that same slow pace. The world isn't perfect, though. Between climate change and fossil fuel peaks, there's good evidence that we can't afford to simply wait around for change to happen on its own. Policy isn't important only because it fosters change on a wider scale at a faster rate. Policy is important because it's the only way we can think about the big picture at the same time that we're considering all of the little snapshots. Energy change is something we will have to deal with, one way or the other, whether we're prepared for it or not. We can tackle this intimidating task of planning our future, or we can deal with the consequences of not planning. Personally, I'd rather be prepared.

CHAPTER THREE

....

THE EFFICIENCY PARADOX

When October comes to the Upper Midwest, it brings along a few predictable signs of change. The air turns prickly. The grass fades and then is coated in a layer of crunchy yellow and brown leaves. The squirrels become morbidly obese. October is far from the coldest month, but in Minneapolis, we'll usually have the boiler turned on already. In every room of my house, cast-iron radiators will transfer heat from the scalding water inside to the air all around. Still a little chilled, I'll throw on a knit cardigan and some socks and coax a cat or two off the radiator and into my lap.

Meanwhile, in Urbana, Illinois, another homeowner named Bernice Dallas won't have to turn on the furnace to push back against the chill. In fact, she doesn't even have one. Throughout the autumn and again in spring, Bernice's entire two-story house—built in 2009 without a central heating system—will, instead, keep itself warm.

How's that work? Pretty well, according to Bernice. She's the first to tell you that her house is different from other houses. It's not *only* missing a furnace, there have been a few things added as well. Bernice's house was built using a design standard called Passive House. Developed in Germany, Passive House design creates homes that use much less energy to produce the same comforts and conveniences as their traditionally designed counterparts.

If we want to reduce our annual fossil fuel use by 20 quadrillion BTUs during the next twenty years, the buildings where we live and work are a great place to start. The Energy Information Administration (EIA) is the federal bureau that keeps track of our energy use and figures out what benefits we get from that energy. In the EIA's databases, all of the quadrillions of BTUs we consume in a year are gobbled up by either homes, commercial buildings, transportation, or manufacturing. Of the 94.6 quadrillion BTUs we consumed in 2009, 21.21 quadrillion BTUs were used to heat and cool homes and keep our gadgets and appliances running. Another 18.5 quadrillion BTUs went to commercial buildings, such as schools, offices, and shopping malls.[1]

You might be used to thinking of transportation as our biggest energy problem, but, at 27 quadrillion BTUs, the energy consumption of cars is dwarfed by the combined demands of all of our buildings. This is why Bernice Dallas's house is so special. Passive Houses aren't common in the United States, but they offer us a good solution for building homes that use a lot less energy without being uncomfortable or off-puttingly strange. Dallas's house isn't a geodesic dome. It's not an off-the-grid hippie compound made out of Coke bottles. Instead, it's just a house that was built with energy use in mind. That house makes it easier for Dallas and her son to use less. By looking inside, you can start to see why changing a system can make a bigger difference on the amount of energy we use than changing a personal habit would.

This is important, because, in the United States, we use lots and lots of energy. Some of that is necessary, so to speak. It's the price we have to pay to get a quality of life that includes warm houses, refrigerated food, and the ability to quickly travel from one side of a major city to the other. You can argue against those amenities if you want. They are, after all, simply lifestyle choices, and plenty of people, all over the world, get by without them. But taking a stand against the really awesome parts of modern life is not going to make you terribly popular. More important, it's not going to foster a whole lot of change. Only a limited number of Americans—probably a limited number of people anywhere—are going to intentionally make a choice to have lives that require more sweat, more discomfort, and more frustration. Everybody likes the benefits we get from using energy. No amount of cajoling or wishful thinking is going to change that.

Yet this doesn't mean we can't get those same benefits for *less* energy. The fact of the matter is that we not only use a lot of energy in the United States, we also *waste* a lot of energy—burning through resources that don't need to be consumed, with no corresponding improvement to our way of life. It's like going out for a delicious dinner and then throwing all of the leftovers in the trash, for no good reason. The only difference is that when it comes to energy, we aren't being willfully wasteful. People don't wake up in the morning, temple their fingertips, and chuckle to themselves as they think about all of the ways they'll needlessly squander valuable resources today. Instead, the waste just kind of happens, without our much being aware of it. Waste happens when we make electricity. It's built into our houses and office buildings, designed into our cities, and grown along with our food. It doesn't take any effort to be wasteful. It's how we were raised. If you remember the way people left their lights burning all night in Appleton, Wisconsin, then you realize that nobody is likely to be efficient without an incentive. In many cases, even if the efficiency is required, people don't know what to do to get it. Reducing waste takes a lot of thought. To do it successfully, we have to fight against our own behavioral instincts and the very structure of our world. That's individual decision making, and it's hard. Systemic changes can help.

How do we know? Because there are people in the world who enjoy the same quality of life as Americans but who use a lot less energy than we do. It's no coincidence that the Passive House design system that was used to create Bernice Dallas's home is intellectual property imported from Germany. In Western Europe, in general, people waste less energy, while simultaneously benefiting from the same level of comfort and convenience as us.[2] They have TVs. They have malls. They travel regularly around the city, the country, and the continent. Europeans have fancy appliances, nifty electronic gadgets, and high-quality clothing that they use to express themselves, not merely to cover up. They work in offices. Their homes are bright, warm, and plumbed and do not house an entire extended family in one room. If you look at the big picture—the wealth we have, the services we expect, the products we use, and the luxuries we have access to—Europeans and Americans lead very similar lives.

The average European, however, uses 50 percent less energy than the average American.[3] How do Europeans do that? It's not because they are magic, and it's not because they're somehow just that much more virtuous than we are. Just as Americans don't get up every day plotting to waste energy, Europeans don't hop out of bed flush with plans to save energy. Frankly, Europeans waste energy, too. They simply waste less of it.

Europeans live more energy-efficient lives not because they are better people than Americans are, but because their lives and social norms have been structured around very different pressures. Here is a newsflash: The European continent is significantly smaller than the continental United States. It's also been developed and carved into cities for a much longer amount of time. Those differences are rather obvious, but they're important. Because Europe is smaller and has been developed longer, there is less land available, and it is more expensive. That, in turn, played a role in shaping the density of cities, which affected car ownership. The availability and cost of land forced Europeans to design shared systems—cities, transportation networks, homes, and offices—that just happened to be energy efficient.

Americans weren't bound by the same constraints as Europeans, and U.S. history is reflected in the systems we built and the energy we use. During the course of the twentieth century, Americans used our continent's largely untapped resources—water, coal, oil, wood, metal, and, most important, land—to create our convenient and comfortable modern way of living. We did it in large, sprawling cities, spread around a large, sprawling continent. Had Europeans been in our shoes, it's likely that they would be using every bit as much energy as we do today. At the time, each continent's different methods of growth made sense. One way of developing wasn't inherently better than the other, and they both got the job done.

The trouble is, in a world threatened by climate change and perilously dependent on one type of energy, the way we Americans built our world has come back to bite everyone square on the rear. At a time when wasting energy can no longer be shrugged off, we find ourselves stuck with systems that are prone to waste, simply because no one had to think too much about energy efficiency when the systems were being built.

• • •

Today, we live in metro areas that are difficult to navigate unless we drive our own cars, we work in buildings that are dark and uncomfortable unless we use artificial light and central heating, and we come home to houses that waste energy in big and small ways—some that are completely incomprehensible to us and others that we see but don't think we can do anything about. We can make our houses more energy efficient. We can screw in some new lightbulbs, pop on some less-leaky windows, or maybe swap the old refrigerator for a shiny new one. That approach does work. It will reduce energy use. But it's not systemic change. If you build a house with energy efficiency in mind, to begin with, then you can get big energy-use reductions for less hassle.

This is what the Passive House design method is all about. It's what makes Bernice Dallas's house different from my house. In Europe, where most of the research on Passive Houses has been done, studies have found that Passive Houses use as much as 60 percent less energy than standard homes.[4] Passive House design isn't a legal requirement anywhere. In Europe, it's a legally defined but voluntarily applied standard. In the United States, it's a voluntary certification process. Yet either way, in order to call your house a Passive House, you first have to hit some very stringent energy goals. For all of the comforts and conveniences of home—heating, air-conditioning, hot water, and lighting—a Passive House can't use more than the equivalent of 11.2 kilowatt hours of electricity per square foot, per year. That ain't much. An average detached home in the Midwest uses twice that amount.[5] Passive House is like a serious, rear-end-kicking diet—the kind of regimen that forces you to spend your time running on a treadmill while eating freeze-dried carrot sticks. Only, in this case, the diet isn't painful. If energy services are frozen Little Debbie Zebra Cakes, the Passive House still gets to eat all it wants. It's just that every cake now contains far fewer calories. But that doesn't mean that a Passive House has to *look* particularly different.

This fact took me a bit by surprise. Before I met Dallas and visited her home in August 2010, the only Passive Houses I'd seen were clearly interested in making avant-garde statements. Although there are tens of thousands of Passive Houses in Europe, fewer than twenty exist in the United States. Because Passive Houses cost more money to build, most of the American examples were made for wealthy home-owners with high-design tastes.[6] That's just fine, if you like houses with flat roofs and exposed concrete walls, loft-style living spaces, and cool, detached modernist styling, but those aesthetics aren't for everybody.

Earlier that same summer, I'd gone on a tour of a Passive House that was for sale in Kansas City. That house had stood out in its neighborhood, a towering alabaster box on a street full of decay-ing Victorians and dumpy mid-century contractor specials. While I was there, a family that lived nearby had come over to see what was inside that gleaming edifice. They were clearly impressed, but the same way you're impressed by a museum—a very pretty museum that you nevertheless find a bit silly. The mom took one look at the master suite, delicately hovering like an open tree stand with a view straight down into the other two bedrooms and the living room, and she laughed.

Bernice Dallas's house isn't like that. It sits at the intersection of two streets that form a T near downtown Urbana. The neighboring houses are predominately boxy, four-square cottages from the sixties and the seventies. There's a lot of scallop trim and tidy chain-link fences surrounding well-kept front yards. Dallas's house is bigger than the others, but it's not out of place in this setting. Her house is just a simple, peak-roofed rectangle, with butter-colored lap siding on the first floor and a solid tan finish above. The windows that face the street are small and square, about the size that you'd normally see in a bathroom. Around back, on the south side of the house, the windows look more normal—even larger than average. That's your only clue that there's something funny going on here.

Dallas is a tiny African American woman. To be fair, I'm almost six feet tall, so my gauge of what constitutes short is often out of whack. When Dallas opened the door, though, I had to actively tilt my head downward to look into her eyes. She greeted us looking very much the active mom on the go: track shoes and jean capris contrasted with a lace-trimmed eggplant-colored blouse; her tight-clipped hair offset by dainty silver earrings and a necklace. This is the first house Dallas has owned, and she'd been in it for only a little more than a year when I visited. She led the tour, beaming. Occasionally, while the Passive House architects who designed the place were talking about its impressive features, I'd catch her looking at the room, with a justifiably smug smile that said, "Yup, and it's all mine."

She didn't set out to buy a sustainable house. Dallas's home was built by the Passive House Institute United States, as part of an effort to prove that the houses—which, in the United States, are normally the domain of upper-income folks who've hired fancy private architects—could be built for a price that would fit the budgets of working-class and middle-class families. Dallas stumbled across it during an open house. Inside the front door, the main part of the house is one large L-shaped room. The kitchen is in the bend, to the right, and the living room is spread out straight ahead. The floors are warm brown concrete, cut into big squares that look like stone tiles. There's a little nook, where she keeps her TV. The living room features a huge picture window that looks out onto the sprawling backyard.

Dallas can't quite explain why, exactly, she chose this house. It was simply love at first sight. She walked in the door and felt, down to her bones, that this was going to be the first house she ever owned herself. "I just knew it was mine, you know? It was just one of those things," she told me.

In general, the house looks like a modest, cozy tract home, but there are differences. I mentioned the undersize windows on the north side of the house. The polished brown concrete floor is also unusual for a home in the United States. Once you're inside, you can see that all of the doors and the windows are set into foot-deep pockets, as if somebody planned for the house to be full of window seats. All of these differences are the features of Passive House aesthetics that you can't change. You'll find them in almost every Passive House out there, from the fancy, gleaming tower in Kansas City to Bernice Dallas's modest home in Urbana. These physical details are central to how the house works.

Passive Houses are designed to maximize the amount of sunlight and heat that can get in during the cold months, to be sealed airtight, and to bulk up the mass of the structure, overall. They're also super-insulated—four times more exterior wall insulation than an average American house, which explains those thick window sills. The north windows on Dallas's house are small, partly to reduce the amount of heat from the sun that gets into the house in the summer, and partly because Passive Houses use windows that are different from the ones we're used to. At my house, which was built in the 1920s, each window has one layer of glass. Newer windows usually have two layers, which helps insulate the house a little better. Passive Houses use windows with three layers of glass. These windows are more expensive than double- or single-paned windows, so, to build a Passive House that somebody like Dallas could afford, the Passive House Institute cut down the cost by shrinking the window size.

It is a little darker in Dallas's house than it is in mine, but the result is a building that holds its own temperature—whether hot or cold—without having to use much energy. Simply burning a single candle or baking a batch of cookies is enough to keep the entire 1,450-square-foot, four-bedroom house comfortable in the fall and the spring. Dallas stays cool in the summer and warm for much of the winter using only a small air-to-air heat pump.

This system looks like a little room-size air conditioner, mounted on a wall in the stairwell, and it works a lot like your refrigerator. Basically, refrigerators don't make cold, they remove heat. Your fridge is simply a sealed box with most of the heat pumped out of it. Both your refrigerator and Dallas's heat pump work by trapping heat in a liquid, then making that liquid release the stored heat outside. Her heat pump can also run backward, bringing heat from the outside in, as long as the outside temperature stays above freezing. When the weather gets really cold, she turns on electric baseboard heaters. So the house does get *some* help in maintaining a comfortable temperature, but this setup uses a lot less energy. Over the course of a year, Dallas's house averaged only 8.46 kilowatt hours of energy per square foot.[7]

If Passive Houses are so great, why aren't there more of them in this country? Because they do cost more to build. It's sort of like driving a Prius. You spend more up front, betting that the cost of energy will keep rising and you'll save money in the long term.

Dallas does save money on her utility bills, but the Passive House Institute, which built her house, says the building costs 10 percent more to build than a comparable traditional house.[8] She bought it for $120,000 in May 2009, about $10,000 less than median home value in Urbana at the time.[9] Yet that was possible only because the city of Urbana donated the lot the house was built on, and other donors helped supply construction materials.[10]

The design of a Passive House also results in a few weird side effects. For instance, Dallas's house has a washer and a dryer. They're upstairs, stacked one on top of the other in a hall closet between the bathroom and the bedroom that she uses for the foster kids who sometimes stay with her and her son. Both units are small, about the size of what you'd see packed into a small apartment, rather than in a four-bedroom detached house. The washer is just like any other, but the dryer is different. Passive Houses avoid what are known as "thermal bridges"—really just anything that cuts through the exterior wall, leaving a fast path for heat to escape in the winter or infiltrate in the summer. You'd be surprised how many of these bridges exist in an average home, and they're a big part of why your house feels chilly in the winter, even with the heat on.

A normal dryer vent is a thermal bridge. The machine runs hot air over damp clothes and dumps the resulting moist, warm air out the vent that's cut into the side of your house. To get around that necessity, Dallas uses a condensing dryer, which recycles the warm air, using a little air from inside the house to trigger condensation, similar to when it rains. The water gets pumped away with wastewater from the washing machine. The now mostly dry air gets reheated and used again. Generally, it works fine, unless Bernice is trying to dry something big, such as a heavy quilt. That kind of load might need to be run through twice or hung up after it comes out of the dryer.

Having such a tightly sealed house also seems as if it would be a problem, in and of itself. In fact, that's usually the first question Americans ask about Passive Houses: "What about the radon?" We're well aware that a house that's impervious to airflow will also trap the radioactive gas that naturally seeps into basements in some parts of the country, but this isn't as big of an issue as you might think. Passive Houses aren't stagnant pools of incarcerated air. In fact, they're better ventilated than most traditional houses. How does that work? Passive Houses bring in a ringer, in the form of mechanical ventilation. One of the very few holes punched through the house is used to draw in and circulate fresh air. Stale air, as well as the smelly stuff from kitchens and bathrooms, is sucked out. As the mechanical ventilation system exhales, it absorbs heat from the outgoing air and transfers that heat to the incoming side—making sure that bringing in fresh air in the winter doesn't mean letting in the cold. The ventilator also controls the humidity, preventing the house from getting too dry in the winter or too sticky in the summer.

The Passive House is meant to handle the job of energy efficiency on its own, without residents having to do much backseat driving—hence the name. But there is a bit of a learning curve. In a house that generally keeps itself cool and warm with the seasons, there are no thermostats, but there are control panels for the ventilation system. This can lead to confusion when daily life in the Passive House crosses mental wires with behaviors learned over years of living in traditional buildings. During their first winter in the house, Dallas found her son trying to turn up the ventilator as if it were a temperature setting for a furnace.[11] This is understandable but is about as useful as trying to speed up your car with the radio tuner.

I didn't meet Dallas's son. He was visiting his dad the day I toured Dallas's house, but, like most ten-year-old kids, he left a pretty solid presence even when incorporeal. There was laundry on the bed in his upstairs room, and his wide Passive-House window ledge was crammed with a stack of books, a jumble of small plastic objects, and a baseball hat. It reminded me of the way my own childhood bedroom looked, when I spent summers away from home with *my* dad. Kids leave their fingerprints on household energy use, too.

I'd arrived at Dallas's house with two big tests of its success in mind: first, could it still feel like an American Dream Home to someone who wasn't necessarily dreaming about eco-living, and, second, did it actually make a dent in Dallas's bills? The house passed both tests, but I thought Dallas's answer to the second question contained some tingly little details, hinting at a trouble that haunts energy efficiency like a rattling ghost.

Her bills had indeed gone way down. In her old apartment—much smaller and with fewer bedrooms—it hadn't been unusual for electricity bills to hit $210 a month. In the Passive House, the highest they'd gotten was $164. That, she told me, was in the dead of winter, with her godson visiting—who brought along his own TV—and with both boys spending tons of time on the computer and playing Xbox.

I have a point here, and it is not that tweens are inherently bad for the environment. No, the issue is this: Passive House design—and every other method we have of standardizing energy-efficient building design—is based on reducing the amount of energy used by the shell of a building: the heating, the lighting, the conveniences that come built into the structure, helping to create the environments where we live and work. If you combine all of the buildings in our lives—from houses and apartments to office complexes and grocery stores—they account for 49 percent of all of the energy used in the entire United States.[12] Passive House standards aren't the only way to reduce energy use in buildings. LEED, or Leadership in Energy and Environmental Design, a U.S. building standard, will do that, too. There's even an Energy Star certification for energy-efficient houses, just like the Energy Star labels that show up on appliances. Whatever standard you decide to judge a building against, though, what it won't address are all of the ways individual people use energy after they've taken up residence inside the shell.

Building codes can control only how the shell of a building works. That slice of the U.S. energy pie? It includes the shell—and everything that everyone who lives and works inside those buildings plugs into the wall outlets: computers, appliances, and every little techie-tacky gadget you ever found yourself mindlessly stroking in the aisle at Best Buy. Fifty years ago, this "plug load" factor wasn't too big a deal. Today, it is an entity unto itself.

"We can go back and look at the energy codes over the last twenty years," said Kent Peterson, the vice president and chief engineer at P2S Engineering and a former president of the American Society of Heating, Refrigerating, and Air-Conditioning Engineers. "Codes today mandate 35 percent less energy use in a building than codes did in 1975, but when we look at the actual buildings being built, the average energy use per square foot is the same as it was back then."[13]

Between 1978 and 2005, the shells of American homes became a lot more energy efficient. Compared to the houses of the polyester pantsuit generation, today's American homes are likely to have far more insulation in the walls, double-paned windows instead of single-paned, heaters and boilers that use less energy, and compact fluorescent lightbulbs. All of those changes, combined, have led to a 31 percent reduction in per-household energy use, and that's great.[14] We all deserve a hearty pat on the back for such an impressive achievement.

The trouble is, we haven't reduced the amount of energy used by the housing *sector*—a figure that includes plug loads—by nearly as much as we've reduced the amount of energy used by our houses themselves. Although the energy used per household plummeted, the total annual energy used by the U.S. housing sector every year only stumbled a bit, dropping from 10.58 quadrillion British thermal units in 1978 to 10.55 in 2005.[15]

It is very clear that plug load is to blame for this disparity. During that same time period—as houses became more energy efficient and even while government programs such as Energy Star promoted more energy-efficient appliances and gadgets—the energy use attributable to home appliances and electronics nearly doubled. In 1978, we spent 1.77 quadrillion BTUs of energy a year powering the modern devices we plug in. In 2005, that number had jumped to 3.25 quadrillion BTUs a year.

When Americans started to build houses that were more energy efficient, we were making personal choices that, multiplied by millions, added up to serious reductions in energy use. Yet along the way, we made other choices, too. If personal choices can help make this nation more sustainable, they can also make it less so.

This is a bit startling, but it shouldn't be a surprise. The energy-efficiency gains and losses we've seen since the late 1970s are related to problems that researchers have argued about for decades. In fact, the first person to rain on the energy-efficiency parade was a fellow named William Stanley Jevons. In 1865, England was a coal-powered giant. It was the world's largest economy, and everything it did depended on coal. Coal ran the factories and the trains. It heated homes and cooked food. Little English children probably ate

Coalios for breakfast. Yet already, some people were starting to think that England might not have infinite supplies of coal, and they were worried about what might happen if the all-important energy source ran out. The generally accepted solution: improved technology that would make more efficient use of coal.

Jevons is the guy who made the inconveniently awkward observation that an improved, more-efficient model of the coal-fired steam engine wasn't actually reducing coal consumption the way everyone thought it would. In fact, the new engine simply allowed people to do more work with the same amount of coal, which made coal cheaper—which inspired people to burn *more* of it.

Today, a Jevons paradox is what happens if you invent some new piece of fuel-efficient technology that ironically ends up prompting people to use even more fuel than they'd used before. For instance, what if you made a car so fuel efficient that the price of gas became less of a deterrent and people drove more than ever, racking up even more total gallons burned than they had in their old, inefficient cars? That's a simple way of explaining how a Jevons paradox might happen, but it doesn't have to be that direct. Instead, people might take the money they saved on gasoline and spend it on a plane flight or a hot tub—or on hiring new employees who can then afford to burn more gasoline themselves.

That sounds damning for energy efficiency, but there's a lot of debate over whether a full-on, pooch-screwing Jevons paradox is really all that common. Some experts say it's simply obvious. When there's more of any resource available, we use it. *Some* people might look at that windfall and see a moral imperative not to consume—but for every person well-off enough to make that choice, there are several others somewhere who would rather be more comfortable and have a life that's more convenient and clean.[16] Those people will take advantage of a drop in demand and the corresponding drop in prices in order to get the lives they want. All of the gains made in energy efficiency are, inevitably, completely counteracted by the energy associated with increased production, travel, or standard of living. It's common sense.

Yet if there's one big lesson I've picked up from being a science journalist, it's this: just because something sounds like common sense doesn't mean you can assume it will match carefully measured reality. That's essentially the argument of the opposing researchers in this debate, who say that the evidence for energy efficiency's demise has been greatly exaggerated. For one thing, the Jevons paradox—this tendency for energy-efficiency improvement to boomerang back into increased energy use—is actually a *feature* of energy efficiency, not merely a potential bug. The Jevons paradox certainly is frustrating if you're concerned about reducing fossil fuel use or combating climate change. On the other hand, though, it's also the very mechanism that allows our economy to grow so successfully. Even if we're not seeing any benefit at all from energy efficiency in the form of lowered emissions, we are seeing economic benefits as companies and families are able to invest and improve themselves by saving money on energy. In fact, pretty much everybody agrees on this. What's being argued over isn't the utility of energy-efficiency improvements—it's whether energy-efficiency improvements can actually do more than simply make us richer.[17]

Certain economists argue that there are other benefits to energy efficiency. After all, the logic of the Jevons paradox is based on the idea that markets and people are pretty strictly rational, and that doesn't necessarily bear out. The real world is more complicated. Gains in efficiency aren't the only factor that affects the cost of our energy, they say, and the cost of energy isn't the only issue that affects our decisions about what we buy or how we live. In practice, they say, a Jevons paradox isn't as inevitable as it may seem. Instead, you're much more likely to get something called a "rebound effect." You can think of the rebound effect as an incomplete Jevons paradox— *some part* of the energy you've saved through efficiency is lost again to increased consumption, but, overall, you've still reduced energy use.[18] You get the economic benefits and you get an environmental benefit, only not as big of an environmental benefit as you might have liked. In fact, that's exactly what we saw in the way that energy use in American homes changed between 1978 and 2005. Overall, energy use did go down; it simply didn't go down as much as it would have if plug loads hadn't increased so much.

At the level of *direct* rebound effects—where the energy-efficiency gains and energy-consumption losses happen in the same sector of the economy—there's good evidence that these researchers are right. For instance, the fuel efficiency of cars increased between 1966 and 2001, and there was a rebound effect, as Americans drove more because it cost less to drive every mile. Yet the rebound effect didn't completely undermine the total energy use reduction. Over the long term, energy use rebounded 22 percent—that is, for every reduction in fuel use caused by low gas mileage, 22 percent of the reduction was lost to a corresponding increase in miles traveled.[19] This isn't stellar news for the environment. But it's also not enough of a rebound to make fuel efficiency standards environmentally pointless.

Zoom the picture out, though, and everything goes foggy. That's because rebound effects and Jevons paradoxes don't have to be direct one-to-one situations, where cars travel more because they've become more fuel efficient. They can be indirect as well—a more energy-efficient house saves you money that you spend on driving more. They can also be economy-wide, at which point the issue gets really confusing.

I'll come back to this a bit later, but, suffice to say, there isn't a clear answer. Here's what we do know. Economists have studied how the Jevons paradox and the rebound effect play out in real life. Some studies that looked at energy efficiency from the regional or national level have suggested that the Jevons paradox isn't inevitable—but rebound might be. It's also not clear whether these studies reflect what happens on a global scale, where the environmental impact of carbon emissions and climate change happens.[20]

Other economists have built computer models that show Jevons paradoxes occurring as a matter of course, but they're based on some heavily questioned assumptions about how consumers behave. Overall, the state of the research is unsatisfyingly complex. This is usually the point where scientific debate gives way to a bunch of people sitting around and arguing about their personal beliefs and economic philosophies—it's like a freshman-year college dorm, but everyone has a better résumé.[21]

I can't give you a hard answer on the Jevons paradox, because there isn't one. That said, the rebound effect is very real, and it truly does seem to be significant. The important lesson: if we want our energy use in 2030 to be about the same as our energy use today, meeting that goal will involve more than simply reducing fossil fuel energy use by 20 quadrillion BTUs during the next twenty years. In fact, we'll probably need to save a good bit more than that, because we're likely to see some of our energy savings head out the door on the back of the rebound effect.

....

CHAPTER FOUR

THE EMERALD CITY

The municipal airport outside Taylor, Texas, is like any other. Minding the gap between the farmland and the edge of town, it has a long, straight asphalt runway, a couple of arched hangars, and apparently enough traffic to warrant its own Tex-Mex bar and grill, Best Western, *and* car rental franchise. If you follow Airport Road around the corner and past the pad sites, though, things start to look a little strange, as in an eight-foot-high, spike-topped fence surrounding what appears to be a perfectly nonthreatening office complex.

Inside that intimidating barrier, however, they don't exactly seem to be sweating an imminent guerrilla attack. The buildings are noticeably sturdy, but they're also noticeably trendy—artfully placed windows, orange paint, sleek squares and rectangles stacked together into architectural sculpture. The sidewalk to the glass-walled entry is lined with flowering trees, metal path-lights that appear to be stolen from Starfleet Command, and a series of pug-size shrubs trimmed into little domes. Looking out from the front door, here's the view: carefully maintained formal garden; scary, scary security fence; Cessna touching down; Texas high plains spreading out into nothingness. Clearly, something is going on here. The only real surprise is that this place is actually even a little more important than its exterior implies.

Behind that deceptively jaunty, pumpkin-colored paint lies the beating heart of Texas's electric infrastructure—one of the three segments of America's electric grid. Power plants generate electricity. They are obvious and important and easy to spot. (Too easy to spot, some might argue.) Yet without this building, all of the electricity generators in Texas would be completely incapable of working together. A lot has changed in the 130 years since H. J. Rogers and Thomas Edison built the first electric grids. Those grids were like islands, isolated systems that weren't connected to one another at all. They had to be self-sufficient. If demand for electricity exceeded production, people went without. Today, however, the grid is more like a continent. No city stands alone. Every place is linked, in some way, to everywhere else.

This means that every single light switch is really part of a collective—joined to a network of wires, switches, and outlets running through a building. Look out the window, and you can see the wires that tie that little network into an even bigger system. Power lines string together houses, offices, and industrial buildings like a strand of Christmas lights—miles and miles and miles' worth of glowing, buzzing electricity demand, all feeding off the same generators. When one Christmas light burns out, it affects all of the others in the chain, and the same basic principle applies here. Every light that's turned on, every air conditioner that's cranked up, every busy day at the factory have an impact on one another and on the system. Ditto with the generators. Problems at one power plant affect what happens at your house and at a different power plant in another state. There are hundreds of thousands of points along the line where things can go wrong. In fact, things go wrong all the time. Remember, energy is built around systems, and those systems are imperfect. Some of the flaws aren't a big deal. Others require careful, constant management to keep the system from imploding. Yet either way, you, the consumer, don't see what's wrong. All you see is what happens at your link in the chain. All you know is that when you flip a switch, you can trust that a light will shine.

There's a curtain between the reliable electricity service you experience and all of the work that goes into making sure it *stays* reliable. From our side—the customer's view—everything that happens behind the curtain may as well be magic, guided by the hand of a wizard. And the compound in Taylor, Texas, nestled into its little triangle between the airport and the Mas Fajitas? That's the Emerald City. Or, at least, one of them. The Taylor site is the control center for the Electric Reliability Council of Texas, or ERCOT. There are similar places scattered all across the country. Thanks to their rather large role in keeping our collective lights on, they're all pretty heavily locked down—I was under more security here than at some military bases I've visited.

It wasn't always that way. Behind the gleaming, modernist building I saw when I arrived at ERCOT, there's a smaller, blue, metal-clad rectangle—like a shed or a pole barn—connected to its fancy younger sibling by a ligament of hallway. This was the old control center. Modest and utilitarian, it once sat out in the fields near Taylor without so much as an intimidating fence for protection. September 11 changed the level of security expected at facilities such as ERCOT's, but it also changed the character. That old tin block feels like the kind of place where behind-the-scenes maintenance is meant to happen. It looks as if you're supposed to ignore it—the equivalent of the way stagehands at a play dress all in black. They're a part of the show, and you know it wouldn't run without them, but at the same time their outfits send a message—"Pretend you don't see this. It's not something you have to care about."

The new face of ERCOT—with that attention-grabbing architecture, the incongruously urbane landscaping, and the obvious security perimeter—represents more than just a simple response to the threat of terrorism. As you shift your focus from ERCOT's old building to its new one, you're seeing a reflection of the growing recognition of the work that's done here. The wizards have always been a part of the electric system. They've always been important. As we look toward alternative ways of generating electricity, however, and as Americans become increasingly aware of energy in general, the curtain between our world and this one has begun to lift.

The public can no longer afford to ignore what happens here. In fact, if we want our country to be less dependent on fossil fuels, then we have to pay a lot of attention to electric grid control centers everywhere. These are the places where the old dirty technology and the new sustainable technology meet. These are the people who force those very different systems to play nice together. That's not an easy job. Alternative energy can grow only as fast as the wizards can incorporate it into the existing mix. If their alchemy doesn't work, then the electric system fails.

Think back to that 94.6 quadrillion BTUs we used in 2009. Thanks to the rebound effect, it's going to be difficult to keep that number from continuing to rise, though we'll look at some potential solutions later. Meanwhile, the same problems that make energy efficiency so important, despite its complications—climate change, peak oil, rising prices for fossil fuel energy—make low-carbon energy sources important, too. Yet how much we can actually increase our dependence on energy sources such as the wind and the sun hinges on more than how quickly we can build windmills. As with energy efficiency, energy generation is more complicated than that.

Joel Mickey has worked behind the curtain for twenty-five years, controlling the flow of electricity first for the Houston Light and Power utility company and now for ERCOT, where he's the director of market operating systems. He was my ticket inside this seldom-seen world and my guide to understanding what it's really like to control the grid. Mickey is a well-preserved, middle-aged white guy: good skin with a few smile-related wrinkles; sandy-blond hair, only slightly receding. The day I arrived, he was sporting the French-blue, cuffed, button-up shirt that I've always thought of as the unofficial uniform of American upper management. I point this out because although "wizard" is a nice shorthand for describing what guys like Mickey do, it's not a very good metaphor for explaining who they are. Joel Mickey is a leader of wizards, but Joel Mickey is not your Dungeon Master.

Like a lot of controllers, he worked his way up the pole, literally, starting out as an eighteen-year-old lineman—one of the people who show up on your block whenever a rogue tree branch takes out an electric wire. On Mickey's desk at ERCOT, there's a black-and-white photo of a very young kid in a hard hat, with a leather harness cinched around his hips. Linemen are a noticeable part of the electric system, but, at least when Mickey started working, they weren't considered terribly special. Along with maintenance workers at substations and power plant operators, entry-level jobs such as this were lumped together under one bad pun—"Plant Life," the single-celled algae at the bottom of a Great Chain of Being, which regarded the wizards of system control as the epitome of creation. It was possible to evolve your way up the chain, but it wasn't easy.

To become a system controller, Mickey had to vie against a hundred-odd applicants for one single job. His first year, he mostly just traveled from place to place throughout the utility's territory, learning a controller's craft by watching what the experienced guys did. In fact, Mickey didn't get to touch much of anything for the first *five* years. It was an almost-medieval apprenticeship, designed to produce a feudal lord of the electric grid, who would be all-knowing and always right. That last part was especially important. Back then, each utility company generated its own power, owned its own lines, and controlled its own chunk of the grid, which was still, at that point, mostly walled off from other chunks. A system controller had to make sure there was enough generation to meet demand, but he was also in charge of turning individual power lines on and off for maintenance. At a big utility such as Houston Light and Power, that could mean fifteen or twenty lines in flux during the course of a single day. The controllers had to keep electricity flowing to customers, make sure certain lines were deactivated and reactivated at the right times, and do both of those jobs while simultaneously managing everything else going on in the system. It was a lot like being an air traffic controller, Mickey says. There were lives in his hands.

"A thunderstorm would come through, and a lot of the distribution circuits would trip off from the weather," he says. "And we had to make decisions on closing the connection back down or not. I mean, occasionally, those lines go down in someone's backyard and a kid goes out to play. You know, you always have that in the back of your head while you're just pushing these little buttons. It's scary sometimes."

The job comes with a little less pressure now, and thus less of a god complex. In Texas, what was once a utility monopoly has been chopped up into three parts—power providers that generate electricity, utility companies that distribute it through local networks, and an independent system operator that coordinates the movement of electricity over long distances. ERCOT is the independent system operator. Its controllers help set the prices utility companies pay power providers. They keep the river of electrons flowing at a constant depth and speed. They also make sure that power providers and utility companies know what the other is doing and avoid accidentally shutting the lights off two counties away. In the modern world, though, system controllers can't directly kill anybody at the push of a button—a fact that has drastically improved Mickey's on-the-job stress level.

System controllers are no longer absolute monarchs, and they no longer consist only of Plant Life that evolved to be the best of the best. Today, Mickey says, a new hire is just as likely to be an electrical engineer, fresh out of college. Mickey has a new nickname for guys like himself. They're the DOUGs: Dumb Old Utility Guys.

Of course, as the people who could black out an entire state if they're not good at their jobs, even the DOUGs still think pretty highly of themselves. Mostly men, the system controllers I met were all dressed in some variation of business casual, just a little more casual than what Mickey wore. There were a lot of plaid shirts, a lot of rumpled, pleated khakis, and each ensemble was finished off with a white laminated photo ID card, hung on a lanyard. When I talk about the wizards, don't let your mind jump to hooded robes, mystical minds, and long, pointy goatees. Instead, imagine an elite fighting force that's been decked out for a weekend business conference at the Dallas Sheraton.

It's the little ID cards that really made ERCOT look like a sea of conventioneers. Those cards are also part of the sense of importance that surrounds everything at the site. Everybody wears a card—from the system controllers down to the secretaries. I got one to pin to my shirt when I came in. More than simple name badges, they are passports. Without a card—without the *right* card, in fact—there was no way to move beyond the lobby. Mine was just a dummy, printed with the word "Guest." I went nowhere but for the grace of Joel Mickey and his real, authorized card. From the lobby to Mickey's office and from there through a tour of the facilities, every door we encountered was locked. Offices, training rooms, even perfectly boring hallways—they all required the swipe of a card to enter. The closer we got to the control room itself, the more persnickety the security became. It took two swipes of Mickey's card just to enter the antechamber full of cubicles where system controllers do their paperwork and eat their lunches. Even if controllers weren't already inclined toward a bit of personal mythologizing, it would be hard to pass through all of that, every day, and not think of yourself as kind of a big deal.

Yet the last barrier was the most impressive. From the brightly lit cubicle space, I could get a glimpse of the control room, dark and more than a little foreboding, through a glass-walled cell that separated the two. The door into the cell opened with Mickey's pass card. The door out of it required a bit more interaction. To the left and the right of that second door were shiny silver pillars, about waist-high. Each was topped with a narrow strip of glowing light, like a blue-eyed Cylon sentry. To open the door, Mickey slid his finger over a biometric reader, then we walked between the blue lights—he and I and the public relations woman traveling with us. The sentries recorded the number of people who came in, tethered, as it were, to Mickey's fingerprint. He'd have to scan his finger again to get back out. If his group left with one person short, the sentries would sound an alarm.

All of that security prepared me to be impressed, but the actual control room was overwhelming. When I go back and listen to the audio recordings I made, I can tell when we stepped into the control room, because that's the point where everybody stopped talking and started whispering. It has that effect on people. Cavernous, dimly lit, and cold, it felt full of ritual significance, almost holy.

From where we entered, the opposite wall was at least two stories tall and stretched the width of a large movie theater—and it was covered in video screens. There were eight of them, each showing something different: a map, a graph, or long lines of black and red numbers arranged on a spreadsheet. On either side of that looming video wall, closer to eye level, was an extra-large, flat-screen television, silently playing the news. On the far right, a stack of what looked like digital scoreboards from a high school gymnasium ticked up and down and up and down—running back and forth over the decimal fractions around either side of 60. Spread out beneath all of that were the system controllers—the wizards themselves. There were seven of them, and they all sat at semicircular desks, each man surrounded by squadrons of eight or ten computer monitors. If this were a sci-fi novel, the wizards might easily be mistaken for the chinos-bedecked acolytes of some strange Windows-based religion.

They certainly spend enough time here to appear seriously devoted. Each shift lasts for twelve hours. A controller gets bathroom breaks, of course. Occasionally, he'll wander back out into the antechamber, blinking under the bright fluorescent lamps, and have himself a bite to eat—maybe hunted out of the vending machines that flanked a hall near the bathroom or gathered from the communal trays of cookies, cheese, and fruit that sat along the top of a filing cabinet on the day I visited. That meal might be at noon, or it might be at two in the morning. The desks in the control room are always filled, unless the staff is working out of ERCOT's other control center. Either way, the work is always being done. Twenty-four hours a day, seven days a week. People spend Christmas Eve in this place. They ring in the New Year under the glow of the video screens. When that crew goes home—to sleep and spend a day off—there's another ready to walk through security and take their places at the desks.

That makes the experience sound dull. It can appear that way, too—to somebody like me, who didn't know what all of the numbers meant or what the graphs and charts were showing. A trained eye, such as Joel Mickey's, can see the chaos that is just barely contained. The job of a controller cycles between periods when everything is relatively calm and times when a hundred things are going wrong all at once. I saw the ERCOT control room at a relatively low-key point, but even then, Mickey said, the wizards who sat casually sipping coffee or soda at their desks were simultaneously putting out lots of small fires. There is no bell, no flashing light to tell controllers when a problem needs fixing. If such an alarm existed, Mickey told me, it would be ringing so often that the warning would pretty much lose all meaning.

That's because the grid—that network of wires connecting the people who make electricity to the people who use it—is surprisingly fragile. Remember that the river of electrons has to move at a constant speed. It must be a constant depth. Imagine a channel of water, running in a loop. Every power plant is like a spigot, filling the channel with water. Every electricity consumer—from your house to a factory to a casino—is a little drain, sucking water away. Controllers are in charge of making sure that the amount of water dumped into the channel is equal to the amount of water being pumped out of it. Back in Appleton, grid controllers such as A. C. Langstadt watched a lightbulb to monitor the state of the system. Modern controllers have their high-tech temple. Yet either way, the job is the same—keep the system balanced. Because if balance isn't maintained, bad things happen. For instance, say a bunch of drains open at once, and there's suddenly a lot more water going out than there is coming in. If that happens, you'll end up in the shallows, and some drains will run dry. Or, consider the flip side of that—only a few drains are open, but the taps are running at full bore. Eventually, the water level will creep too high. The overwhelmed drains will back up, and the flood will spill over the edges of the channel itself. In the real world, both of these scenarios—too much demand for electricity or too much supply— lead to the same place: Blackout City.

The gymnasium scoreboards I saw in the ERCOT control room keep track of the balance between supply and demand. Controllers call that measurement the grid "frequency."[1] I told you that the numbers on those displays would climb and then fall and climb and fall—always hovering around 60. That's because 60 hertz is the grid frequency. Or, at least, that's what the grid frequency is supposed to be. The fact that it never stays at exactly 60.00 for very long should tell you everything you need to know about why controllers have to be on the job all of the time.

The rest of the equipment in the control room is, in some way, all related back to that 60 hertz. The charts are used to keep track of trends in demand over days and weeks and how well various power plants are functioning. The spreadsheets document imme- diate demand and supply at various locations all around the state. The maps show damaged power lines and trace weather patterns, both of which can have an impact on the frequency. The controllers really control only the supply side—they have their hands on the spigot, while the drains function independently, for the most part. Yet if demand increases, they can pump up supply to meet it, and if demand falls, they can cut supply back. A good chunk of the job is actually predictive—looking at demand trends, weather conditions, and historical patterns and using all of that information to guess how much supply will be needed in the next day, the next hour, the next minute. This is what happens all the time, every day, all over the country. All of it works together so that on your side of the curtain, a light can come on when you flip a switch.

When I first started thinking about the supportive skeleton of America's energy future, I had a lot of trouble figuring out where to focus. The more research I did, the more I felt as if I'd been backed into a corner by a growing horde of sugar-besotted kindergartners, all talking over one another, trying to get my attention. The problem: there's really more than one energy infrastructure. From electricity to liquid fuels to public transportation systems—all of the various infrastructures are important. Yet I kept coming back to the wizards behind the electric curtain.

To explain why, first I have to tell you about my favorite way to look at energy and emissions data. Every year, the Energy Information Administration (EIA) releases reports that explain how much energy Americans are using, where we get that energy from, what we use it to do, and how much emissions we produce in the process.[2] These reports are important, but they're also dense and not much fun to read. So, the EIA and other groups also take those numbers and convert them into something visual. Suddenly, the rows and the columns of a very boring spreadsheet take on shape and weight, as though a flat man plugged his nose, drew in a breath, and inflated into the third dimension. It can be really tough to understand the big picture of energy—to think about multiple uses and sources for it and put both of those factors into some kind of emissions context—but these charts help you figure it out. When you look at them, you notice what makes electricity different.

For instance, in 2008, the World Resources Institute turned EIA data on greenhouse gas emissions from 1990 through 2003 into a colorful and easy-to-read flowchart.[3] This image starts out looking at those broad, technical categories of energy use we've already talked about, such as "transportation" and "industry," and shows how much each one contributes to our national emissions footprint. Then each category is teased apart and broken down, to show something closer to the way you and I think about energy. Transportation splits into road transportation, air travel, rail, and ships. We see that the fuel being burned directly at industrial factories is being used to make steel, chemicals, paper, and food. Finally, these divided streams reconverge to show various types of greenhouse gas emissions. Working backward, you can see that carbon dioxide accounts for 85 percent of our total national emissions, and that road transportation contributes 21.6 percent of that CO_2. You can also tell that road transport, from cars to semitrucks, produces most of the emissions in the transportation sector.[4]

From start to finish, the path of transportation emissions is pretty much a straight line. Industry branches a bit more. Electricity looks like a tree, however, with branches reaching into almost every part of the chart, twining over and under the other bars. It powers buildings; it contributes to industrial production; it's used to produce the fuels that make cars run. Add up all of those uses, and you'll find that electricity doesn't *only* account for the biggest portion of our energy use in the United States—it also produces more emissions than any other sector, even transportation.[5] The fossil fuels we burn to make electricity are playing a bigger role in climate change than the fossil fuels we put in our gas tanks.

I've talked about this a little earlier, but it's worth repeating: we use more energy to make electricity than we use for transportation. The wires over your head account for more greenhouse gases than the tailpipe of your car. That's why I decided to have this book focus on the infrastructure of power lines and electric generators, more than on the infrastructure of vehicles and highways. That's why the energy wasted by conversion losses at power plants is such a big deal—if more than half of the energy we use to make electricity doesn't actually make electricity, then we have a great opportunity to reduce emissions without changing our levels of comfort and convenience. That's why the buildings we live and work in matter so much—they're the biggest consumer of electricity. Electricity will only get more important, as it becomes more intertwined with transportation via electric cars and trains. If the future of energy is really going to be a world with fewer fossil fuels and climate-confounding emissions, it will mean drastically changing the way we produce electricity.

In fact, that was what brought me to Texas. The United States is riddled with electric grid control centers, but ERCOT is different in a couple of really important ways. For one thing, it's the sole manager of a geographic area that is both quite small and quite segregated from the rest of the country. The U.S. electric grid is split into three parts. There are connections among the three kingdoms—dedicated transmission lines that function sort of like drawbridges—but in emergencies, each segment can get by on its own. These three sections are the Eastern Interconnect, which includes most parts of Canada and the United States that lie east of the Rocky Mountains; the Western Interconnect, which covers the other side of the Continental Divide; and, finally, Texas. Let's be clear: there is no *technical* reason why Texas needs its own fiefdom. But come on. It's *Texas*—the state that started out as an independent nation and would prefer that the rest of us never forget it. It's a cultural thing, like the predilection for unnecessarily large hats or the tendency to equate truck ownership with state citizenship. Honestly, it would be weirder if its grid *wasn't* separate.[6] You're much more likely to be surprised by where the Texas grid is getting its electricity from.

See, we do a great disservice when we take alternative energy and slap it with a big label that reads, "Lefty, Coastal, Pinko Thing." In reality, the middle swath of this country has some serious renewable resources and is making significant efforts to harvest them. Texas, for instance, has the highest installed wind power capacity of any state—more than 10,000 megawatts.[7] What's a megawatt? That's an important question. I'm going to talk about megawatts a lot in this book, and you've probably run across the word often before—in newspapers, in other books, whenever somebody comes on TV to discuss electricity. A megawatt is a unit of measurement that describes an amount of electricity, with the number of megawatts usually being the maximum amount a power plant is capable of making at any given point in time. It's a metric thing. "Watt" is the actual unit. To give you an example, 1 watt is the amount of electricity it takes to power a bicycle lamp. If you run that lamp continuously for an hour, then you've *used* 1 "watt hour" of electricity. If you run two lamps for two hours, that's 4 watt hours. You get the idea.

"Mega" is simply a prefix that tells you about the scale of measurement.[8] When we talk about "megawatts" and "megawatt-hours," we usually are referring to the scale at which cities and states make and use electricity. Go down a step on the scale and you'll find kilowatts, a smaller unit that's normally used to refer to the electricity you and I consume at home. Your electric bill, for instance, is measured in kilowatt-hours. Up a step from megawatts are gigawatts, pronounced with a "j" sound, as it was in the movie *Back to the Future*. The entire United States uses electricity on the scale of *terawatts*—one step up from gigawatts. In 2009, we used 3,741 terawatt-hours of electricity.[9]

Technically, the 10,000 megawatts of capacity that Texas has is enough to power millions of homes.[10] I say "technically," because ERCOT doesn't really get to use all of that potential power on a daily basis.[11] Less than 8 percent of the electricity Texans use came from wind in 2010, according to ERCOT. Yet in a country that is, overall, around 2 percent wind-powered, that's enough to place Texas among the top ten wind-using states.[12] Combine that with the walled garden of the Texas Interconnect, and you've got a nice model for the future of the electric grid as a whole. The grid control wizards of Texas are on the forefront of learning how to work with renewable electricity.

This is not necessarily an easy skill to pick up. Why? Because wind does not work the same way as a coal fire, which can be built up or cooled down as you like. Nobody creates wind or even controls it. Instead, wind is a resource that you harvest when you can. If there isn't enough wind blowing, then the turbine blades—each often as long as a jetliner—can't turn. If there's too much wind, they could buckle and snap if they aren't shut down. Days when the wind slams doors shut and forces you to walk at an angle are, ironically, just as bad for wind power as the calmest doldrums are. The amount of useable electricity ERCOT can actually get out of those 10,000 megawatts of installed capacity varies, minute by minute.

That natural variability is what makes renewable energy generation a little tough to work with. Remember, the controllers are really only in control of the electricity supply. Demand happens, and they alter supply to match it. Yet that process—how the electric grid has functioned since it was built—won't work with wind. If a thousand people turn on their air conditioners in the middle of the day, the wizards can't ask a wind farm to produce more electricity than the wind will supply. And if there's more wind than there is electric demand—which happens pretty much every single night—there's nothing they can do except disconnect the grid from the turbines and let the wind go to waste. If the wizards are lucky, the weather forecast and the electric demand predictions are both right, and everybody can go about his or her business. On February 26, 2008, however, they weren't.

That night, like most winter nights, millions of Texans came home, flipped on the lights, turned on the TV, cranked up their heaters, and made themselves some dinner. Yet they did all of that a little sooner and a little faster than ERCOT's controllers had predicted. Meanwhile, out in West Texas, where wind farms straddle the buttes, a storm was moving through. Everybody knew the storm was coming, and everybody knew that the wind speed would fall just before the storm passed over each farm. But, again, it happened a little earlier in the evening than expected. During the course of three hours, wind power that everyone thought would be rising instead fell and fell far. Demand that was expected to climb rose faster than predicted. At the same time, several fossil fuel power plants failed to produce as much electricity as they'd told ERCOT they would. The careful balance shifted, and the grid frequency fell. In the dark and quiet control room, the scoreboard numbers dropped from 60, to 59.85.

That doesn't exactly sound like a tumble off a towering inferno, but a dip like that is enough of a big deal that even the calmest wizard will set down his RC Cola and pick up the phone in a hurry. In that kind of situation, when supply slips briefly out of his control, what he does, essentially, is call in a few favors. There are big customers—factories, usually—that can reduce their electricity use or shut off the power entirely when the grid needs their help. They're paid by the utility companies to be on call, a single point where wizards can control demand, used only when the supply side fails. As they have in countless other near emergencies, these demand-response customers saved Texas from blackouts that night in February.

In the weeks that followed, Joel Mickey told me, the incident got blown a bit out of proportion in the press.[13] Without the context—if you didn't know that little panics are rippling across the grid all the time or that cutting power to demand-response customers isn't a particularly rare occurrence—it's easy to see the events of February 26 as something uniquely horrifying, but they weren't. In fact, just a few months earlier, three fossil fuel power plants simultaneously failed and took the grid frequency down even lower, to a thoroughly disconcerting 59.787. So, the moral of this story isn't that Texas has more wind power than it can handle. No place in the United States has more wind power than it can handle. Likewise, you shouldn't come away thinking that variable renewable electricity is horribly faulty, whereas fossil fuels and nuclear power plants are always totally stable.

Instead, think about it this way: The wizards have this dragon. They got it a long time ago, when it was very small. Over the years, as it grew bigger and fatter, they learned how to make it obey them. Today, the dragon is huge, but it's mostly well-mannered. Recently, the wizards went out and picked themselves up a new dragon, a baby. It's not a bad pet, but it's not the same as the older animal. It behaves differently. It makes different mistakes. The tricks they used to tame the big guy don't always work in this case. For the most part—for right now—that's okay. The little dragon is getting along just fine. But it won't always fit in so well. As it grows, problems that seem small today will become a much bigger deal.

There's not really a problem with controlling the amount of renewable electricity we have now, but someday we'll have enough that variability could become a serious limitation. If we want the electricity grid of the future to work, we have to start fixing it now.

....

CHAPTER FIVE

A BOX FULL OF LIGHTNING

O n the Great Plains, wind prefers the night. As the sun sets, the wind rises. I didn't always know that, but it was a fact that made sense to me, as soon as I heard about it. Kansas is a pretty windy place. In some states, they cancel school in the winter on account of heavy snowfall. Where I come from, we were much more likely to get a "wind day," when the temperature itself wasn't too bad, but the wind chill and the heavy gusts convinced authorities that it wasn't safe for a kid to stand out on the corner, waiting for the school bus. In college, when I lived in a dorm, it sometimes took two people to push open the big glass lobby doors when we wanted to leave for class in the morning. I was in my twenties and living far from home before I ever owned an umbrella that lasted more than one year. So there was plenty of wind blowing during the day, to be sure. Yet in my mind, windy days seem to come and go. More constant are the memories of the last sounds I usually heard as I went to sleep—the wind rattling the panes of my bedroom window, scraping branches across the roof or plowing into the side of the house in bursts. Night was when people went to bed, and the wind ran wild.

The behavior of wind gets varies from place to place and season to season, but in general, across the Plains states that are our wind power "breadbasket," there is more wind at night.[1] That's a bit of problem, because the grid can use electricity only right as it's gener-ated. When the wind comes thundering across Kansas at two in the morning, it could produce some serious power, but nobody is awake to use it. If you take the daily trends in electricity demand and average them out into a graph, what you'll see is a flat plain, a large hill, and a little divot notched out of the right-hand side of the hill. The plain is electricity demand at night. The hill starts to form at around eight am and peaks at roughly four in the afternoon. The notch is the small drop in demand as everybody heads home from work, followed by another short rise as we settle in to entertain ourselves for the evening. By ten p.m., we're decidedly on the hill's downward slope, heading back to the plains.

If you graph the average trends for wind energy potential, you'll see a hill form over time there, too, but, in general, it forms in almost exactly the opposite hours. When there's a plain in demand, there's a hill in potential generation, and vice versa, so the wind goes to waste. The wind turbines we already have installed could be a lot more useful to us if we had some way of storing the electricity they are capable of producing overnight—but we don't.

That isn't precisely true. Storage isn't impossible. It's simply not done, at least not at any scale that would be useful. Sure, batteries exist. Those are the first devices most of us think of in terms of energy storage. From a limited, layperson's perspective, it also seems as if they ought to work pretty well. After all, batteries have been happily pumping electrons into our cars and toys and cell phones for years. Couldn't you just slap a bigger battery on the grid and call it good? Not exactly.

The batteries that sit under the hood of a gasoline-powered car are a vintage technology, virtually unchanged for a hundred years. Like all batteries, they work through a chemical reaction. The black box you see contains two metal plates—one made of lead and another made from lead dioxide—which sit in a tingly bath of acid. The chemical interaction of lead and acid releases free electrons, which are attracted to the lead dioxide. The electrons flow through the acid and build up around the lead dioxide plate, where you can pull them out and use them later.

This is called a lead-acid battery. The good news: lead-acid batteries are cheap, as far as energy storage goes. Yet they also have some limitations that make them a bad fit for the grid. For one thing, lead-acid batteries have an awfully short life span. You've run into this problem every time you've had to replace the worn-out battery in your car. Three to five years is all you'll get out of one, and that's if you play with it nicely—never draining its reservoir of electrons below 40 percent capacity and never charging it up above 60 percent capacity.[2] There's a very narrow range left in which to work. It's fine, if what you're doing is starting an engine and running some small electronics. But if you're trying to store as much energy as possible during the night and disgorge as much as possible the next day, the persnicketiness of lead-acid batteries becomes a problem.

Batteries are also hard to scale up. Think about the teeny little AAAs that power a remote control and how much bigger the battery has to be just to power an electric lantern. By the time you're lighting up headlamps and a car radio, the battery has become Godzilla-like in comparison. Now, with that in mind, think about how big a lead-acid battery would have to be if you needed it to store megawatts' worth of wind-generated electricity overnight. The prospect quickly becomes a bit intimidating.

Ultimately, these problems were what kept storage from being built into the grid from the beginning—the batteries that were available simply didn't work well with the system. Combine that with the fact that the storage wasn't strictly necessary, and nobody saw much reason to worry about it. Fossil fuel and nuclear generators don't work perfectly. Demand for electricity doesn't always follow the wizards' predictions. The job of controlling the grid has always involved its fair share of scrambling and scraping—far longer than wind and solar generation have been popular. Yet the flexibility of demand-response customers could handle some of the trouble. Other problems could be solved by natural gas–powered generators, which can ramp electricity production up and down fairly easily. When none of that worked, everybody could deal with a certain amount of failure. Remember, the energy infrastructure that we have got that way because of incentives. In this case, the economic and technological incentives led people to build a grid with almost no storage capacity.

In fact, the little bit of storage that was built was more about business than about balancing out electric demand against electric supply. Some utility companies constructed pairs of lakes—one at a higher elevation than the other—with electric turbines built in between. At night, when electricity produced by the turbines has few buyers and is, thus, cheap, the utilities use that electricity to pump water to the upper reservoir. Then, during the day, that water can be released to flow downhill, into the second reservoir, generating much-more-profitable electricity along the way. In this case, the "battery" was a water-filled reservoir.

That's the historic relationship between the grid and electric storage. Yet as we add more wind and solar resources, the situation will have to change, and not only because of what the grid itself needs. There's evidence that in certain places, a lack of storage means renewable electricity won't be able to reduce greenhouse gas emissions as much as it should. Without storage or some other way to balance the load, the more renewables you add, the more you could be reducing their overall effectiveness. This is a tricky little counterintuitive problem, but it's easy to follow once you know a couple of key facts about the electric power plants that exist today.

First, nuclear power plants and coal power plants are meant to produce steady, constant levels of electricity, with only slow-moving changes in output. These systems ideally shouldn't be ramped up and down, up and down. Now, neither kind of plant will explode if you use it in a more erratic fashion, but if you want to get the full life out of that plant, you need to run it as if it's a station wagon, not a hot rod. In particular, rapidly changing the amount of electricity generated by coal plants can make them produce more carbon dioxide emissions and air pollution than they otherwise would.

Second, natural gas power plants can quickly change the amount of electricity they produce, but when you do that, they also run less efficiently. If you take a natural gas–fired generator and force it to spend a lot of time rapidly changing the amount of electricity it makes, you'll find that every watt you generate produces slightly more emissions than there would have been if that watt had come from a gas generator running at a more stable pace. The penalty isn't as large as with coal, but it's there.

Thanks to these two facts, electricity produced by variable renewables isn't always as clean as it looks in theory. The entire frustrating chain of events works like this: Because the "fuel" is free, and because many states have set mandates on how much of their electricity should come from clean sources, utility companies choose to take electricity made by variable renewables when it's available. Renewable is the first choice, and that's good. Yet because of the inherent variability, the utilities also have to have backup—coal- or natural gas–powered plants that are running at a low level and can be quickly ramped up when the renewables aren't available. That's an inefficient way to run a fossil fuel generator. The more a given region of the grid relies on variable renewables for first-choice power, the more backup it has to have available, too.

I should clarify: this does not mean that combining variable renewable first-choice electricity with fossil fuel backup produces more emissions *overall* than if you'd simply stuck with using only fossil fuels. It's certainly been spun that way, by biased interests, but emissions-per-watt produced by a single fossil fuel plant isn't the same as total emissions produced.[3] Instead, this problem is more likely to mean that adding lots of wind and solar won't cut emissions *as much* as you might think. Essentially, there's a bit of a rebound effect.

That said, though, we can probably agree that increasing the emissions-per-watt of a fossil fuel plant—even if we're producing fewer emissions overall—is not an ideal situation. If we want electricity that's really and truly clean, then we have to find a better way to balance variability.

Even in places where the backup power is also renewable, variability can still cause problems. The Pacific Northwest, for instance, produces a lot of electricity with the power of water moving down its rivers. Those generators can provide emissions-free backup power, but they also have their own limitations. For instance, on a Saturday afternoon in October 2009, this chunk of the grid experienced what's known as an "upside" event—producing too much electricity, rather than not enough. Saturdays are often lazy days for electricity use. Office buildings sit empty. People spend more time outside and away from their home electronics. On this particular Saturday, the weather was mild—further reducing electric demand—but the wind was high and blustery. Across Oregon and Washington, wind turbines pumped out electricity at full capacity.

To balance the load, controllers asked the hydroelectric stations to generate less, but there's only so much less those power plants can make. You can't completely turn off most hydroelectric generators. To do that, you'd also have to shut off the river itself. That's bad for fish, and environmental regulations won't allow it. The backup generators could have helped, but it wasn't enough.

Next, controllers tried to sell the excess electricity to other regions. Unfortunately, the weather was nice all over, and this left the Pacific Northwest in a bind. California didn't want its electricity. Idaho didn't want it. Nobody nearby would purchase the excess, not even at a discounted price—not even if they were paid to take it. In that situation, the controllers had no option but to call up the wind farms and tell them to shut down. "It was a Saturday, and some didn't answer the phone," said Rob Pratt, a senior research scientist with the Pacific Northwest National Laboratory. "Some said, 'No,' because they were making good money on sales. Enough complied, but it was a real operational problem on the upside. They just couldn't get rid of the power."

In the Pacific Northwest today, the government-owned hydroelectric system has actually started to tax wind farms, to pay for the cost of providing backup and the problems of variability.[4] The people who owned the wind farms weren't the same ones who owned the hydroelectric dams, and they weren't the same as the people trying to manage the grid. Competing interests created a massive snarl. Ultimately, the controllers were able to untangle the knot, but if they hadn't, the excess electricity would have overwhelmed the system. When there's too much supply and not enough demand, the resulting surges can fry appliances and other electronics that customers own. To save themselves, the generators have to shut down, and then you have a blackout. "We haven't experienced anything like that up here yet," Pratt said. "But it would be interesting. You can't just dump excess electricity. Without storage, 'dump' means 'to consume.' All you could do is turn the wind and solar off."

This makes the situation sound a little dire, but it's not. At least, not yet. In order to really be a serious problem, you'd have to have a lot more variable-renewable generation on the grid than we currently do—either nationally or in any given region. It's not something anybody's dealt with before, so no one knows exactly how much variability is too much—but the vast majority of scientists, grid controllers, and utility companies that I've spoken with have all come back with estimates of somewhere between 20 and 30 percent. That is, if you don't have storage or some other way of balancing the load, you can get between 20 and 30 percent of your electricity from variable renewable generation. More than that and the problems will outweigh the benefits. This is true on a regional level—think about the Texas grid or even the less-isolated Pacific Northwest—and it's true on a national level as well. We've got a ways to go before anybody hits that barrier—remember that Texas is currently one of the best, at less than 8 percent wind energy use—but some parts of the United States will get there faster. Eventually, we'll have to find a way around the barrier.

Energy is essential but also complicated. Awareness and once-a-year events aren't enough to solve the problems we have with it. System-wide efficiency can help, but the rebound effect means that there's not always a direct connection between saving energy and saving the planet. Saving energy in one part of our lives doesn't necessarily mean we get an energy savings of equal size in the big picture. Wind-generated electricity is clean, but our grid isn't set up to store it. Right now, we can't rely on wind and solar alone, because it's far too easy to end up with too much or not enough. When it comes right down to it, no single energy solution is as good a solution as it sounds. That doesn't mean there's no hope, but it does make the short-term goals outlined by groups such as the Intergovernmental Panel on Climate Change, the IGSM model, and McKinsey and Company a lot more daunting.

Back when I was in grade school, my mom signed me up for swimming lessons at the Topeka YWCA. It turns out, I was not the most athletically gifted child. I could float on my back just fine. I dog paddled all right. But mastering a nice, face-down breast stroke was a bit beyond me. My frustration only grew during swim tests, when my instructor would tell me to swim to him—and would then slowly back away, forcing me to swim farther and farther into the deep end. I remember thinking that he wanted too much. I could make it halfway down the length of the pool. Why did he keep trying to force me to go the whole distance?

Energy feels like that sometimes—as if the goal keeps moving, as if we're being expected to do more than we are capable of. So it's reasonable to ask, "Can we change the goal?" Earlier, I told you that the prediction made by the IGSM model—twenty quadrillion BTUs' reduction in annual fossil fuel use in twenty years—is based on what it would take to hit a goal of 550 ppm carbon dioxide concentration in the atmosphere on a global scale. So, what does that really mean?

Ppm stands for "parts per million"; it's one of the ways scientists talk about chemical mixtures where one substance is diluted in a large amount of something else. In this case, molecules of carbon dioxide are spread throughout the other gases that make up our atmosphere. Right now, our global atmospheric carbon dioxide concentration is around 390 parts per million, or 390 ppm CO_2.[5] This is a place where you can really start to understand the scale of the problem, because, in absolute terms, 390 ppm CO_2 isn't really a *huge* quantity. For instance, 1 ppm is equivalent to putting one drop of water into a car's fuel tank. If I put 390 drops of water into my car's 13-gallon tank, I'm still going to have mostly gasoline in there, but those 390 drops can make the difference between a smooth-running engine and a big, expensive mess.[6] And 390 ppm is the highest atmospheric CO_2 concentration this planet has seen in 800,000 years.[7] Prior to the Industrial Revolution, our atmospheric CO_2 was less than 200 ppm.

More greenhouse gas in the atmosphere means a hotter planet.[8] What's not entirely clear yet is *exactly* how much warmer Earth will get for a set atmospheric CO_2 concentration, but scientists do have some good estimates. At 390 ppm CO_2, we've probably already committed ourselves to 1 degree Celsius of warming, compared to pre-Industrial temperatures, and quite possibly to 2 degrees. That matches up with what we've observed. Since the 1880s, the global average temperature has gone up .8 degrees. Warming lags behind CO_2, so even if we stopped burning fossil fuels tomorrow, the temperature would continue to rise for a long time.

Climate change cannot be prevented. It's already happening. So when we set targets such as that 550 ppm CO_2 ceiling for emissions, we are being somewhat arbitrary about where we draw the line. Technically, we could just as easily decide to set the cutoff at 650 ppm CO_2 or even higher. The higher we go, the easier it would be for us to meet the goal. We could make smaller changes to the way our energy systems work, and we could take longer to make them.

In some ways, that option is pretty appealing. To hit the global goal of 550 ppm CO_2, the United States would probably have to stabilize its annual emissions at somewhere around 6,000 million metric tons of CO_2 per year. We already produce more than that—6,576 MMTCO$_2$e in 2009.[9] (CO_2e means "carbon dioxide equivalent.") So, to hit the goal, we'll have to reduce the amount of fossil fuels that we already use *and* stop emissions from growing annually. That's an important distinction to make, because it means that the change we need is larger than it first appears. You might think that we simply need to cut 576 MMTCO$_2$e from our annual emissions. Yet because emissions usually increase year after year—especially in times of economic prosperity—we actually have to reduce more than that to produce a long-term stabilization in our emission levels. It means that it's not enough to build a bunch more new energy-efficient houses. We have to make the old ones energy efficient as well.

Beyond that, 576 MMTCO$_2$e isn't actually a small number when it comes to the impact on your daily life. You can see that most clearly when you understand what a number such as 576 MMTCO$_2$e really represents. Let's put it into some context. One way to reduce our annual greenhouse gas emissions by 576 MMTCO$_2$e would be to take 112,940,928 cars off the road. That's almost half of all of the cars that existed in the United States in 2007. To lock in that 576 MMTCO$_2$e reduction, you'd have to keep them off the road permanently. Half of the drivers in this country would have to put their vehicles up on blocks and never drive again.[10]

Another option: you could shut down 137 coal-fired power plants. Now, this might sound appealing, but it's really not. Not for a change to be made in a year. Not if you like living in a First World country. In 2007, according to the EPA, there were 464 coal-fired plants in the entire country.[11] Remember, coal supplies 48 percent of our electricity, so we can't *only* jettison 137 coal plants. We have to find some other way to produce that electricity. Do we get it from nuclear power? If so, we need to build 66 new nuclear power plants— and good luck with that. Do we get it from wind? If so, we need to build more than 2,000 new wind farms. Of course, as you're figuring out, simply swapping wind for coal doesn't quite work as smoothly as we'd like it to. At least, not yet.

These examples make the situation we're stuck in seem depressingly hopeless, and they make setting ourselves an easier-to-reach goal seem a lot more appealing. Be careful, though. The cutoff line of 550 ppm CO_2 may be arbitrary, but that doesn't mean there aren't consequences for crossing it. Really, scientists say, the actual goal is to lower our emissions as much as possible as fast as possible. Even 550 ppm CO_2 isn't a "safe" line. As the global average temperature inches upward, it creates a diverse array of local changes. The planet is already warming. We've committed ourselves to 1 degree Celsius, at least. If we limit atmospheric CO_2 concentrations to 550 ppm, we'll be setting ourselves on a course toward 3 degrees of warming.

We're not talking about minor changes at that point. Reports by the National Academies of Science say that the situation will get exponentially worse for each additional degree. For instance, there's evidence that we should expect wildfires in the Western United States to increase two to four *times* for each degree of increase. The Southwest will also become drier—between 5 and 10 percent less rain for every degree of warming—threatening water supplies, at the same time that the Midwest is experiencing more heavy, destructive downpours. Meanwhile, Arctic ice keeps on melting, so that by 3 degrees, millions of people will be at risk from coastal flooding.[12]

If we put off energy change or set ourselves a less stringent goal, then the job becomes easier and we don't have to worry as much about how we're going to coordinate all of these complicated, imperfect systems into a single energy solution. Yet if we do that, we'll also be forced to deal with climate consequences that are a lot more dire. The longer we put off change, the more difficult and more expensive it becomes to avoid those increasingly worse consequences. Energy is a hard problem to work out. It's never going to be easy. Yet intimidating or not, it's a problem we'll need to tackle, because the only thing worse than dealing with it is what happens if we don't deal with it. Again, change is inevitable. The question is whether we're going to take control of what kind of change happens to us.

Right now, we can't simply shut down 137 coal plants, replace them with 2,000 new wind farms, and expect our electric infrastructure to work as well as it now does. If we want a more wind-fueled future, we'll need storage of some sort.[13] The good news: there are lots of options. The bad news: as with everything related to energy infrastructure, those storage systems are all imperfect, and they're all expensive.

We know that lead-acid batteries won't solve the problem, but there are other batteries we could use. The same basic system that operates the lead-acid battery—a chemical reaction creates free electrons that move through an electrolyte and collect around an electrode—can be created with a lot of other different chemical combinations. Some of those combinations will give you a battery with a longer life span and the ability to fill and discharge more of its total electron capacity and will provide both talents in a smaller package. There are many improved batteries that look promising, but the one that's furthest along and that utilities are really putting to the test right now is called a sodium-sulfur battery.

Instead of lead and lead dioxide electrodes, this battery uses molten sodium and sulfur. Where your car battery has a liquid acid electrolyte, the sodium-sulfur battery uses solid ceramic. Each sodium sulfur battery will last for twenty years and can be both filled and emptied completely. These batteries are definitely smaller than lead-acid batteries of a similar capacity would be, but they aren't what you or I would call petite. In Minnesota, 30 percent of the electricity produced by our main utility company, Xcel Energy, will have to come from emissions-free sources by 2020. We've already had short periods up here where as much as 13 percent of the electricity being consumed was renewable—and most of that was from wind. So Xcel Energy is experimenting with sodium-sulfur batteries. In 2009,

Xcel hooked a sodium-sulfur battery up to a wind farm in Luverne, Minnesota. The battery has a 1 megawatt capacity, and can power five hundred homes for seven hours. Each sodium-sulfur battery is as big as a semitruck. From the outside, it looks a lot like a row of white metal lockers from a high school for giants.

The more you want to store, the bigger the batteries get. Presidio, Texas—a small town lost out in the far West near the Mexico border—has a 4-megawatt sodium-sulfur battery that is, literally the size of a house.[14] The largest sodium-sulfur battery installation in the world is in Japan. It serves as a backup for wind power and has a capacity of 34 megawatts in seventeen batteries that look like massively oversized versions of the white marble vaults in a New Orleans cemetery.

Size is still something of a drawback for sodium-sulfur batteries. It limits where we can use them and what we can use them to do. These batteries have a big future as on-site wind farm storage, slurping up electricity overnight and discharging it into the transmission grid the next day. Yet they aren't as likely to be common right near cities or for balancing minor fluctuations in power on the distribution scale within towns. The size also helps make them expensive. As of December 2010, there still aren't any companies making sodium-sulfur batteries in North America. They're all made in Japan, and must be shipped—semi-size battery by semi-size battery—across the Pacific Ocean.

At the other end of the battery spectrum are lithium-ion batteries—the kind that power your laptop and sit under the hood of some hybrid and fully electric cars. These batteries are a little different. The name doesn't come from the chemicals used for electrodes or electrolytes—in fact, you can make lithium-ion batteries using several different chemical combinations. Instead, "lithium-ion" refers to the substance that moves around inside the battery. The electrons belong to atoms of lithium.

At first glance, lithium-ion batteries don't sound like a very good fit for the grid. You can't charge or discharge them completely, and their life span is very short, compared to sodium-sulfur batteries—the ones used in cars will last only a few years, although scientists are working on ways to make lithium-ion batteries more long-lived. Yet although they wouldn't be much use for capturing the power of the night wind or sucking up a big chunk of excess electricity on a windy day, lithium-ion batteries *could be* a handy tool for balancing the minor frequency fluctuations caused by minute-by-minute shifts in wind speed and customer demand. What's more, lithium-ion batteries offer an opportunity for utilities to get those storage benefits without necessarily having to buy the storage units themselves.

When people talk about incorporating lithium-ion batteries into the grid, they, for the most part, mean using the lithium-ion batteries in electric cars on double-duty. See, our cars aren't as busy as we are. Ninety-six percent of the time, personal vehicles are just sitting there, doing nothing—in a parking lot at work or in a garage at home.[15] If you installed the right technology in the right places, you could easily plug an electric or hybrid vehicle into the grid and make that downtime useful. Instead of cooling their metaphorical heels, the lithium-ion batteries in those cars could spend the day giving and taking small amounts of electricity from the grid. Collectively, a lot of small batteries would become one ginormous battery.

This idea really does work, from a technological standpoint. The state of Delaware and its regional independent system operator are doing it right now. Seven electric cars, owned by the state, have been outfitted with everything they need to plug in at charging stations located at government buildings and at the University of Delaware campus. As long as the cars are at a charging station, they are connected to the grid. All of the cars are bundled together by an aggregation system, which becomes the middleman between the grid controllers and the cars. The controllers tell the aggregator how much electricity they need or how much they have to dump. Each car knows its upcoming energy needs and driving schedule, either from learning the driver's habits or from a driver-updated calendar. The aggregator figures out how many cars are plugged in and what it's allowed to give or take from each battery. Then the aggregator splits the controllers' order up among all of the cars it can reach. The charge in each individual battery changes by only a very small percentage, but the controllers get a very useful service—the kind that they normally have to pay demand-response customers a healthy fee for. Someday, individuals could sign up for a program like this and make a little extra money off their electric cars.[16]

Unfortunately, "someday" is likely to be a long way off. The downside of using privately owned electric cars for grid storage is that you have to wait for enough people to buy electric cars, and that glacier moves slower than you might realize. Think about it this way: The Prius was released in the United States in 2001. By 2011, a million Priuses had been sold in the United States. That's a lot, but it's not the kind of critical mass you'd need to make a car-based grid storage work. Add to that the fact that lithium ion–powered plug-in hybrid and all-electric cars are so far a lot more expensive than the Prius. You can assume *at least* two decades before you could turn Delaware's small experiment into a national norm.[17]

After that, you'd still have to convince enough vehicle owners to sign up for the program. You'd also have to convince utilities to install all of those networked charging stations in all of the different places they'd need to be located for the program to work. This isn't an impossible scenario. It doesn't invalidate car batteries as a legitimate source of grid storage in the future. Yet it's important to understand that the plan isn't easy or quick. A lot of regions are likely to get to 20 percent renewable penetration before they could even hope to set up something like this. Sometimes, even if the technology works, there's still a devil in the details.

So, the wind and the sun don't work like coal. Batteries can be a good solution for the variability of renewable power—if you pick the right battery and match it to the right sort of use. You should remember, however, that we're talking about *a* solution, not *the* solution. None of the batteries that exist today are perfect or particularly generalizable, and that isn't likely to change. The electric infrastructure problems of the future will probably not be solved by one does-it-all battery. At the very least, we'll need two specialized types of batteries: one that can pick up large blocks of energy and shift them from night to day or from a sunny day to a rainy one and another type that can even out the constant small fluctuations in energy, like a man balancing in the center of a teeter-totter. More realistically, we'll wind up with a whole Dr. Seuss book of battery types that we use—big ones, small ones, cheap ones, tall ones, light ones, fast ones, always-on-call ones. It just depends on what matters most at each specific installation. In fact, some of the storage that we'll use in the future won't come from batteries at all.

Take compressed air energy storage, or CAES, for instance. This is a very boring name for a very nifty energy storage system. Even scientists who understand its limitations get sort of giddy while describing CAES because it's just that much fun. Why? It starts with a cave.

To make CAES work, though, you can't turn to just any old cave. It's got to be something air-tight. Usually, this means that the sort of cave you've toured while on vacation isn't an option. Instead, you have to find a hollowed-out space underground that used to hold something naturally—such as a drained aquifer or a natural gas reservoir that's had all of the gas pumped out of it. Once you've identified your cave, then you build a wind farm nearby. These turbines have to be connected into the grid, but they're also connected to big air compressors. During the day, the system works like a normal wind farm, but at night, when the wind is plentiful and electric demand is decidedly not, the turbines stop sending electricity to the grid. Instead, that electricity is used to power the air compressors. During the course of the night, the compressors pump the cave full of air. Then the next day, as electric demand rises, that compressed air is released and used to help run on-site electric generators.[18] CAES converts wind into electricity, converts electricity into compressed air, and then turns the air back into electricity again. In a lot of ways, it's very similar to those pumped-water storage systems that utility companies have used for decades. Only, instead of storing energy as water in a reservoir, it is storing energy as compressed air in underground caverns.

This is very basic stuff from a technological standpoint. Compressing air and using it to run an electric generator isn't much different from the way your car mechanic uses tanks of compressed air to run power tools. Yet despite the simplicity, CAES can be expensive. There's just so much you have to buy to put the system together. The caves have to be prepared to hold air. Then you have to build the wind farm. The air compressors are extra. So are the generators. On top of all that, there's the cost of finding and buying the land. CAES systems take up a lot of space, and there aren't many places where you'll find a suitable cave that also happens to be a good site for a wind farm, and that is close enough to an urban area that you won't have to build a lot of transmission lines, which would jack up the price even further. Right now, there are only two operational CAES systems in the entire world—one in Alabama and one in Germany. Neither is actually used to store wind power. They're simply backup for the grid, in general.

Even so, scientists say that wind-powered CAES is one of the more promising storage options. You're going to see more of it in the future. In fact, at the limited number of locations where all of the right conditions come together, CAES has the potential to actually be cheaper—both up front and over the life of the system—than any other storage option.[19] Again, though, it's *a* solution, not *the* solution.

Electricity isn't as simple as turning on a generator and letting the electrons do their thing. The unhappy ghost of H. J. Rogers could tell you that. To generate enough renewable electricity, we can't just swap out fossil fuel generators for wind turbines and solar panels. Today's grid-control wizards are learning that they can't tame the new dragon with the old dragon's toys. So it shouldn't come as a shock for us to find that the problem of grid storage won't be fixed next week by rounding up a bunch of batteries we already have on hand. There are three factors at play here: the high cost of building this new infrastructure, the desire to get the infrastructure built right the first time, and the need to build the infrastructure quickly. The first two factors do not play well with the last one.

Remember the sins of the Appleton electric system. Given the choice between good, cheap, and fast, they chose—poorly. As we build the grid of the future, we don't want to make the same mistake. Our priority has to be on quality and reliability. Along the way, we'll figure out ways to do good for less money, such as using CAES for storage in some places, instead of sodium-sulfur batteries. We'll create better storage systems and lower the cost of the ones that already exist, but we won't be quick about it. There's a fundamental dichotomy driving the development of alternative energy. We need it, and we need it yesterday. If you try to build an electric infrastructure at that pace, though, what you'll get is a system where the only thing standing between you and a city-wide blackout is a guy in a shack down by the river who stares at a lightbulb all day.

There's really only one way to reconcile these conflicting interests: we have to be in two places at once. Mentally, I mean, but also in terms of how we build and plan infrastructure. When we think about a world with no coal-fired power plants—or even a world with significantly fewer—we need to plan what we have to do now to make that infrastructure work for our children and grandchildren. Adding storage to the grid, in amounts that allow us to shut down coal plants and replace them entirely with wind and solar, is a goal that will play out on this long-term scale. That's good, and it's necessary. Unfortunately, it doesn't do a whole lot to help places such as Texas and Minnesota, which are on track to get 20 percent of their electricity from variable renewables in a decade or so. That's why we can't *only* think long-term. The short game matters, too. To make this work, we have to play both sides at the same time.

In forty years, maybe thirty, we'll be on our way to getting grid storage under control. What happens in 2030, though? How do we balance the grid, reduce greenhouse gas emissions, and continue to expand our energy options—and do it fast—when we're facing a limitation that won't go away as quickly as we need it to? This used to drive me nuts, but then I realized that I was stressing out about the wrong problem. The answers to this conundrum aren't all that mysterious. They simply aren't popular.

CHAPTER SIX

···

GOOD AND GOOD ENOUGH

One ferociously hot day in the summer of 2010, I found myself standing in a sandy clearing on top of a hill near Tuscaloosa, Alabama, staring intently at a white Styrofoam beer cooler. The cooler was upside-down over the top of a short pole, sitting off-kilter like a lampshade on the head of a cocktail party guest. All around me were about two dozen other people—mostly middle-aged men, plus a handful of twenty-somethings from both sexes—who were also under the beer cooler's thrall. Together, we milled around it, sweat pooling on the fronts of our shirts and dribbling out from beneath our white hard hats. The hike to this spot was short—less than a half-mile from where the air-conditioned vans had dropped us off—but the upward trajectory and the merciless sun exposure had turned this Appalachian foothill into a sort of hell. None of us had climbed that gravel road for fun or exercise. Instead, we'd come to see the future of coal power in the United States. This hill was one of the few places in the whole country where carbon dioxide was being pumped beneath the earth, never to be heard from again.

At least, that was the idea. Researchers were using this spot to run experiments to put that theory to the test. If you followed the gravel road farther uphill, you'd find another clearing, where a tanker truck was parked alongside the black hulk of a natural gas derrick. A jointed line of skinny, rust-flecked pipes led from some electric-blue machinery near the tanker to a wider pipe—about the size of a residential plumbing stack—that burrowed into the ground just in front of the derrick.

During a couple months in 2010, a team of scientists from the Geological Survey of Alabama and the University of Alabama had pumped 278 tons of compressed carbon dioxide, a little at a time, into that wide pipe. Far beneath the hilltop, the liquidlike CO_2 became a gas that could flow into a series of narrow coal seams. Bound by layers of air-tight rock, the seams had trapped large amounts of natural gas—methane—chemically locked to the coal. The bonds that tied the methane to the coal weren't very strong, though. Carbon dioxide and coal are much more attracted to each other. Because of this, carbon dioxide can push the methane aside and take its place. Once freed, the methane can be pumped up just like a normal natural gas well. The Alabama researchers weren't capturing the methane they released, but the same basic technique has been used in commercial natural gas drilling projects.

The beer cooler that had so mesmerized me was an important part of that system. A cheap and easy insulation against the summer heat, it protected a small computer, which compiled data from sensors all over the hilltop. The computer made sure that wherever CO_2 was put into the ground, it didn't sneak back out. So far, the researchers told me, it looked as if the plan was working. Carbon dioxide that went down, stayed down. Their experiment in carbon capture and storage was going almost exactly according to plan.

Most of the people on that Alabama hilltop were geologists or folks who worked for various branches of the fossil-fuel energy industry. For me, though, seeing carbon capture and storage in action was part of separating reality from fantasy. I mentioned earlier that energy efficiency is more complicated than it seems on the surface. The rebound effect bungles our best-laid plans. Wind and solar power, too, are limited by their own inconvenient truths. Building a sustainable energy infrastructure will involve more than simply constructing a couple thousand wind farms. If these imperfect partial solutions sound too messy—if you're still looking for a silver bullet—carbon capture and storage can start to look awfully appealing. If the problem is atmospheric carbon dioxide, why not prevent CO_2 from getting into the atmosphere? If the problem is supplies of liquid fuel, why not turn coal into synthetic "oil"?

Clean coal is sold as the best of both worlds. Every debate I've ever heard on the subject seems to start with the premise that carbon dioxide could be scrubbed out of coal smoke and stored away at any time. This was something we knew how to do. The kinks had already been ironed flat. From media coverage I'd seen in recent years, I'd even gotten the impression that clean coal was happening already.

It's not. The reality is that clean coal is every bit as complicated as any other energy issue. First off, although clean coal is a real technological innovation, it's real in same way that stem cell medicine is real. In places such as Tuscaloosa, scientists are researching clean coal, taking important baby steps, but it's not yet a proven technology, and it's definitely not ready to roll out on a broad commercial scale. Second, when people talk about "clean coal," they're really referring to two processes: removing all (or most) of the carbon dioxide from the exhaust of a coal-fired power plant, and then doing something with that carbon dioxide so that it never has an opportunity to escape into the atmosphere—which usually means storing it underground. Indefinitely. This combination process has never been accomplished anywhere—at least, not at a real-world scale.

In fact, the site I visited in Alabama was testing only half of the system. The carbon dioxide trapped beneath that hill didn't come from a coal-fired power plant at all. Instead, it came from a company that extracts naturally occurring carbon dioxide from rocks and sells it for use in industrial processes. Right now, it's a lot cheaper simply to buy this CO_2 than it is to rig a power plant up with a collection system. The Alabama experiments are a model, not the real deal, and models should always be cheaper than full scale. In this case, that means carbon dioxide is being taken from underground, shipped cross-country, and then pumped back into the ground. For now, the model is actually *producing* atmospheric carbon emissions, rather than reducing them. Clean coal—more accurately called "clean*er* coal"—is still an experiment in progress. It's a concept car, not the minivan in your neighbor's driveway. It won't be cheap, and it's unlikely to ever solve our energy issues on its own.

That said, however, cleaner coal isn't something we can just write off.

The future of energy isn't only about what we want to do; it's also a question of what we *can* do—and what we can't. During the course of a century, from H. J. Rogers to the wizards of Taylor, Texas, America has cobbled together an electric infrastructure built on fossil fuels. This system is a wonder. That a fragile web of wires and machinery can reliably keep our houses bright, our hearths warm, and our gadgets blinking is nothing short of fantastic. The balance is repeatedly being upended and restored. The strength of the web is regularly put to the test, but it holds fast—more or less. The grid is imperfect. It is both beautiful and terrible. As much as it serves us, we are also at its mercy. This infrastructure we have built now controls what we can build next and when. Ultimately, with electricity, it's hard to tell where infrastructure ends and energy generation begins. Infrastructure determines the kind of generation we can use, and generation has its own infrastructure, beyond the transmission grid I've focused on so far. It's possible to talk separately about infrastructure or generation, but the two ideas bleed together at the edges, and the former controls the latter.

This leaves us in an uncomfortable position—whatever our values on energy, the infrastructure we have is going to force us to make compromises. Remember the rules we're dealing with: our energy infrastructure isn't ideal, we waste a lot of energy, what we do with energy is governed by economics and social incentives, infrastructure is always expensive, and nobody gets exactly what he or she wants. In particular, we physically cannot just drop everything and immediately shift over to a world powered entirely by wind and solar generation. Not if we want to maintain the comfortable, convenient, modern lives that precious few of us would be willing to give up. You've probably heard that wind turbines or solar panels covering a relatively small square footage, in just the right part of the United States, could provide enough energy to power the entire country. Infrastructure— infrastructure and engineering—are the reasons that plan, which looks so good on paper, wouldn't work in real life. I think this is an important fact to highlight. If we're going to successfully adapt our world to mitigate climate change and reduce our reliance on fossil fuels, then we have to be as realistic about the solutions as we are about the problems.

Scientists, engineers, and grid controllers across the country are learning how to build an infrastructure that will work with a wind and solar future, but that's a slow process. In the meantime, we have to do the best we can with what we have. What does that mean? A lot of different things. It means tweaking the current grid, using strategic technological upgrades to make it a little friendlier to renewable energy in the short term. It means that we have to acknowledge the realities of the grid and know that just because we don't like a natural gas, coal, or nuclear power plant doesn't mean we can always afford to abandon the constant, controllable electricity that plant provides. It also means that we need to support research that could make those less-than-ideal energy sources cleaner and safer, so that even if they aren't unequivocally good, we are at least making them a little better.

That's why I think cleaner coal is valuable. The scientists who are burying carbon dioxide beneath a mountain in Alabama aren't solving our energy problems, but they are taking steps toward changing our energy infrastructure in ways that will reduce our carbon emissions while we wait for the *real* solutions. From that perspective, cleaner coal—flawed as it is—really could be part of the way forward.

I've shown you how the electric grid was built, how it works today, and why it won't be able to support an emissions-free future without some major changes. So, what do we do in the meantime? Just because the grid can't yet be clean doesn't mean it can't be *cleaner*.[1] There are several ways of working toward that goal, and none of them are perfect. Yet not all of them are as experimental as cleaner coal, either. In fact, the best of the bunch involves widely available technology and might actually be able to save electricity consumers money.

You've probably heard about "smart grids," but there's also a good chance that you aren't quite sure what that term refers to, exactly. Don't feel bad. "Smart grid" is, first and foremost, a buzzword—one media-friendly phrase that's used to describe many different ideas. In general, though, they all boil down to a similar concept. Smart grids are about taking existing twentieth-century infrastructure and giving it some twenty-first-century upgrades. Similar to cleaner coal technology, smart grids allow us to use the infrastructure we already own in a more environmentally friendly way. Some smart grid concepts are more ready-for-prime-time than others. Conveniently, the one with the most real-world experience is also the one that applies most directly to the problems I've been talking about in this book. This type of intelligence can actually help dumb old grids support more wind and solar power than they otherwise could. Yet at the same time, it's not completely outside the realm of the grid controllers' previous experience. In fact, the smart grid I'm talking about is really just a clever system for turning average electricity consumers into super-powered demand-response customers.

Today, demand-response customers are necessarily big customers. Usually, they're factories or other industrial campuses, which are paid a monthly stipend in exchange for being willing to turn off their electrical use when the wizards of grid control need help. On that stormy night in February 2008, when ERCOT found itself without enough electricity to go around, it was the demand-response customers who answered the call and shut down their own power to protect the grid. That's not all that distinguishes them from normal customers, however. There's also another side to how demand-response customers interact with utility companies. They also pay for their electricity in a way different from how you or I do.

Most household electricity bills are added up based on an averaged flat fee—you pay the same rate for every kilowatt-hour of electricity you use, no matter when you use it. Yet big businesses, including demand-response customers, pay different rates for every kilowatt-hour, depending on the time of day and the time of year. For them, electricity costs more whenever more people want it—such as on summer afternoons, when air-conditioners run full-tilt. Likewise, their electricity costs less when electricity is not in demand—such as at night. Demand-response customers are paid to be on call, but they also pay extra if they want to use electricity at the same time that everybody else wants to use it. The system is meant to encourage them to help lower the peaks in electric demand, which, in turn, helps reduce the amount of backup generation capacity that has to be available.[2] These customers are the wizards' only means of controlling demand. If there were more of them in more places, then the wizards could fine-tune their control a little better. That's where the smart grid comes in.

There's a nice, simple way to understand how the smart grid works in this context, and it starts with a typewriter. When I was in grade school, my dad, an art professor, owned an electric typewriter. I liked to feed paper in around the roll, lock it into place under the metal bar, and then spend thirty minutes of a summer day pretending that I was writing something very important.[3] When I was twelve, though, he replaced the typewriter with a word processor—a clunky, green-screened computer that wasn't much more sophisticated than the electric typewriter but *was* more expensive—and more fragile. I wasn't allowed to play with it. Today, when my father sits down to type up a syllabus, he does it on a computer that is linked, via the Internet, to lots of other computers.

There are benefits to the Internet-connected computer, obviously: instant access to research, the ability to communicate with students and other artists. Yet there are drawbacks, too. The typewriter didn't come with a monthly fee for Internet service (itself a frequently distracting confection that simultaneously makes it easier for people to collect information about my dad that he doesn't want them to have). And neither the typewriter nor the word processor was particularly at risk of catching a virus.

My dad—and pretty much everybody else in America—left the typewriters and word processors behind, anyway. That's essentially the same transition a smart grid asks us to make. Only this time, we're talking about major home appliances.

The Pacific Northwest GridWise Demonstration Project, an experiment that ran in 2006 and 2007, took 150 clothes dryers and 150 hot water heaters and rigged them up with little computer circuit boards—similar to the chips you find when you open up the back of a cell phone or a hand-held video game. Called Grid Friendly Appliance Controllers, the chips could sense what was going on with electricity as it passed through the wall outlet, and they used that information to monitor grid frequency—that balance of demand and supply that should always be as close to 60 hertz as possible. Whenever the frequency dipped too low or pushed up too high, the chips would automatically shut off the dryers and the water heaters or turn them on. The result was instant demand response that didn't even have to wait for the wizards' command. It worked far faster than asking a power plant to ramp up production of electricity or cool down and produce less, and it worked faster than traditional demand-response customers could turn off their power. That's great for the grid, but what if you needed to tumble the wrinkles out of a shirt at the same time the wizards needed your dryer to shut off? And what happens when the program expands beyond the dryer—to heaters, refrigerators, and everything else in your house? This is usually the point where people start objecting.

In this particular situation, however, the smart grid wasn't really all that oppressive. Customers lost some of the control they'd had over their own electric use, but they didn't lose all of it. For one thing, like the traditional demand-response customers, participants in the GridWise Demonstration Project were paid for the services they offered. In addition, even though the chips took control of the appliances hundreds of times during the study, most of the people said they didn't even notice. That's because—on or off—the zombie states never lasted more than a couple of minutes. That isn't how all of the similar programs have been designed, but this study did show that it's possible to get the benefits of having small-scale demand-response without overly inconveniencing the small-scale demand-response customers.

More important, another part of the same GridWise Project showed that it's possible to have household customers pay demand-based rates for electricity without completely pissing them off. This is really the tough part. Most people are happy to be occasionally inconvenienced for short periods of time if they get paid for it. It's harder to get them to cheerfully pay *more* for electricity at exactly the times they're most accustomed to using it—especially if they find they can't change the way they consume and end up with higher electricity bills.[4]

The GridWise test case automated the energy systems inside peoples' homes and programmed those systems to respond to constantly fluctuating electricity prices—with the prices updated every five minutes. Participants could decide for themselves how expensive was too expensive—basically, drawing the line where they wanted their appliances to shut down. When the cost per kilowatt hour passed that point, everything from thermostats to water heaters went dark. The programming wasn't one-size fits all, and it wasn't done on a speak-now-or-forever-hold-your-peace basis. Participants could change their minds about whether they preferred comfort or cash, and they could take short time-outs from demand pricing entirely. Yet few did. In the end, the combination of automation and demand pricing *saved* people money—about 10 percent, on average, compared to the year before, when electricity had been priced at the normal flat rate. The program also worked for the grid. During the course of the year, the peak in electric demand dropped by about 15 percent.[5]

For all of that effort, the GridWise smart grid itself didn't directly reduce greenhouse gas emissions. That's a point I see people getting confused about a lot. This isn't about smart grids versus alternative generation—the issue is what smart grids can do to *help* alternative generation work. A larger number of faster-responding demand-response customers can both balance the little fluctuations of variable power and help shift demand for electricity away from peak periods—meaning that we can avoid building new fossil fuel power plants, *and* that we need fewer of those same plants sitting around as backup, increasing and decreasing electricity production in an inefficient way. Although it's expensive to buy compatible appliances, install the control chips, and network everything so that the automation works properly, it's a lot cheaper to do that than it is to buy a bunch of sodium-sulfur batteries, or build a new natural-gas power plant. (This is a key point you shouldn't overlook. You can't just slap a smart chip on your current dryer. You need a smart dryer that works with the chip.) The relative cost is important.

Researchers say that smart grids don't cancel out the need for storage, but they can make wind and solar power cheaper. They can also extend the limits of how much wind and solar generation we can install before the problems of variability overwhelm us—

reducing emissions more and faster than we could without them.[6] The drawbacks still exist. Networked electricity systems are vulnerable to cybercrime. In the future, your thermostat could get a virus, just as your computer can now—and those viruses would have the potential to cause blackouts. It's also clear that not every utility company would set up its smart grid program with as much forethought and customer education as went into the GridWise trial. Depending on how it's implemented, a smart grid could increase utility bills or take away too much customer control. It could also give your utility company the means to collect a lot of information about the way you live and what you buy—information that not all utility companies will protect. Smart grids are going to make some people angry and for good reason.

I used to think that the benefits of smart grids weren't worth fighting for. But knowing what I know now about how the grid works and how variable renewable generation fits into it, I think we're going to have to put up our collective dukes. The technology for this is here, ready to go, and it's cheaper than our other options. We know it *can* be done responsibly, from a privacy and control perspective. As with Internet-enabled computers, we can protect the smart grid, to a certain extent, against attack. Despite our best intentions, we will be taking some risks here, but they are risks that, I'm pretty sure, need to be taken.

Shoring up the existing grid with intelligence is one key change we can make while we wait for grid-scale storage. The other big problem we can tackle: find ways to make most of the generation that already exists—the coal, the natural gas, and the nuclear power—a little better than it is currently. This takes us back to that mountaintop in Alabama, but it also forces us to look with fresh eyes at a couple of big news stories—the meltdowns at a nuclear power plant in Fukushima, Japan, and the ongoing concerns about how certain natural gas drilling techniques affect water supplies and geology in America.

All three sources of electricity have major drawbacks and associated risks. Even if you don't care about climate change, there are still very good reasons to question whether we want to rely on these fuels. Coal, for instance, has a rather high body count. In fact, many studies have shown that coal kills more people, per unit of electricity produced, than any other kind of electric generation.[7] It also causes more serious illnesses. This is true if you look solely at the deaths and the illnesses caused by air pollution, and it's true if you also include the deaths caused by accidents.[8] Most of the people whom coal kills die because of air pollution—from lung disease and cancer. A 2007 study, done in the European Union, found that air pollution from burning coal killed almost twenty-five people per terawatt hour of electricity produced. To give you a sense of what that means, the EU gets around 1,000 terawatt-hours of electricity from coal every year. We can assume that coal kills twenty-five thousand Europeans a year.

Although natural gas and nuclear power are generally considered less deadly, they come with their own problems.[9] In order to collect natural gas, you often first have to release the gas from a geological prison. Forcing carbon dioxide into the gas well—as the cleaner coal researchers in Alabama are doing—is one way to free the natural gas. Another is called hydraulic fracking, pumping enough liquid into the ground that the pressure fractures rocks, allowing natural gas to flow through the earth and up the well. Hydraulic fracking hit the news in the summer of 2010, when people in Pennsylvania started posting videos of burning tap water, suggesting that fracking techniques were allowing combustible gas to seep into their wells. There's some debate over whether that phenomenon can actually be attributed to fracking, but it's never a good development when your tap water becomes flammable.[10] This single, memorable image brought attention to a number of other downsides to fracking, including more generalized contamination of groundwater with dangerous toxins such as arsenic.

Meanwhile, in March 2011, the world got a reminder that the risks of nuclear power can't necessarily be summed up in numbers of deaths. On March 14, Japan's Fukushima Daiichi power plant was damaged by an earthquake and a tsunami and began to leak radioactive particles from four of its six nuclear reactors. As I write this, it isn't yet clear what long-term effects those leaks will have on the land around the power plant, but the disaster has brought up a couple of big issues. It's possible that as at Chernobyl, some of the land closest to the Fukushima power plant will be uninhabitable for decades to come. Fear of radiation has proved to be a concern as well. Japanese people who lived near the power plant or even simply in the same prefecture, have found themselves socially ostracized and in some cases verbally attacked.[11] Some researchers think that the psychological impact on people who lived near the site of the Chernobyl disaster was as damaging as the radiation exposure.[12]

These are just *some* of the side effects we chose to accept as we built the electric system that serves us today. The trouble is, although the risks of using these energy sources are serious, so are the risks if we choose to *stop* using them—at least, for now. Coal, natural gas, and nuclear energy support us and our way of life. In 2009, 45 percent of our electricity came from coal, 23 percent from natural gas, and 20 percent from nuclear.[13] The limitations of the grid mean that of the 88 percent of our electricity that comes from risky sources, only 20 percent or so can be replaced by renewables until a better storage option exists. Those limits hold fast, even as, every year, our demand for energy goes up. And still the grid must always be fed the exact amount of electricity it craves.

If you understand the grid, then you can see why the question of which power plants we shut down and when has to be carefully considered. Location matters, because the national limitations to how much wind and solar we can feed the grid apply at a regional level as well. Money matters, because coal and natural gas power plants are the two cheapest electricity options around.[14] The megawatts that were produced by a shuttered plant must be made up somewhere. They can come in the form of negawatts—efficiency and conservation efforts that reduce demand—but they're also likely to come from the construction of new power plants. If you close a nuclear plant, it's most likely to be replaced with a coal or a natural gas plant. If you close a coal or a natural gas plant, it's most likely to be replaced with a newer version of itself.

If you don't replace the lost megawatts at all, you get blackouts. In Japan, they've faced this recently. Before the earthquake and the

tsunami, Fukushima Daiichi had a capacity of 4,700 megawatts—
megawatts that vanished from the grid when the power plant turned
into a disaster zone. Although Fukushima Daiichi is likely the only
power plant to go offline permanently, others were damaged and
had to shut down temporarily. All told, Japan lost more than 18,000
megawatts of generation capacity. What happened next was a crisis-
within-a-crisis, as grid controllers balanced the country's megawatt
debt by intentionally cutting power to different cities and regions
at different times of the day, in what's called a "rolling blackout."
Behind the scenes, utility companies scrambled to figure out how
they were going to meet electricity demand for months to come.

The real threat was summer. Electricity use hits its highest peaks
in the hot months, pushed upward by millions of people turning up
their air conditioners at roughly the same time of day. So demand
would be highest at a time when supply was still likely to be lower
than normal. To make up the difference, Japanese utility companies
had to turn to several different solutions. In April 2011, the *Economist*
reported that increased production at several natural gas generators
and hydroelectric power plants would help somewhat.[15] So would
the private companies that started to make their own electricity on
site, a job that is usually done with diesel-powered generators. After
all of that, though, Japan was still likely to be 3,000 megawatts in
the hole, and that deficit would have to be made up by efficiency,
conservation—or more rolling blackouts.

An earthquake created that energy crisis, but it took the man-
made electric grid to make the crisis tragicomic. See, there is enough
electricity being produced in Japan to make up for the shortfall. The
problem is that Japan, like the United States, has a grid that can't do
what that country needs it to do. You know that our grid is divided
into three parts, like walled cities—the Eastern Interconnect, the
Western Interconnect, and the Texas Interconnect. Japan's grid is
split as well, but the walls between its two parts are much taller and
much thicker. In fact, the two halves of the Japanese grid function
on entirely different grid frequencies. Passing electricity between
them is like trying to have a conversation with someone who doesn't
speak your language, and you don't speak theirs. So, instead of the
eastern half of Japan sharing electricity with the western half, western

Japan was forced to generate more of its own—generation that came primarily from fossil fuels.

If the risks of producing electricity keep you awake at night, you should probably devote a couple of sleepless hours to pondering what we should do about the electric grid that keeps forcing us to take those risks.

So, what do we do? If we're held hostage by our own infrastructure, how can we reduce carbon emissions and diversify our energy supply?

This is where the compromises I talked about earlier have to be made. If we can't get to "good," then we'll have to settle on "good enough for now." To do that, we'll have to implement as much efficiency and conservation as we can muster and get as much renewable generation as we can into the grid. Where those fall short, we'll probably want to look to natural gas, our first choice out of the bad bunch. I say that because, although natural gas does have risks, it also has a few benefits that make it more appealing than coal or nuclear power. New natural gas power plants are cheaper—in levelized cost— than coal or nuclear power plants. They also do a better job of balancing the up-and-down variations in electricity output produced by wind and solar; a grid with more wind, solar, and natural gas would produce fewer emissions, and those components would play nicer together. In fact, it's generally accepted that natural gas power plants produce fewer emissions than coal power plants to begin with.[16]

After that point, though, the decisions we need to make start to become a lot harder. Coal and nuclear power aren't all bad. Coal is cheap. Nuclear doesn't produce greenhouse gas emissions. Both are stable sources of electricity that we have a lot of experience using. Where they fall short—the emissions and the air pollution of coal, the risk of nuclear disaster—they can be improved. Yet even with those upgrades, cleaner coal technology, and better-designed nuclear plants that are less likely to fail in catastrophic ways, these two sources of energy share a risk that can't be easily worked around.

Both cleaner coal and advanced nuclear power ask us to create an entirely new kind of infrastructure and do something human beings have never done before—safely store dangerous materials indefinitely.

• • •

If we adopt carbon capture and storage—the plan behind cleaner coal—we will have to monitor and protect underground reserves of carbon dioxide, essentially forever. Some of those caches will be like the one I visited in Alabama, where the carbon is held in place by chemical bonds, as well as by layers of impermeable rock. In others, there's only the rock. These sites are researched extensively. They are tested. There are safety controls built into the machinery that injects the carbon dioxide and into the caps that seal the wells. I trust all of those safeguards. Nothing is ever perfect, but it's important to understand that sequestration isn't done just anywhere, and it isn't done on a whim. If I thought the setup only had to be temporary, I probably wouldn't be all that concerned, but time is powerful. Basically, there are too many unknowns—from the political to the geological to the life cycles of the businesses and the universities tasked with maintenance. Forever is a long time. My concerns about nuclear energy are pretty much exactly the same.[17]

In fact, at a basic level, nuclear energy isn't all that different from fossil fuel energy. The process of generating electricity at a nuclear power plant is really all about making heat, just as it is at a coal-fired plant. Heat turns water to steam, steam moves turbines in the generator.[18] The difference is where the heat comes from—you can light coal on fire, or you can create a controlled nuclear fission reaction. This is a lot like a table filled with Jenga games, each stack of blocks standing close to another stack. If you pull the right block and get one stack to topple, it will fall into the surrounding stacks. As those stacks fall, they crash into others. Nuclear fission works the same way—one unstable core, or "nucleus," of an atom breaks apart, throwing off pieces of itself, which crash into nearby atoms and cause those to break apart, too, and on and on.[19] Every time a nucleus breaks apart, it releases a little heat. Multiply this by millions of atoms, and you have enough heat to turn water into steam.

It can't go on forever, though. The nuclei that produce heat in a nuclear power plant are usually atoms of uranium-235. This element is refined and processed into little black pellets about the size of your thumbnail, which are poured by the thousands into long metal tubes—the fuel rods. Bunches of tubes, each taller than a basketball player, are grouped together into square frames. These tall, skinny columns are what we call fuel assemblies, and they have to be replaced about every five years.[20] That's because, as the uranium nuclei break apart, they leave behind detritus that slows down the heat-producing chain reactions. It would be like putting a sheet of cardboard between one Jenga tower and another. The first falls, but it hits a barrier instead of the next tower.[21] Eventually, nuclei in a fuel rod no longer break apart frequently enough to produce the right amount of heat. The rod's useful life in the power plant is over. Yet the chain reaction doesn't simply stop. Nuclei keep breaking apart, releasing both heat and fast-moving particles that can penetrate human skin and damage our cells.

What we call nuclear waste consists—for the most part—of fuel assemblies whose rods are still producing chain reactions, but which can no longer be used to boil water into steam. They are dangerous. There isn't a whole lot we can do with them. Right now, when a used fuel assembly is removed from the nuclear reactor at a power plant, it's put into a big pool full of water that's been treated with a reaction-slowing chemical. The assembly sits there for a few years, the water absorbing both heat and harmful particles. When the pool is full of rods, the oldest ones are taken out and put into what's called "dry-cask storage." The cylindrical casks are made of metal, coated in layers of concrete. They look like small versions of the silos you'd see on a farm. Just outside of most nuclear power plants in the United States, you'll find a thick concrete pad, dotted with several of these casks. The dry-cask system was designed to safely store spent fuel for a few decades, until it could be transported to long-term storage. Yet long-term storage doesn't exist. There's no facility for that anywhere in the world, and that's a big problem, because the fuel rods will continue to release dangerous particles for tens of thousands of years. It's not forever, but in terms of engineering, it might as well be.

That brings us back to the big question here. Whether we're stocking away nuclear fuel rods or captured carbon dioxide doesn't really matter that much. Either way, we have to decide whether forever-storage is a trade-off we're willing to accept in exchange for a cleaner energy infrastructure. On one hand, if the storage fails, the results could be dire—depending on how and when the failure happened. For instance, a small, slow leak of sequestered CO_2 would add to the greenhouse effect but wouldn't be particularly dangerous in a "run for your life" sort of way.[22] If an injection pipe failed, however, and a lot of CO_2 were released at once on a not particularly windy day, it could accumulate and suffocate any animal or human unfortunate enough to be in low-lying areas nearby.

Although the concept of a leak at a nuclear storage facility is more nerve-wracking, its effects would likely be more isolated than a slow CO_2 leak and less immediately threatening than a bubble of CO_2 rising from the ground all at once. The primary threat from nuclear storage—especially once you've made it past 1,000 years—is cancer.[23] Basically, if the containment barriers break down over time or if an earthquake ruptures them, then the dangerous, cell-damaging particles could escape into the soil and the ground water. From there, the particles would harm anyone living on that soil or drinking that water.

Many smart people have put a lot of hard work into designing storage systems with multiple fail-safes. They've run hundreds of computer models, testing those designs and predicting changes to geology and the environment that could affect the storage sites.[24] The basic conclusion: it's technically feasible.[25] This is how scientists describe an idea that isn't crazy, but also hasn't been proved—can't be proved, in fact, until you try it. What they're saying is that based on everything we know about how the world works, forever-storage should be possible, but we have no way of knowing *exactly* how it will work out. Science has done what it can. The rest is a judgment call.

When we talk about coal and nuclear power, what we're really discussing is how we choose to craft new infrastructure and how we choose to deal with the infrastructure that already exists. To a certain extent, we're already committed to the forever-storage of nuclear fuel rods. The waste already exists, and it will eventually have to go somewhere. Coal-fired power plants also already exist, emitting carbon dioxide into the atmosphere every day. Is it better to let that CO_2 drift or try to catch it? This is the difference between ideal scenarios and scenarios that are relatively better than business-as-usual. I think this matters.

The other thing that matters is proper perspective. If we are going to build the infrastructure for cleaner coal and nuclear power, then we have to consider whether we can implement that in limited ways without allowing it to take over. Nuclear energy and cleaner coal could both help us out during the transition to a renewable energy future. Yet neither is, itself, the future. At the same time, though, they are both more familiar and easier to wrap your head around than the new and diverse world of alternative energy. If we aren't careful, we could wind up treating a stop-gap as the Ultimate Answer.

In the real world, every day, we grit our teeth and work out solutions that aren't what we want but are better than what we have. We embrace the Zen of Good Enough. Are the risks worth the rewards? Is producing less atmospheric carbon than we currently do, in a shorter amount of time, a good trade-off for shouldering the burden of forever-storage? I'll be up front here: I don't know what the right answer is. Yet I do know that the question has to be asked, and I know that when we ask it, we have to think about the real world, as well as the ideal one.

In the real world, infrastructure was, is, and always will be expensive. We have always paid a high price for improving our lives and improving the lives of the generations that come after us. What we build with all of that money has never worked perfectly, either. That was true in Appleton, Wisconsin, in the 1880s. It is true in Taylor, Texas, today. And it will be true tomorrow, as we decide how we want to bridge the infrastructure gap between the dirty, fossil fuel–dominated electricity of today and the more-sustainable, diverse relationship with energy that our children and grandchildren will enjoy.

CHAPTER SEVEN

THE VIEW FROM MERRIAM'S PEAK

If Kansas were a teeter-totter, it would be fundamentally broken. The whole point to that toy is the fun of pivoting up and down, and up and down, on a lever that's balanced at a central point. Yet it works only if weight is distributed equally on both sides of the fulcrum. Two five-year-olds can have a great old time, but one five-year-old and one adult is a recipe for teeter-totter misery.

I was born and raised in Kansas. My home state is, sadly, one seriously unbalanced beam, with the population listing heavily to one side. If you split the horizontal rectangle of Kansas in half, you'd find that most of the people live in the East. In fact, if you look only at Kansas's five major metro areas—all of which are on the eastern side of the divide—those eighteen counties alone hold almost 70 percent of the state's entire population.[1] That end has the sprawling Kansas City metro area, Wichita, Topeka, and several smaller urban centers that might seem puny by some standards but are still definitely large enough to be called "cities." The western end of the state, in contrast, is best known for its wheat farms and a certain kind of stark, panoramic beauty. I spent six years of my childhood out on the edge of the east/west rift.[2] Western Kansas is not devoid of cities, and it's lovely country, but it's no place for anyone who craves the roar of the crowd. Although the population of Western Kansas grew during the first half of the twentieth century, the region has only gotten more sparsely inhabited since the 1960s and the 1970s. In some parts of Western Kansas, population density has now fallen so far that at least two counties could technically be classified as "wilderness" again.[3] The East is the big weight, resting solidly on the ground, while the western end of the state dangles precipitously at the top of the teeter.

Not surprisingly, the people who live in the western half of the state are different, in many ways, from their eastern counter-parts. More of them live in rural regions, rather than in urban centers or suburbs. They are wealthier.[4] They're older.[5] And while a sixty-mile drive is a somewhat rare occurrence for the majority of Eastern Kansans, that same distance might only be a daily one-way commute or even a trip to the nearest hospital out West. Eastern Kansans and Western Kansans have different priorities—including how they think about energy. Those differences, cultural and practical, show up most prominently in state politics, where political punch-outs are frequently divided along urban versus rural lines. That's because although there may be greater numbers of urban and suburban voters, the legislature is still predominately rural and exurban. To give you an idea of what I mean, the two most populous counties—Johnson and Sedgwick—carry, on their own, 37 percent of the entire Kansas population. They're eastern and generally urban or suburban, centered around Kansas City and Wichita. All of those people can make a difference during a statewide election. Even with forty-six house seats between them, however, Johnson's and Sedgwick's representatives and senators are easily outnumbered in the legislature.

In reality, the lines don't break down quite that neatly into Johnson and Sedgwick counties versus everybody else, but the example gives you an idea of how Kansas politics quickly splits into East versus West, urban versus rural, density versus square footage. Those fights remind everybody that they feel just a little cheated by the system. The urban counties are resentful that their greater numbers of con-stituents don't have more pull in the legislature. The rural counties are offended that the urbanites can swing state-wide elections, even though they represent (in land mass) less of the state.

The Climate and Energy Project was born out of one of those tussles. This is the environmental nonprofit I told you about in the introduction to this book, the one that decided to skip the usual arguments about climate change, in favor of focusing on the common ground of energy alternatives. Before the group made *that* decision, however, the people involved—including Eileen Horn—were focused on the very climate-centric legislative debate over a proposed new coal-fired power plant. I can talk until I'm blue in the face about the complexities of energy. I can tell you that energy decisions are driven by economics and other pressures that go beyond "what we ought to do." I can tell you that energy is always expensive, and energy is always being wasted. I can tell you that making our energy systems better isn't the same as building a utopia. Sometimes, though, it's better to show than tell. I've told you about the challenges that stand before us if we actually want to make good on our desire to reduce annual fossil fuel usage by 20 quadrillion BTUs by 2030. Now I want to show you how those challenges play out in the real world.

In 2006, the Sunflower Electric Corporation asked the state of Kansas for permission to build three new generators at an existing coal plant in the Western Kansas town of Holcomb. Each of the new generators would have had a capacity of 700 megawatts.

This stuff can get confusing. In particular, it's often hard to wrap your head around what the steps between the scales of measurement really mean. Here's one analogy I've found helpful: the difference between kilowatts and megawatts is like the difference in salary between somebody who brings home $40,000 a year and someone who pulls down $40 million. That gives you an idea of what we're talking about, but it doesn't really tell you much about the proposed Holcomb generator. One megawatt of capacity is enough to supply all of the electric needs of 750 average American households during the course of a year.[6] Together, all three generators would have had enough electric capacity to power more than 1.5 million homes every year.[7]

To put it mildly, that's a lot more electricity than little Holcomb needed. Its population barely pushes above two thousand people. You'd have to travel more than two hundred miles, in any direction, before you hit a city with more than thirty thousand residents.

In fact, Sunflower Electric itself served about four hundred thousand people, and far fewer homes. So, why build big? Because electricity isn't produced and used in the same place. That's just not how electricity—or, really, any form of energy—works in this country. Historically, it has cost much less to produce a lot of electricity in one spot and ship it over the wires to many other places. If the new power plant had gone according to plan, the electricity it generated would have been sent out into the wide world, far from Holcomb, traveling along transmission lines from one looming skeletal tower to another. That electricity wasn't even meant to light *only* Kansas. Instead, it would have been sold to customers in seven different states, as distant as New Mexico and Wyoming.

Yet producing power for an entire section of the American West doesn't come without some trade-offs. As coal burned in the three Holcomb generators, it would have released carbon dioxide into the atmosphere—11 million tons every year. There are several ways to look at that number. The entire country of Kenya produced only a little more CO_2 than that in 2007, but 11 million tons is just a drop in the bucket compared to America's total CO_2 emissions, which in the same year were somewhere north of 5 *billion* tons.[8] Depending on your perspective, you could use those statistics to argue that the carbon dioxide output of the proposed Holcomb plant was going to be devastating or piddling. The state of Kansas came down on the side of devastating, and that's where the trouble began. Sunflower Electric asked for the air quality permit it needed to move forward with building the three generators, and the state said no.

Now, it's not particularly weird for a state to object to a new coal plant because of the emissions it would produce. Whatever one's position on climate change, nobody—nobody who's honest—believes that coal is benign. We are, after all, talking about a source of power that kills tens of thousands of people every year on the European continent alone. It's just that usually, when states refuse air quality permits, the emissions in question are toxins such as mercury and sulfur or the particles of half-burned coal dust that float out of the power plant's smokestack and into local lungs. Historically, state permit denials have hinged on the sort of pollution that has a more immediate, obvious impact on the environment and on the health of people who live nearby.[9]

In 2007, when the state of Kansas said that Sunflower Electric couldn't build its three new generators, it marked the first time that a state had made a decision like that based on the long-term, slowly creeping health impact of *carbon dioxide* emissions.[10] The battle lines were quickly drawn, right along the old east-west, urban-rural tribal divides. The secretary of the Kansas Department of Health and Environment—the man who'd made the call—was appointed by a Democratic governor, someone who represented urban Eastern Kansans' power in statewide elections. The legislature, on the other hand, was dominated by representatives from the rural central and western counties. Old resentments flared up quickly. Urban Kansans saw pollution and an opportunity for their state to take a historic stand as a leader in the fight against climate change. Rural Kansans saw lost jobs and contempt for their home regions, which—thanks to declining populations—seldom get a shot at serious infrastructure upgrades. In nineteen months, the legislature introduced four bills aimed at allowing construction of the Holcomb power plant to move forward. The governor vetoed each one. Meanwhile, debates over those bills turned the state capitol building into a proxy battlefield for national debates over climate science.

Those fights might have gone on and on, two tribes indefinitely circling, were it not for a major political sea change. In April 2009, Kansas governor Kathleen Sibelius was sworn in as President Barack Obama's secretary of health and human services. Her replacement in the governor's mansion, Mark Parkinson, made a Holcomb compromise his first priority. In the end, both sides got part of what they wanted and a lot of what they didn't want. For the urban Kansans, there was a renewable energy standard, stipulating that 20 percent of Kansas's electricity would have to come from renewable sources by 2020. Rural Kansans got a scaled-down version of the Holcomb power plant—only one new generator, 895 megawatts, one-third of the generating capacity and one-third of the emissions.[11]

Western Kansas isn't in imminent danger of rolling blackouts. But just as we have to start working now to create a low-carbon future for our grandchildren, utility companies also have to plan for the future. Specifically, they have to plan for increased demand. During the next few decades, the United States will need more electricity generation, both to meet growing demand and to provide backup for the electric grid. Unless we implement some major changes in the way we give incentives for energy efficiency, that trend won't go away. Sunflower Electric wants to expand its power plant in Holcomb now so that it won't be caught without enough supply in twenty or thirty years. That's a legitimate concern, and it's one that's driven by the economic messages we send to our utility companies. Even Kansans who don't support the Holcomb power plant use electricity—and use more of it than they did a couple of decades ago.

Yet there are legitimate reasons for opposing a new coal power plant, too. We can't ignore those, either. Let's shift our attention to the other end of the Kansas teeter-totter, to the town of Merriam.

Most people reading this would probably find Merriam, Kansas, very familiar. Not because they've been there, but because it's a lot like home. Merriam is usually described as a suburb of Kansas City—a small town that grew into a residential center for people who worked in the much larger city nearby. Yet the mental images that go with the word *suburb* don't really fit Merriam all that well.

When I think suburb, I imagine something like Levittown, treeless insta-villages where rows of identical houses dot gleaming new cul-de-sacs recently carved out of some farmer's field. The greater Kansas City area certainly has its share of developments that would fit that description, but Merriam isn't one of them. In fact, when I was a kid, I didn't even know Merriam existed at all. I thought it was Kansas City. Specifically, I thought it was where Kansas City began, the distinct point where you exit the Interstate and find yourself in the big city. This particular misconception has more to do with my family's regular travel plans than anything else—Merriam's main drag happens to be the same road that leads to the art museum my dad and I went to a lot and to the Christmas light displays I visited every winter with my mom. It also speaks volumes about what Merriam actually looks like, though, and it's tied to some important trends in the way most Americans live today.

Merriam isn't a small town. There's nothing really recognizable as a small town central business district. Instead, Merriam's stores and

offices are mostly concentrated along two major thoroughfares—
Shawnee Mission Parkway and Johnson Drive. These wide, multilane
roads are dotted with clusters of shopping centers and big box stores,
like necklaces strung with fat pearls. The municipal building and
the police station are a couple of nondescript offices that sit off the
frontage of Shawnee Mission Parkway, on a ridge overlooking the
Interstate. Nothing about that says, "Classic Americana."

Yet Merriam isn't a suburb, either—or an urban city. It's too dense
to be the first and not dense enough to be the latter. Merriam has a
mixture of house styles. Drive down one street, and you'll see a 1930s
bungalow standing shoulder to shoulder with a spare little 1950s
Cape Cod. Next to that, there's a 1980s split-level with windows on
the front and the back but none on the sides. More than three generations of the American Dream are living here. Each house sits on
its own little lot, generous by the standards of city dwellers, but those
lots would seem cramped to anyone who grew up on an expansive,
truly suburban range of lawn. Some neighborhoods have sidewalks;
others don't. All in all, Merriam doesn't quite fit in with *any* of the
paradigms we use to describe "place" in the United States, and that
sense of befuddlement extends all the way to the edge of town—if
you can find it. The truth is that Merriam's borders are hazy, known
only to people whose jobs require them to be aware of that sort of
thing. To most people, Merriam bleeds into Mission, into Shawnee,
and into Overland Park. Those towns, in turn, nuzzle up against
others just like themselves. You could almost call them neighborhoods, except that they have their own separate governments. It's
ironic that Merriam doesn't really fit any of the classic American
paradigms, because, quite frankly, most of us have already left those
paradigms behind. We talk about this country as if it's full of neatly
defined small towns, big cities, and tidy suburbs. In reality, the places
where we live are lot mushier than that. Merriam isn't the exception.
Merriam is the rule.

The Brookings Institution calls places such as Merriam metropolitan areas. Each named community is just one part of a larger
symbiotic organism. "Being in a metro means being tied to someplace else," wrote Jennifer Bradley and Bruce Katz, of the Brookings
Institution's Metropolitan Policy Program, in 2008.[12] The collection

of cities in a metro work together, economically and socially, and by the Brookings Institution's tally, this is how most Americans live—as much as 84 percent of the population. That definition of "metro" is wide-reaching, encompassing places that might think of themselves as cities, small towns, and suburbs. That's certainly true of Tonganoxie, where my paternal grandparents lived. Thirty miles from Kansas City, it was a far-flung Hicksville when my dad was a teenager. Today, Tonganoxie is part of the metro—not really *just* a suburb, but not truly its own entity, either. The Brookings definition also includes such places as where I live now—a 1920s streetcar suburb that's been absorbed as a neighborhood of Minneapolis. We aren't urban, as visiting friends from New York City often remind us, but we're not suburban, either.

You can see that the Brookings definition is kind of broad, possibly overly broad. Residents of the places it describes might disagree with it, even vehemently. Yet if you're trying to figure out an objective way to group places by shared economic and social characteristics, it makes sense. This is better than a survey, which would tell you more about perceptions than about what places are actually like.[13] It also makes an important point: Independent, small-town life isn't archetypal America anymore. The interconnected metro is. Like Kansas, the weight of the *national* teeter-totter is unbalanced.

Kansas is full of places that aren't like Merriam. There are also tiny towns such as Quinter—a Western Kansas community with a population of fewer than a thousand—and mid-size cities such as Salina, which is home to more than forty-five thousand people. If you want to know what's at risk in the future of energy, however, Merriam is the place to focus. It's the place that can teach the majority of us something important about the places where *we* live and about the risks we're taking.

As I mentioned earlier, I'm concerned about climate change and about energy diversity.[14] They are the big reasons I think we need to seriously alter the way we make and use energy. Why do I think that? In a nutshell: that's what the majority of scientific studies tell me. When many different, unconnected scientists come to the same conclusions, after decades' worth of research, I listen. You should, too.[15] This isn't to say that the process of science is perfect, that researchers can't be biased, or that what we know about the world today will be exactly the same as what we'll know about the world twenty years from now. Nobody thinks that, least of all scientists. In fact, the scientific process is designed to account for all of those possibilities.

Take climate models, for instance. These are the computer simulations that researchers use to better understand how Earth's climate works as a system and how that system is likely to operate in the future. Climate models are digital laboratories, where scientists can program in all the different processes that make up a global climate system and then watch how that system behaves and changes under different circumstances. The models are based on math, complicated algorithms that spot connections between greenhouse gases, natural phenomena, dust in the air, and changes in climate. The algorithms extrapolate these connections into a vision of what the world could look like in decades to come. The models also rely on input—estimations, such as how high greenhouse gas concentrations are likely to increase in a given amount of time or how many volcanoes are likely to erupt. This input is based on historical evidence and "if/then" scenarios.

No single climate model is likely to be 100 percent accurate. That's why independent groups of scientists create *different* models to study the same situations. Compared to one another, these models use some of the same observational data and some that's different. They each give particular focus to specific factors that could affect the climate system, and each model is run many times, with many combinations of types of input. Unsurprisingly, those different models and various simulations also produce different results. Yet here's the key: all of the climate models that now exist show the same basic trends—the world will keep getting warmer, and climate patterns will continue to change in potentially devastating ways as concentrations of greenhouse gases in the atmosphere rise.

If there were only one climate model, or if all of the climate models were made by only one team of researchers, then those results *could* be a mistake. Bias and fraud would be a very real risk.

That's not what's going on, though. Instead, many groups with different interests, different sources of funding, different mistakes, and different biases are coming to the *same* conclusions. The models may disagree on some of the finer details, but they agree on the big picture. That's how science weeds out human error and human vice and brings us closer to the truth. If one mechanic claimed that you needed a new transmission, it could be an error or a scam, but if thousands of mechanics tell you the same thing, there's a much greater chance they're right.[16] Personally, I'd stop putting off the repairs at that point.

There is obviously much more to climate science than this, but all of the details I'm leaving out here are widely available elsewhere, and they aren't meant to be the focus of this book.[17] I just want you to understand a little about why climate change is one of the main reasons I'm interested in energy. It all boils down to a preponderance of evidence—evidence collected by many different people, in many different ways, during the course of more than three decades. That's what "scientific consensus" really means. It's not only something a bunch of scientists choose to believe in. It's something they've seen. It's what the bulk of the evidence is telling them.

In Kansas, researchers have collected more than a hundred years' worth of data about temperatures, rainfall, and weather patterns. From the perspective of a single year or even a decade or two, you might not notice much of a difference. There are seasons. Winters are still colder than summers. Kansas is one of those states with a reputation for fickle weather, anyway. Don't like this cold winter day? Just you wait a week; you'll be wearing shorts.[18] Yet if you zoom out and look at the century, patterns emerge. The average winter temperatures have gone up by 2 degrees Fahrenheit. Summer has been more stable, with an increase of only .6 degree.[19] In general, during the last century, Kansas has had fewer relatively cold days, while the number of relatively warm days has increased. *When* those increases happen also matters. During both winter and summer, average nighttime temperatures have increased more than average daytime temperatures have.

That doesn't sound like much, but it makes a difference in practical ways. In Merriam, Kansas, there are plants thriving today that probably couldn't have survived thirty years ago. When I was born, home gardeners in Merriam chose the seeds they'd plant outdoors by finding species that were rated to USDA Hardiness Zone 5—meaning that those plants could survive winter temperatures as low as –20 degrees. By the time I graduated from high school in 1999, the Kansas City metro, along with most of Kansas, had been upgraded to Hardiness Zone 6. Winter was no longer likely to be so frigid. If a plant could survive a few days of zero-degree temperatures, it could probably live in Merriam just fine. That opens up more possibilities for creative green thumbs. There aren't a lot of buildings in Kansas that are covered with the trailing green fingers of English ivy, but today, if you wanted a little ivy-covered cottage on the prairie—or an ivy-covered fence surrounding your metro backyard—you could grow it, without much worry of winter killing the plants.

If English ivy doesn't sound like a particularly horrible fate, that's because climate change isn't inherently good or bad, in and of itself. It's all about how those changes affect people.[20] We might like some of the results—English ivy can thrive, and even Kansas's many food crops are likely to grow better, at least in the short term—but we won't like everything that happens. For instance, the same warmer temperatures that favor English ivy are also quite favorable to ivy of another sort. Research shows that rising temperatures—even the small increases seen in Kansas—and rising CO_2 levels in the atmosphere are combining to expand the range of *poison* ivy, allowing it to be active for a longer part of the year *and* making it more poisonous.[21] A walk through local parks or state lands near Merriam is now more likely to involve a brush with the less-than-friendly side of nature.

The warmer climate works in tandem with a wetter one. Merriam and much of the northern and eastern parts of Kansas have become a lot wetter, especially in the winter. This ties in with what I mentioned in chapter 1—the Midwest is experiencing heavier storms more often than it did in the past. Those storms can cause serious damage and cost communities some serious money.[22] That's not all, though. Higher temperatures and more frequent downpours affect metro areas and their residents in a number of ways. When you combine warm water and flash flooding, you get a risk of water-borne disease.

That's because many harmful microorganisms favor higher temperatures. If floods overwhelm water-treatment facilities, those organisms
can find their way into the pipes, out of the tap, and into your glass.
This isn't something that happens only in underdeveloped countries
or other places we can write off as "not like home." The sanitation
infrastructure of American metro areas is impressive, but it's not
infallible. Many parts of the Midwest have experienced increased precipitation from more numerous large storms. This isn't only a Kansas
problem. In 1993, Milwaukee, Wisconsin, suffered an outbreak of
gastrointestinal disease caused by the bacteria *Cryptosporidium*.[23] This
bacteria doesn't merely give you a tummy ache. Instead, it leads to
a week or more of diarrhea, cramps, vomiting, and fever. Fifty-four
people died. Just before the illness struck, the region had received
its heaviest rainfall in fifty years.[24]

Since 1993, researchers have found that heavy rainfalls are associated with higher levels of potentially dangerous bacteria.[25] This
has been measured in drinking water and in recreational waters. It's
also turned up in floodwater. In 2008, when major flooding inundated Iowa City and Cedar Rapids, Iowa, raw sewage came right
out of the Cedar Rapids water-treatment plant and into the flood.
Those contaminated waters sloshed into people's houses, and when
the water finally receded, it left behind buildings full of muck and
mold. The people tasked with cleanup duties suffered from what they
called "flood crud," weeks of fatigue, cough, and other respiratory
symptoms.[26]

Speaking of breathing problems, warmer springs that bloom earlier in the year have also led to longer allergy seasons, and scientists
say that the higher CO_2 concentrations found in traffic-heavy cities
and metros are causing plants to have higher pollen counts.[27] This
means that people who weren't affected by allergies thirty or forty
years ago might be sniffling and stuffy today, and Merriam residents
who have always had allergies now have to deal with them for longer
periods of the year.

Air pollution is another big problem. In the heat of a hot and
sunny day, tailpipe emissions from cars turn into lung-damaging,
heart-straining smog. In any metro area, including Merriam, the more
relatively hot days you have, the greater the risks of smog-associated

asthma and heart attacks.[28] Kansas City, Kansas, and Overland Park—two cities near Merriam—spent more than $13 million on asthma treatment in 2001.[29] The more risk there is of smog-related lung damage, the higher those costs will rise.

During the next thirty years or so, a warmer, wetter Merriam might be, in some ways, a more comfortable place to live—the last few decades have brought longer growing seasons for plants and winter temperatures that are more reliably pleasant. Yet Merriam is also becoming a more expensive place to live and a place where the individual risk of illness and property damage is going up—and up and up. The more greenhouse gases are added to the atmosphere, the higher the global average temperature will eventually climb. As that happens, Merriam and places like it all around the United States will be exposed to risks that are greater and more numerous. Some people talk about thresholds for climate change—how many years we have left to act, how much CO_2 we can afford to release, how high of a global average temperature we can accept before all hell breaks loose. I'm not sure that's really a great way to think about it, though. Our climate is already changing. The risks are already being realized, and every emissions reduction goalpost ever set is somewhat arbitrary. There's not a magic number that can save us. Instead, we should really just be trying to limit the continuation of climate change as much and as fast as possible.[30]

If that isn't enough to worry about, metros such as Merriam are also likely to be hard hit when oil production peaks and higher gasoline prices follow.

There's an increasingly large collection of research telling us it probably isn't a good idea to rely solely on fossil fuels. Why? Because those fuels are finite. There's only so much of them to go around—although it is still open to debate exactly *how* finite the supplies of oil, coal, and natural gas are.

All three fossil fuels come from the same place—ancient plants and animals that died and were buried beneath layers of earth and rock, often millions of years before dinosaurs roamed this planet.[31] Changed by heat, pressure, and the process of decomposition, these dead remains became the substances that make our modern lives possible. The coal that we burn to make electricity was once forests and swamps full of plants. The oil in your gas tank and the natural gas that heats your house are the remains of tiny sea creatures. Turning those plants and animals into fuel takes millions of years, and it can happen only under certain circumstances. Once we burn through these fuels—or, more important, once we burn through the ones that are relatively cheap to collect—there won't be any more. Not on any time scale that would be useful to you or to me.

That's worrisome. All of the conveniences, comforts, and wealth we've accumulated since the late 1800s have been largely based on the availability of relatively inexpensive fossil fuels. Those fuels pack a lot of energy into a compact space. Other fuels, such as cut wood, can't compete with that kind of energy density—a fact that becomes especially important when you need to travel somewhere and must carry fuel along with you. The weight and the volume of fuel definitely matter. More than a hundred years ago, oil, refined into gasoline, solved the transportation-fuel problem, but what happens if oil becomes too expensive for most Americans? What happens, eventually, when it finally runs out?

To answer these questions, we first have to know "when." If we have a hundred years before oil production peaks, then we'll be in a very different position compared to that peak happening next year—or last year. The timing of this peak isn't easy to figure out. The world's supply of oil is harder to measure than carbon dioxide concentrations in the atmosphere, for the simple reasons that nobody owns the atmosphere, and the atmosphere is well-mixed. Oil, on the other hand, is a business. It comes with trade secrets. It also comes without an industry-wide standard for calculating untapped oil reserves. If one company tells you how much oil it has left, you can't directly add that to another company's number and get a reliable total, because both calculations were figured in very different ways. Unlike the atmosphere, you can't just take a sample from anywhere on the planet and expect it to tell you something about conditions everywhere.

Finally, there's no equivalent of the Intergovernmental Panel on Climate Change (IPCC) for peak oil. This matters. Part of what makes the IPCC so important is that it does the job of consolidating many little theories into one big Theory. The IPCC reviews all of the scientific papers published on climate science and the impact of climate change. It looks at methodology and figures out which papers are more trustworthy than others, and it compiles all of that information into realistic estimates of what might happen and when. If there are two competing little theories that should be given equal attention—because nobody knows yet which is correct—the IPCC tells you that.

In contrast, peak oil research is a confusing jumble of individual, often contradictory, papers. To a layperson, it's not easy to tell which little theories on this subject deserve more respect, and it's hard to get a sense of what the overarching scientific consensus is, if one exists at all. That means you have nothing to draw on when it comes time to judge the statements about peak oil that are made *outside* the scientific community. When you read an op-ed that claims oil production has already peaked and that our entire way of life is imminently going to collapse, do you know how much evidence supports that and how much doesn't? When another source tells you that peak oil isn't something to worry about at all, is there a reason to believe this statement? Without an IPCC-like entity, answering those questions requires a lot of time and a not-insignificant amount of scientific expertise.

There's been *some* progress made in solving this problem. In 2009, British researchers put together a sort of micro-mini IPCC aimed at answering the question "What evidence is there to support the proposition that the global supply of 'conventional oil' will be constrained by physical depletion before 2030?" In other words, is peak oil a short-term problem or a long-term problem?

The researchers' report doesn't cover all of the questions surrounding the idea of peak oil. For instance, they specifically avoid predicting what economic, political, or social side effects peak oil could produce, and their research covered only supplies of "conventional oil"—no tar sands or fuels made from coal or natural gas.[32] This group was also much smaller than the one that evaluates the evidence for climate change—only eight experts, drawn from the United Kingdom and the United States. Yet the project is an important first for peak oil: a group with no obvious bias had collected all of the available research, evaluated it in a transparent way, and summarized the whole body of evidence for nonexperts.[33]

Here's what they found. First, peak oil is a real occurrence. We know enough about how oil fields work and what happens during the life of a given oil deposit to say that production of oil will peak, and then it will decline.

Second, figuring out *when* that decline will happen isn't easy, for reasons I've already mentioned and more. Yet although the data on oil supplies are flawed and patchy and the methods used to forecast future supplies have some serious limitations, the researchers agree that there's still enough information available that we can start to form a clear picture of global oil supplies and make some adequate estimates about how long conventional oil will last. These estimates won't be perfect, but they're necessary, and they'll be accurate enough to help us plan for the future, at least until better data come along.

Finally, even if you factor in a wide range of reasonable estimates about the quantity of oil supplies, you're still left with a relatively narrow window of time during which oil production is likely to peak. The peak is probably going to happen by 2030. To claim a later date, the researchers wrote, you have to start getting optimistic in your estimations of global oil supply.[34] When we hit peak oil, it won't mean that gasoline will vanish overnight, or even in a few years. But it would most likely mean the end of cheap gasoline. You may not feel that gas is cheap when you're paying for a full tank. It's never cheap right then. Even when I first started driving, in the late 1990s, and paid less than a dollar per gallon, I still drove away from the pump feeling disgruntled. Today, in early 2011, I pay closer to $4 a gallon, but that gas is cheap, too. Gas has always been cheap in the United States, both compared to other developed countries and compared to the finite supply and the amount of work and convenience we get out of burning it. Gasoline is so cheap here that we built our entire lives around the expectation of being able to burn it whenever we want, no matter the reason. Gas is so cheap, I don't even think twice about driving alone in my car less than a mile to the grocery store, just because I want an errand done faster. Gas is so cheap, my father-in-law can use a snow plow in the winter, instead of a shovel. Gas is so cheap, my mother can go for a ride through the woods on a four-wheeler, just for fun. Peak oil means all of that will likely change. We'll have to start considering whether we can afford certain aspects of our lifestyles that we currently take for granted.

For instance, right now, living in Merriam means owning a car. The whole town is designed around the idea that cheap gasoline will always be available. The main shopping center is a strip mall off the Interstate. Sidewalks—and easily walkable grid street plans—come and go throughout the neighborhoods, following the whims of past developers. Merriam has two bike routes, but one is mostly aimed at recreation. It doesn't follow any path that people travel daily for business, school, or shopping. The other bike route begins and ends suddenly, covering only a small portion of busy Shawnee Mission Parkway. There are bus lines that pass through town, but the service isn't particularly robust. Most of the buses are strictly for commuters, offering a handful of morning trips to downtown Kansas City and evening trips back. The system isn't really meant for general mobility. A trip from Merriam's main shopping center to my favorite Chinese restaurant in nearby Overland Park is a nine-minute drive. By bus, it's forty-four minutes, and you can't go for lunch or a late dinner. The buses don't run between nine a.m. and four p.m., and they shut down for the night after six p.m.. You see the problem here.

As the price of gas climbs, and middle-class Americans have to start seriously thinking about whether they can afford a given trip, the residents of Merriam will find themselves without an easy, all-weather way to navigate the crazy quilt of metro towns that surrounds them. For those who work outside Merriam, it'll be harder to get to work. Inside Merriam, businesses will suffer the loss of the heavy traffic that now passes by twice a day. Metro towns aren't self-reliant. Their fates have been tied to the fates of the towns they touch for decades. That interconnection works now because gasoline is cheap. What happens to a metro town when travel from one part to another is no longer easy and frequent, no longer something that can happen daily or hourly? What happens when the parts of a metro can no longer rely on the direct support of all of the others but are still on the hook for funding shared systems? What happens to the city at the metro's heart when it can no longer count on the social support, the financial investments, and the intellectual capital of people who actually live elsewhere?

Maybe the parts of a metro can break down into tighter-knit blocks. In a world of high fuel prices, Merriam could theoretically band together with the cities of Shawnee, Mission, and Overland Park to make a smaller, more walkable version of the metro experience. Yet it likely wouldn't be as well-off as those places are today, when they can easily trade throughout the larger metro area and far beyond, when a local job doesn't have to be closely tied to local demand, when the cost of food and goods isn't also being driven up by the high cost of the fuel needed to make and transport them.[35] If you think about all of the parts of our lives that rely on cheap oil, it's easy to see how authors such as James Howard Kunstler can believe that peak oil will lead, unstoppably, to the collapse of modern, industrial civilization— where metros will descend into poverty and anarchy, and only independent small towns will be able to survive in a future that shares a lot of similarities with the nineteenth century.[36] You don't even have to go that far, however, to be concerned about the impact of peak oil. In a 2005 report written for the Department of Energy, researcher Robert Hirsch wrote that total economic meltdown wasn't an inevitable consequence of peak oil.[37] Yet he also pointed out that most economic recessions in the United States after 1969 were preceded by a spike in oil prices, and that every jump in oil prices was followed by a recession. There's a key quotation from the paper that really drives home the kind of risks we're talking about: "Economically, the decade following peaking may resemble the 1970s, only worse, with dramatic increases in inflation, long-term recession, high unemployment, and declining living standards."

The 1970s, only worse. That's the pleasant outlook. Even that won't be possible, Hirsch says, if we don't start changing the way we make and use energy now. Remember, oil is most likely to peak sometime before 2030. We don't know exactly when. It could be tomorrow, could be 2029. Yet if we want to really mitigate the impact of peak oil and keep the economy as stable as possible, Hirsch thinks we need at least twenty years of dedicated effort to sufficiently reduce oil consumption and create alternative fuels.[38] As the prep time shortens, the consequences get larger. With only a decade of preparation before peak oil, we're likely to be stuck with ten years of chronic fuel shortage. If we don't start trying to mitigate the effects of peak oil until it actually happens, Hirsch thinks we'll be looking at more than twenty years of hardship.

We have two problems: we need energy, but we also need to avoid the negative impacts of climate change and peak oil. The timeline for action: the sooner, the better. So, the question becomes "Now what do we do?"

....

CHAPTER EIGHT

THE TAKE-CHARGE CHALLENGE

W e like the benefits we receive from our energy systems—light, heat, gadgets, comfort, and convenience. Yet the way these systems currently function, using them means accepting some dangerous side effects. In Kansas and across the United States, the debate over energy has split into a battle between people who worry about having to give up their modern lifestyles and people who are concerned about the long-term fallout. Meanwhile, both sides keep using the flawed systems, and nothing gets done to solve either problem.

That's the conundrum the fledgling Climate and Energy Project (CEP) found itself facing in the wake of the Holcomb compromise. The organization had started out as a public voice against the power plant, but that one power plant wasn't really the issue, only a symptom of it. To produce any real change, both the people who wanted access to energy and those who wanted to avoid the side effects of our current energy systems would have to work together.

"We had to sit down and figure out how we were going to reengage Kansans in a conversation about [climate and energy] now that this controversial decision had pissed everybody off," Eileen Horn said. That's why the man from the Wichita focus group—the one who thought climate change was a scam but was happy to invest his own money in energy efficiency—was so important. He gave the CEP a chance by changing the group's perspective.

The Holcomb power plant debate had divided Kansans into very clear tribes, both of which thought the other was being terribly irresponsible. The two groups had come to an agreement that thrilled pretty much no one. There was a very real possibility that had the CEP started to push climate education as a primary objective, the group members would have found themselves welcome only among the people who had also heavily opposed the Holcomb plant. Worse, that same course of action might have alienated a lot of folks in the middle—the ones who weren't sure what to think about climate change *or* power plant construction but who were definitely sick and tired of being yelled at by the true believers on both sides of the aisle. "Instead, we decided to just kind of ignore the elephant in the room and focus on solutions, instead," Eileen told me.

All of the work the CEP did in the wake of that decision was centered on the revelations that came out of their focus groups. It turned out that a lot of Kansans already cared about energy. By accepting their personal reasons for caring and by honoring their concerns, the CEP could sidestep the most contentious part of the process. Instead of continuing the fight over climate science, the CEP set out to help Kansans take action on energy in ways that aligned with what those Kansans already cared about. Because of the research I've read, the scientists I've interviewed, and the evidence I've seen, I think that climate change and energy diversity are the most important issues. Those are my reasons to care about energy, but there are other reasons you might care about energy.

For instance, the CEP's focus groups found that a lot of the people who said they were Christians also said they were interested in Creation Care—the idea that part of worshipping God means respecting and protecting the world he made.[1] Basically, your Heavenly Father wants you to clean up after yourself.

Some of those people thought about climate change as a part of Creation Care, while others were focused on the more obvious kinds of pollution, and on conserving limited resources for future generations.[2] Either way, Creation Care was closely connected to energy, and the CEP used that connection to establish Kansas Interfaith Power and Light, a faith-based nonprofit that now distributes energy-saving tips and tools, helps make church buildings more energy efficient, and provides resources for pastors who want to communicate the idea of Creation Care to their congregations.

Yet that's only one example. I mentioned earlier that there are a lot of reasons people care about changing the way we make and use energy. The CEP tried to create a variety of programs to match the various reasons. Kansas Interfaith Power and Light had its place, but it wouldn't be enough to inspire the entire state. The organizers of the CEP had already decided that they weren't going to get very far trying to convince everybody to care for the exact same reasons. Now they took that a step further. They decided that no energy program could be one-size-fits-all. Reaching the largest segment of the population meant talking about energy from as many different perspectives as possible. On the one hand, you had Christian churches hoping to touch the divine, and on the other, you had groups of people who were interested in much more earthly concerns.

When the CEP asked Kansans why the future of energy mattered, another popular response was the desire for self-sufficiency and more homegrown power. To these people, relying on oil from the Middle East or even coal from West Virginia was antithetical to pioneer values. If you depended that much on resources from far-away places, then you lost control of your own destiny. Making energy could be a source of pride and money. Both Kansas and the United States ought to be able to stand on their own two feet—or, at least, be a little more stable on the one foot.

A lot of the people who felt that way were also farmers and ranchers, Eileen Horn told me. They'd been raised with the idea that America could and should feed itself, and energy self-sufficiency was simply an extension of that. Plus, if you know any farmers, you've probably noticed that the job often goes hand in hand with a love of machinery and homemade fix-it solutions. Farmers dig DIY. It's often occurred to me that rural mechanical tinkerers, such as my step-father and some of my cousins, really have a lot in common with the urban digital tinkerers and hackers who congregate on BoingBoing. The main difference is the medium. Either way, you're talking about people who like to make things more than they like to *buy* things and who love to build and improve on the stuff they *do* buy.

To reach out to those folks, the CEP helped found the Blue Green Alliance, a group that brings together farmers, rural associations, labor unions, and energy activists.[3] Together, they work on making Kansas a politically friendly place for wind power and other local energy sources.

Yet that still leaves one of the biggest motivators out there: money. Most people notice when their utility bills go up. Most people see what happens when city budgets fall short. Likewise, everybody in the focus groups worried about the rising cost of energy and wanted to make sure that both Kansas and the United States would be competitive in a global, energy-conscious economy. This was a big motivator for the man on the first page of this book, who changed the CEP's way of thinking, and the Take-Charge Challenge was made for people like him.

The Take-Charge Challenge is the biggest and most well-known of all of the CEP programs. It emphasizes energy conservation and efficiency—reducing demand for electricity by cutting out waste and doing more with less. If you turn off a lightbulb in a room you aren't using, that's conservation. If you replace your old lightbulb with one that provides the same amount of light for less energy, that's efficiency. These changes can save you money directly, but they matter in larger ways as well.

If you reduce energy use enough, you can put off the need for a new power plant or reduce the size of what you need to build.[4] It's a lot cheaper for a utility company to encourage conservation and efficiency, compared to what it would cost to build a new power plant, and the company then passes those savings on to customers. Individuals save money by using less electricity, and the utility company saves money by not having to invest in new construction. It's the same idea behind smart grid programs such as GridWise.

The trouble is that using less energy doesn't sound like much fun. It sounds like deprivation—Jimmy Carter, in his infamous sweater, telling people to keep their houses cold all winter long. Events such as Earth Hour tell people that reducing energy use means sitting in the dark. If the Take-Charge Challenge was going to work, it couldn't be only about saving money by saving energy. It also had to show people that the savings didn't have to hurt.[5]

So, the CEP turned conservation and efficiency into a game. They picked seven towns across Kansas and divided those towns into five teams, pairing up the smaller ones that needed to share resources. From the summer of 2009 until the summer of 2010, everyone would do everything he or she could think of to get schools, municipal governments, and residents to use less energy. At the end of the year, the CEP and local utility companies would add up the savings and see how much each team had reduced its town's energy use compared to a year earlier. The winner would get a wind turbine to power a local school, some solar panels to attach to a civic building, and cash to invest in even more energy efficiency.

Some of the places that signed on for the contest were in Western Kansas—such as Quinter, that little town I told you about earlier, nestled between the parallel bars of an old U.S. highway and the modern Interstate 70, two hours from the Colorado border. At the other end of the scale—and the state—is Merriam. These towns couldn't be more different. The physical footprint of Quinter hasn't changed much in a hundred years. In that same time, Merriam grew from a small railroad town to a popular summer resort to a mushroomed expanse of American domesticity. Quinter is the kind of place where everybody knows your name. More people commute *through* Merriam every day than live in Quinter. You get the idea. The legislative battles over the Holcomb power plant had been split along tribal lines between places such as Quinter and Merriam, but a mutual concern about the high cost of energy brought them together.

Although it literally has ten times the population of Quinter and an annual budget that Quinter would likely envy, Merriam isn't particularly large or wealthy compared to its neighbors. Cash is tight, and the municipal staff is small. The city council wasn't inclined to waste either resource on sustainability initiatives, such as alternative energy, just because its members might feel a bit of empathy for woodland creatures. In that setting, Chris Evans Hands, the city council's self-described hippie member, actually reached the same conclusion about how to motivate energy change that the CEP did but without the help of a formal focus group. The council *was* her focus group. "Early on, I learned that you don't say, 'We're trying to save the planet,'" she told me. "Instead, I say, 'We're trying to save you money. We're trying to save the city money.' That was really the only way to solve it."

The Take-Charge Challenge fit right in with why the Merriam city council cared about energy. If the council members could reduce the amount of money they spent on electricity to light city hall or run the computers at the police station, then that money could be used in other ways—ways that the residents of Merriam would be more likely to notice and appreciate come election time. If homes and businesses in Merriam could reduce the amount of electricity they used, then the local utility company might not have to build its own new power plant, which would help hold down the cost of electricity in Merriam and make it a more appealing place to live and work. When the city council gave Evans Hands the go-ahead to take part in the Challenge, it had the immediate state of the city coffers in mind.

Evans Hands told me she was okay with that, although it seemed to frustrate her a little. I'm okay with money as a key motivator for energy change, too—up to a point. Money, just like fossil fuels, is a limited resource that we have to use wisely. I think we need to drastically change the way we make and use energy, and we should do that as cheaply as we can.[6] Yet often when I see money used as a motivator, the people involved are focused only on the short term. Just as the cities of Quinter and Merriam did, most individual Americans will jump on an opportunity to change the way they use energy if they know they'll see the results next month in their utility bills. That works great for certain kinds of energy change, but it's less helpful when we need to spend a lot now, so that our children and grandchildren can save even more money fifty or a hundred years into the future. The way we think about energy and money sometimes is like deciding not to fix your roof because the repairs will be expensive. Ultimately, the *real* issue is how much more you'd have to pay in a few years, and how much more of your house would be damaged, if you didn't fix the roof now.

We can't rely on the thrill of an immediate cash savings to push the United States toward all of the different energy changes it needs— at least, not if we want to be honest about it. Worse, there's good reason to think that if we make only the kind of changes that come with instant gratification, we'll regret it later. Places such as Merriam and Quinter have a lot to gain by saving money on energy now, but they also have a lot to lose if we don't start *spending* money on energy change soon.

Out of five teams, all vying to be the energy-efficiency capital of Kansas, Merriam came away as one of the two big winners—compared to the previous year, the town used 5.5 percent less electricity.[7] When I tell Kansas friends this, their first response invariably is incredulity. They know that greater Johnson County isn't the kind of place where the majority of the population would jump at the chance to fight climate change, and they wonder how a place like Merriam could possibly organize its residents around such a hippie-ish goal. I could have treated myself to a very nice meal if I'd earned a dollar every time someone asked, "*Merriam* won that? Really?"

To be fair, Merriam's Take-Charge Challenge leadership—city council member Evans Hands and her staff—seemed a little surprised by the win themselves. Everybody figured Merriam was at a disadvantage, both because people assumed the twelve thousand– odd Merriamites didn't care that much about energy and because they knew that civic life in a metro doesn't work like civic life in independent small towns.

Quinter, for example, kicked off its participation in the Take-Charge Challenge by throwing a party. Half of the town was there— literally. Another example is Salina. Almost exactly in the middle of the state, Salina has a much larger population than Quinter does, but it's an independent entity, not part of any bigger metro. In Salina, they could promote the Take-Charge Challenge on local radio stations or the Fox TV affiliate and know that the advertising dollars were well spent. The people who heard the message were likely to be the people whose actions contributed to the contest. More important, both Quinter and Salina had a sense of themselves as distinct places. Even if they were apathetic about energy savings, the people who lived there could be rallied behind the idea of winning the prize *for* Salina or *for* Quinter. They cared about their town being the best—like a scaled-down version of flag-waving patriotic pride.

None of that would have worked in Merriam. Like most metros, many of its residents work in other places—and vice versa. Because it sits at the junction of several major arteries through the Kansas City area, you can't even assume that most of the people who shop in Merriam live in Merriam. The local population drifts in and out of the city limits multiple times every day. Although they may know their neighbors, their social circles don't revolve exclusively around the town where they live. Evans Hands laughed at the idea of getting half of Merriam's residents to turn out for anything. What's more, that interwoven, multicity economy, combined with shared media outlets, meant advertising was all but pointless. At least, pointless to the purposes of the contest. *Somebody* would have heard the energy-efficiency message, but there was no guarantee that the money spent would do anything to change how people used energy in Merriam. When Hands and her staff set out to plan their strategy for the contest, they knew that plenty of Merriam residents didn't even know they lived in Merriam.

How does a city like that win an energy-efficiency contest? The solution is deceptively simple. All you have to do is stop assuming that small-town ways of building community and motivating people are the only ways for a community to exist or for people to be motivated. So, pulling together a big turnout for a Take-Charge Challenge Kickoff Party wasn't realistic? And there's not really a downtown where everyone gathers? Okay. Instead, Hands and her staff showed up at long-standing community events. The people of Merriam still get together, they simply don't do it all at once, and it happens in places such as Merriam Marketplace—a small park and a farmers' market venue—or in the nearby county parks. The Turkey Creek Festival, for instance, has been around for twenty-six years. It already draws thousands of people from Merriam and surrounding towns. With the help of Thermie the Thermostat—Kansas City Power and Light's odd, yet surprisingly kid-pleasing, mascot—Merriam organizers blanketed the festival with Take-Charge Challenge fliers, passed out energy-efficient lightbulbs, and signed people up for home energy–reduction services that KCPnL already offered all of its customers.

As for advertising, Evans Hands says that the city didn't spend a single dollar on advertising for the Take-Charge Challenge. Instead, the city council took the energy-saving message directly to niche groups that were likely to pick up the information and spread it around—like, say, kids. Local Boy Scout troops went door to door, passing out lightbulbs. There were also grade schools serving mostly Merriam families that were already incorporating energy and sustainability messages into the classroom. All that the Take-Charge Challenge had to do was step in with specific activities that could help families reduce energy use and get the kids fired up about how they could help the city win. Because that was the other thing: even though Merriam couldn't count on the kind of civic pride that goes along with high school football and an independent city mind-set, that didn't mean there was *no* civic pride, and it didn't mean the people of Merriam couldn't get caught up in the thrill of competition. It's just that the competitions—similar to the message about the challenge itself—had to be more narrowly targeted. Classrooms and schools were pitted against one another. Local hotels faced off to see who could reduce the most. Merriam's small business community also jumped at the opportunity to distinguish itself from competitors in nearby towns.

Instead of casting one wide net, Merriam threw out a bunch of little ones, and the strategy paid off. "From listening to what some of the other cities in the challenge did, they pigeonholed themselves in what their efforts were," says Elliot Lahn, a Merriam city planner and one of the people who worked closely with Evans Hands on the Take-Charge Challenge. "We [took the message everywhere] from community park events to school reading functions to pizza parties to the Boy Scouts to working with the hospitals. We really got our fingers into everything."[8]

Despite the stereotypes and the skepticism, the Merriam city organizers knew that their town—and other metros like it—wasn't devoid of community and social connections. This intermingling simply happened at different places and in different ways than in a small town. People who live in a metro don't lack local pride. You just have to harness it differently. The city of Merriam won the Take-Charge Challenge because instead of lamenting what the city wasn't, the organizers took advantage of what it was.

Yet what does that win really mean? Merriam reduced its electricity use by 5.5 percent. That's not an insignificant amount. When you're dealing with large numbers—and U.S. energy use always comes in large numbers—even small percentages add up fast. For instance, if the United States as a whole cut electricity use by 5.5 percent, we'd be saving more electricity than the entire country of Mexico uses in a year.[9] At the very least, Merriam's win shows that the simple act of reducing our greenhouse gas footprint doesn't require any fancy technology and doesn't have to be particularly expensive. Installing compact fluorescent lightbulbs and programmable thermostats made up the bulk of the changes.

At the same time, though, you have to keep Merriam's success in context. This was a onetime reduction, after all. At the end of the Take-Charge Challenge, the CEP actually had to split the first-place title—dividing it between Merriam and little Quinter—because although Merriam had the largest single-year energy reduction, the people of Quinter had invested in changes that were likely to pay off with larger energy savings than Merriam's over the long term. Merriam changed its lightbulbs. Quinter insulated houses and installed energy-efficient air-conditioning systems. There are no data on how the citizens of either town spent the money they saved, so we don't know what the rebound effect for this event was like. It's also worth noting that all of this happened during a recession. Would the citizens of Merriam have been as motivated to reduce their energy use and save money if the economy weren't so flimsy? Evans Hands admitted that she's not sure, and energy change that's dependent on Americans being worse off financially doesn't paint a particularly inspiring image of the future.

Even the success itself is rather subjective. Remember how the 11 million tons of carbon dioxide that would have been released every year by the original full-scale Holcomb power plant could be thought of as both a lot of CO_2 and not that much, depending on the comparisons you chose? It's the same here. On one hand, reducing electricity use by 5.5 percent is a success. On the other hand, it's nowhere close to being *enough* of a success, not if we're concerned about climate change and energy diversity. It's definitely not enough if we want the big changes to happen fast. In fact, energy efficiency and conservation, in general, aren't enough to create the kind of change we need, not on their lonesome.

We could theoretically put climate change on pause right now—lock in atmospheric accumulation of carbon dioxide at its current level and stop the process from getting worse. Efficiency and conservation could do that. But you wouldn't like the outcome very much, says Stephen Pacala, the director of the Carbon Mitigation Initiative at Princeton University. To solve the problem that way, we'd have to adopt a very strict and meager rationing of greenhouse gas emissions—just one ton of emissions per year, per person. A ton sounds like a lot, but in this case, it's not. The resulting budget would look less like a prudent belt-tightening and more like the work of Ebenezer Scrooge, pre-Christmas. One ton of greenhouse gas emissions buys a year's worth of heat for one average home in the United States, Pacala says. That's not including electricity, clothes, food, or transportation. Do you travel a lot for business? Maybe you could spend your one ton of emissions on airline flights instead. On that yearly budget, you can afford to fly ten thousand miles in coach. Of course, again, that leaves you with no food to eat, no clothes to wear, and no house to come home to.

So, there's saving the future, and then there's actually being able to enjoy the future we saved. If you want the latter, it's clear that simply reducing energy demand won't be enough. In fact, no *one* change will be enough. Pacala made this point about efficiency and conservation not because he's a killjoy or because he doesn't think those efforts are worthwhile. He made it because he's convinced that no single change can solve our energy problems. You can't do it only with efficiency and conservation. You can't do it with nuclear power alone. You can't do it with only biofuels or wind and solar generation or a smart grid.

Instead, Pacala and many other experts say that you'll need all of those elements. As with scientific theories, many little solutions have to come together to create one big Solution. In some ways, the little solutions can't work at all if they aren't used in tandem with others. A good way to think about the future of energy is to imagine it as a three-legged stool. To keep it from wobbling or breaking, you need a strong foundation in three key areas—energy efficiency, energy infrastructure, and alternative generation, all three at once. To get the most environmental benefit from energy efficiency, you also need to have alternative generation.[10] America's electric infrastructure needs smart grid technology, natural gas, cleaner coal, and nuclear power to stay stable during the next few decades. Alternative generation needs a smart grid to work, and it needs efficiency to lower electric demand. All of the parts support one another. If we really want to reduce our fossil fuel use by 20 quadrillion BTUs a year in only twenty years, then we need to embrace as many ways to change energy as the CEP embraced reasons to care about energy.

More important, this is how we have to do it if we want to make a difference in the time we have. There are many reasons to care about the future of energy, and I think we can find enough common ground to get the ball rolling by respecting everyone's concerns. Frankly, given a perfect world, I'd be happy to just sit back and let people move on energy change at their own pace, but the world isn't perfect. Between climate change and fossil fuel peaks, there's good evidence that we can't afford to let the future of energy slowly evolve. The risks are too big, and they get bigger the longer we wait. We don't know exactly when oil will peak, and the economic fallout is likely to be worse and last longer the less prepared we are for it. The climate is already changing. The more greenhouse gases we add to the atmosphere, the hotter the planet will get, and the longer the effects will last—even after we do finally reduce our reliance on fossil fuels. That's because the excessively high levels of greenhouse gasses currently in our atmosphere won't quickly drop back to normal once we stop adding to them, just as your body doesn't instantly sober up when you pass on a seventh beer. The impact of climate change—the hangover—will take even longer to vanish. Even if we somehow stopped burning fossil fuels tomorrow, researchers say we could still be living with the results of choices we've already made for a thousand years.[11] The longer we wait, the bigger the problem gets and the harder it is to do anything about.

This brings me to another key lesson about energy, something I hinted at earlier but didn't really shout about yet: you can't do this yourself. Coordinating lots of different solutions on the level of systems, as fast as we possibly can is something that requires a group effort directed by policy, not volunteerism.

Think about it this way: energy is like public health. There are small acts you can perform to protect yourself from disease, choices you can make that have a minor impact on your little corner of the world. Yet these actions alone won't prevent you from getting a disease, and they definitely won't solve the problem on a larger scale. Smallpox was a scourge that humankind is better off without, but we didn't get rid of it because individuals decided to quarantine themselves. You don't fight a systemic problem on an individual level. Eradicating smallpox required us to make big societal investments in the research and development of vaccines and in the infrastructure to get those vaccines to every corner of the globe. Individuals mattered in that process: people did the research, people administered vaccines, and people chose to get vaccinated. The plan worked, however, because those people were acting as a part of something bigger. On their own, with nothing to connect their efforts, individuals trying to eradicate smallpox couldn't have made a difference, even if lots of individuals were separately working on it at the same time.

Energy is a system, just like public health. Changing that system will require something bigger than what you and I can do at home and even bigger than what one metro can do during the course of a year. That doesn't mean there's no point to changing our personal lifestyles. My husband and I have made a number of changes because we are concerned about energy. We bought a house on a heavily traveled bus route, so that we only have to own one car. The house we chose is smaller than average, on a small lot, so that it takes a lot less energy to heat it, and we can easily take care of the lawn with a push mower, instead of a gas-powered one.[12] Our house is also older. Basically, we recycled, rather than building new, and we've updated it to make it more energy efficient. We opted into a program from our utility company that allows us to pay a little extra every month to help fund wind power projects.[13] We recycle. We compost during the summer. When we have to buy appliances, we choose Energy Star. Since my husband started working as an energy consultant, we've made a lot of little changes to the way we live. We do this because energy is important to us, and we want to express those values. Yet we also know that our actions aren't really helping the United States get off fossil fuels.

My husband and I certainly aren't the most energy-conscious Americans ever, but even if we were, that wouldn't change the fact that individual actions aren't the solution. In *Powering the Dream,* journalist Alexis Madrigal's book about the history of alternative energy technologies and what it can teach us about energy today, Madrigal cites an MIT study that does a very good job of expressing the limits of individual choice. In the study, researchers looked at the energy impact of eighteen different types of American lifestyles, ranging from a homeless person and a Buddhist monk to a U.S. senator and a multimillionaire. The homeless person and the monk used a lot less energy than the senator and the multimillionaire did, to be sure. Yet when you take the energy they did use and add to it the energy embodied in our shared systems—roads, schools, the military, and so on—even the Americans with the most Spartan lifestyles still consumed more than *double* the average global energy use.[14]

In other words, you could beat your own lifestyle into submission with a ten-foot club—you could do more to save the planet than almost anyone is willing to voluntarily do—and it still wouldn't be enough. This isn't about you, and it isn't about me. It's about the systems that we share. The answer to the question "So now what?" has to be "Now we change the systems." No other option makes sense.

CHAPTER NINE

....

THE OLIVE GREEN
REVOLUTION

It was a bright, hot July day in northern Florida—the kind of day when birds pant, black asphalt parking lots turn sticky underfoot, and your scalp gets sunburned beneath your hair. It was the sort of day that could change your energy habits in an instant. Back home, in Minnesota, I hardly ever used air-conditioning. Opening a window and turning on a fan were usually enough to make my house feel comfortable. When the air conditioner in my car had slowly drifted toward producing more hot air than cool, I hadn't felt the need to pay for a repair.

In Florida, things were different. Here, the heat was oppressive. Within ten minutes, it had shoved you aside, knocked you down, and pressed a boot into your face. Time seemed to crawl. I was aware of every bead of sweat that dribbled down my neck. I felt a strong, instinctual drive to sit under a tree and stop thinking until sundown. Here, the line between the real world and the air-conditioned one was sharp and clear, and I knew which side I'd rather be on. Every time I stepped into an air-conditioned space, it was like receiving an answer to a prayer I hadn't realized I'd been reciting. In Florida, air-conditioning was a miracle. Yet it was also more than a bit ironic.

After all, I'd come to this part of the country precisely to investigate an impressive example of Americans learning how to function on *less* energy. I wanted to see how our lives, our jobs, and the buildings where we live and work might change if we got serious about reducing the amount of electricity and liquid fuels that it takes to power our daily lives. I had not imagined this tour taking place from inside a crisply chilled van, and I *really* hadn't expected to be this grateful for the cold conveyance. Frankly, though, that surprise was in keeping with the irony of the larger story.

This place I'd come to tour, where the act of reducing energy use was becoming an important way of life, was a military base. Leaders at the Naval Air Station in Jacksonville, Florida, had decided that sustainability was going to be a major goal, as much a part of daily military discipline as shiny shoes or a neat buzz haircut. That didn't mean the twenty-three thousand sailors and support staff at NAS Jacksonville were going to stop working. Pilots would still be trained. Planes would still be repaired and sent out on missions of war or of mercy. Yet NAS Jacksonville had committed itself to doing these same jobs while consuming less energy.

Stretched along the bank of the St. Johns River, NAS Jacksonville is walled off against the outside world by miles of razor wire–topped, chain-link fence. The main gate is imposing. The line of cars waiting for approval to pass through that gate is intimidating. Once you're actually inside, though, the Naval Air Station resembles nothing so much as a slightly dumpy suburban industrial park. Block after block of low-slung concrete buildings—available in gray or tan—sprawl on wide green lots. The sameness is broken by a scattering of metal sheds and a few stands of palm trees and tall, bare-trunked pines. Near the waterfront, aircraft hangars, some as large as a shopping mall, loom against the sky.

This is not what a sustainability-minded community looks like. Or, at least, it's not what we expect a sustainability-minded community to look like. Glancing around, you won't see well-tended gardens or a farmers' market. There's no stylish architecture that speaks of modern ideals or trendy aspirations. The buildings are set far apart from one another, baking under that Florida sun, which also completely burns away any thought of going for a walk. NAS Jacksonville doesn't look like a place that cares about energy, and, historically, that's pretty much been the case. Military bases such as this one were not designed or built with conservation in mind.

With all of the planes, the tanks, and the trucks; the feeding and housing of thousands of people; and the actual job of conducting war, the military uses a lot of energy. In fact, the Department of Defense (DOD) is the single largest consumer of energy in the nation. Every year, roughly 1 percent of America's energy use, give or take, can be traced directly to the military.[1] That might sound like a small number, but when we talk about U.S. energy use, even single-digit percentages represent incredibly huge amounts of energy. One percent of the 94.6 quadrillion BTUs we used in 2009 is still 946 trillion BTUs. The DOD uses more energy every year than the entire country of Denmark.[2] American energy use goes up almost every single year, and military energy use increases right along with it.

For a long time, nobody lost much sleep over that fact. Energy use was simply a given. The military had to work, so energy had to be used. Whether the DOD had to use quite *so much* energy to do said work was a question that very few people bothered to ask, but that's changing. Today, energy used represents more than simply work accomplished. You've seen this in the civilian world. When you think about your utility bills, you know they represent more than the comfort of a warm house or a month of quiet evenings watching TV. The bills also represent negative consequences such as pollution, reliance on foreign nations, the risks of climate change, and—last, but not least—how much money all of that gas and electricity costs you. This is one place where the military mind-set isn't that much different from your own. During the course of the last decade or so, the DOD started to think long and hard about what all of the energy it was using really meant.

The implications were not pretty. Not only does the DOD have to consider the same sort of problems that haunt civilian energy use, it's also got a few key issues all its own. For instance, in a war zone such as Iraq or Afghanistan, the amount of energy used can actually equate to lives lost. That's because the diesel that powers a tank and the fuel oil that runs a generator don't simply appear on the battlefield by magic. They have to be transported there, and the delivery convoys are prime targets for attack. To protect them, the military has to divert combat troops from other places to serve as chaperones. If less fuel had to be shipped, fewer soldiers would be at risk, and combat soldiers could be used where they're really needed.

These military-specific concerns matter at home, too. Although most of the DOD's energy use is tied up in making cars, tanks, trucks, planes, and other vehicles move, its stationary buildings also consume a lot of energy. Military bases, such as the Naval Air Station at Jacksonville, account for almost a quarter of the DOD's energy use.[3] When natural disasters happen, the military can be an important part of helping communities stabilize. Yet if that same natural disaster has cut off the military's energy supply, it becomes a lot harder for the military to do its job.

Finally, climate change holds special challenges for the military. The extreme weather that occurs as the planet gets hotter—causing wildfires in some regions, flooding in others, droughts and famines someplace else—has an impact on political stability. Ongoing climate change is likely to mean a military that's stretched thinner and thinner, responding to requests for help at home and abroad and dealing with conflicts that heat up along with the temperature. This is really something the DOD is concerned about.[4] The navy has even joined in on climate research.[5]

You can think about the DOD as exhibit number one in the case for self-interest, rather than moral or ethical concerns, driving a cleaner energy future. Once you know that, it's not really surprising to find that the DOD is embracing ideals and ideas that were once the sole domain of granola-crunching, back-to-the-land hippies. Maybe the reasons a military base cares about energy are different from the reasons your local food co-op cares—but their actions are similar. Maybe a sustainability-minded community looks different at NAS Jacksonville than it does in Portland, Oregon, or Madison, Wisconsin, but that doesn't mean the military isn't busy making its communities more sustainable. Since the 1990s, the DOD has invested heavily in alternative energy. One of the largest solar arrays in the Americas supplies one-fourth of the electricity needs at Nevada's Nellis Air Force Base. Navy and air force planes are fly-ing laboratories where scientists test fuels made from algae, grasses, and animal fats. In 2007, 12 percent of the electricity used by mili-tary facilities came from renewable resources.[6] In contrast, 8 percent of the energy used by the nation as a whole came from renewable sources in 2009.

Beyond taking the lead on renewables, the military is also paying enough attention to energy to know that you can't solve the energy problem through renewable generation alone. The military isn't only thinking about new ways to make energy; it's also thinking about how it can use less energy to begin with. The best way to do that is to make the kind of changes I went to the Naval Air Station at Jacksonville to check out. The goal is to do the same amount of work as we've been doing and enjoy the same comforts and conveniences we've enjoyed for decades—but simultaneously reduce the amount of energy it takes to get those benefits. That's what people mean when they talk about energy efficiency—getting the goods and services we want for less.

It's an exciting concept, but energy efficiency doesn't normally make for a very exciting tour. As I drove around NAS Jacksonville in my air-conditioned van, accompanied by a group of naval officers and civilian engineering contractors—my entourage of men with very good posture and very severe haircuts—nothing I saw would have stood out as special to the untrained eye. Energy efficiency is not sexy. You'll rarely notice from the highway that a building has become more efficient. There aren't many energy-efficiency projects that will catch the eye and spur the imagination as a wind turbine or a solar farm can. In addition, although overhauls to the energy infrastructure tend to involve cutting-edge, gadget hound–pleasing technology, you can produce a remarkable amount of energy efficiency using nothing more complicated than a particularly thick wall.

Yet efficiency is essential to making the future of energy work.

Right after college, I married a great guy who is an architect and an engineer and incredibly smart. Like me, he also has a tendency to get obsessively excited about new ideas. So when he got a job as an energy modeler—using computer simulations to make buildings as energy efficient as possible, for the least amount of money—and our dinner conversations began to gravitate toward the importance of energy modeling, I wrote it off as a consequence of his finding a career he really enjoyed. It took a couple years and a lot of research before I realized that pretty much everybody—scientists, politicians, even utility company executives—was just as excited about the power of energy efficiency as my husband. From coast to coast, experts told me the same thing: if we want to tackle climate change or even simply reduce our dependence on fossil fuels, energy efficiency has to come first.

Get the benefits we want for less energy. Reduce our carbon footprint and our dependence on fossil fuels for less money. That's what makes energy efficiency so powerful. How do you make efficiency happen? As you saw at Bernice Dallas's house in Urbana, Illinois, you can change people's behavior, but it's a lot more effective to change the larger systems where they live and work and then watch their behavior naturally adapt. Think about it as the bottom-up approach versus top-down direction.

My tour of NAS Jacksonville started at the top—at a new aircraft hangar that had been designed and built to create an environment where people could easily use less energy, while still doing the same jobs. Yes, an energy-efficient aircraft hangar. No, that is not an oxymoron. Energy efficiency is inherently a relative concept. We aren't talking about reducing energy use down to nothing. Instead, we want to cut waste and find better ways to work and live so that we can use less energy than we currently consume. That distinction isn't always totally clear, but it's an important one to make. If you don't get it, you'll miss the real meaning behind all kinds of "green" and sustainable news.

Case in point, this aircraft hangar—Hangar 511. It wasn't built simply to be energy efficient; it was built to meet the standards of a specific program, the United States' Green Building Council's Leadership in Energy and Environmental Design certification. Like Passive House, LEED is voluntary, but earning LEED certification means a building has to meet certain requirements. During the last few years, more and more buildings have earned their LEED seal of approval. You probably live near a LEED building. Maybe you've even been inside one. The brand is popular and well-known, but what it really means is kind of confusing. LEED, you see, is relative. Essentially, it's a tool that helps people put together buildings that are more sustainable. LEED assigns point values to all sorts of different decisions—from offering bicycle parking and showers for sweaty riders to choosing heating and air-conditioning systems that use less energy than average. The idea is that as you add up more points, you're creating a building that has less of an impact on the environment, compared to its peers.

The advantage with LEED is that it gives you a metric. Instead of having to trust that any building labeled "Green" really is, you can look at the LEED rating and know there's more going on than a coat of viridian paint. On the other hand, you have to look at what's being compared here. It's not *just* apples to apples. It's juicy Minnesota Honeycrisp to juicy Minnesota Honeycrisp. In other words, a LEED-rated building is not necessarily the most sustainable building ever. It's simply more sustainable than other buildings of a similar type and function and size.

That's why you can have a LEED-rated, energy-efficient aircraft hangar. Any building that can bed down a whole fleet of blue whale–size jet planes is going to be on the large side. Hangar 511 is definitely big—in that "filling up your entire frame of vision and causing you to momentarily forget what you meant to say" sort of way. It's a giant rectangle encompassing more than 280,000 square feet of land. The size is part of what this building does. You can't really scale it down much and still have it serve the same purpose. If you measured Hangar 511 against your house, it would look like a fat, snort-y energy hog. At the same time, though, this building is also very different, in some extremely important ways, compared to the other aircraft hangars with which it shares a runway.

In order to earn a LEED rating, Hangar 511 had to be built with a wide variety of energy-saving measures. Some of these changes could be seen from afar; others, you'd never see without a guided tour of the building's mechanical systems—the machines that kept it warm in the winter and cool in the summer. To me, however, the most impressive example of how energy efficiency could change a building this size was best viewed from the perspective of a landing airplane.

As my van rounded the corner of Hangar 511 and drove out onto the tarmac, I found it increasingly difficult to focus. Outside the right-hand windows, the hangar loomed, its bay doors thrown open to reveal seemingly tiny crew people scurrying over, under, and through enormous silent aircraft. To my left—and a little closer than I would have preferred—a lumbering gray elephant of a prop plane shuddered to life and began to move distressingly fast for something so awkward-looking. I was pulled back out of wide-screen view only when one of my guides paused in his explanation of the hangar's elaborate mechanical systems to point out a simple energy solution that was visible inside those gaping hangar bays. "Notice the white floors and white walls," said Mike Blair, a quiet, friendly, round-faced petty officer—and the youngest person in the van besides myself. From the driver's seat, he gestured to our right. "It really helps during daylight hours with not having to have the lights on. You can see that they're only running minimum security lights."[7]

It did seem plenty bright in the hangar. You'd have had no trouble reading the tiny print on a maintenance manual in there. When I looked up at the ceiling, I could see that most of the light fixtures hanging from the structural beams were indeed dark. Yet I didn't get what a big difference the change in color had made until our van passed by the hangar next door, number 30. The bays on this building were almost as big as Hangar 511's; their doors, too, were wide open, and they faced the same direction, so there shouldn't have been any less daylight. Yet Hangar 30 was dim, almost dingy. Toward the back wall, shadows set in, creating the sort of reading environment that—if moms across America are to be believed—would absolutely *ruin* your eyesight. This, despite the fact that every light in the ceiling was already blazing. The only difference: the walls and the ceilings of Hangar 30 were painted beige. Change the paint color, and the lights could go off in there, too.

This is the second important fact you have to understand about energy efficiency. What I saw when I compared Hangar 511 to Hangar 30 is the difference between energy efficiency and conservation. The top-down changes that the navy made to the environment of

Hangar 511 were designed to encourage energy efficiency. Without those changes—if you're the guy working in Hangar 30—the only way you can save energy is via conservation. It might sound as if I'm being redundant, but that's not the case. These two concepts, energy efficiency and conservation, are related, but they aren't the same. Efficiency does something that conservation can't.

See, when you conserve, you simply stop. Maybe you shut off a light, or you choose not to drive your car somewhere. It's a superficially easy choice to make, but it can put some serious limits on your life. Turning off a light works great during the day or in a room you aren't in. At night, though, you have to choose between using the energy or not using it and being stuck sitting quietly with your thoughts in a pitch-black living room. Likewise, sometimes, and in some places, it's easy to simply choose not to drive. In our world, though, that's not always an option. At least, not without sacrificing your job.

Conservation is solely about using less energy. Efficiency is about using less energy, while still being every bit as productive as you were before. Turn off a 60-watt incandescent lightbulb for an hour, and you've saved 60-watt-hours of electricity. Swap the pear-shaped bulb out for a 15-watt compact fluorescent, however, and you'll get just as much light, while simultaneously saving 45-watt hours. On the road, efficiency might mean covering the same miles in a smaller vehicle or one that gets better gas mileage. Yet it could also mean the difference between simply not driving—and thus not going anywhere—and having the local infrastructure to make riding a bicycle a safe and easy alternative. Either way, energy use gets reduced, but the job still gets done.

If what's going on in Hangar 511 were *only* about conservation, then those massive, totemic airplanes would never leave the runway. Flip off the lights in a beige hangar bay, and energy gets saved, but engines can't be serviced in the dark. By painting the walls white, the navy made it possible to simultaneously save energy and do the job. In fact, compared to Hangar 30's beige pit of despair, the working environment has actually been improved. Conservation says, "Don't do it." Efficiency says, "Do it better." That's a really, really, really important distinction, because it gets to the heart of where we—human beings, that is—have been, where we're going, and what we're afraid of.

My maternal grandparents were farmers. They raised corn and soybeans, pigs and cows, and experienced firsthand America's shift from family farming to the industrial kind. My grandfather once told me about how he'd been the first guy in the county to take a risk on the new, modern fertilizers. That was an expensive step in the 1940s. People thought he was nuts, but he convinced *his* dad that those ag science boys knew what they were doing, and it paid off.

By the time he retired, my grandfather owned his land and the house—not a given, in a small county with a lot of big Catholic families. He had a blue air-conditioned tractor with massive tires that grade-school me could crawl inside, and a combine whose catwalk became a tree fort and sometimes pirate ship for my cousins and me. I remember sitting on his lap in the combine, listening to the radio, while he drove around the fields. A hundred years earlier, farmers would have broken their backs over that same land for lower crop yields. There were downsides to the rural Industrial Revolution, but given the benefits industrialization brought his family—free time, health, educational opportunities, financial security—I don't know that my grandpa would have traded those drawbacks for a less energy-intensive world where he'd have had to work harder at an already hard job and maybe not done as well.

For my grandfather and a lot of other people, the consumption of fossil fuels has been directly tied to a better life. Experience, from the nineteenth century until today, has taught us that the more greenhouse gas emissions we produce, the more we can do, and the happier we are. Tell us that we need to cut our use of fossil fuels at all—let alone by 20 quadrillion BTUs—and we can't help but imagine a rough, grimy world we don't want any part of. That assumption is a brick wall standing between a lot of Americans and a more sustainable future, and we aren't alone in that misconception.

"Developing countries have a right to develop, and they see carbon dioxide emissions as a part of that, because we've chosen to use fossil fuels as the way we energize our economies," said William

Moomaw, Ph.D., a professor of international environmental policy at Tufts University's Fletcher School of Law and Diplomacy. "What we have to do is help people see that they don't really care about the energy and emissions. What they want is the services—light, base comforts, mobility, electronics. If we can provide those services and expand them, in a manner that ties to reduced greenhouse gas emissions, combating climate change will work better from a political standpoint." That's essentially the same sort of concerns the people who supported a new coal power plant in Holcomb, Kansas, had. Efficiency—doing more with less—is the first step in dealing with those legitimate fears.

Yet to get that benefit, you first have to start paying attention to energy, and that's harder than it sounds. I don't know, off the top of my head, what it takes for my boiler to keep my house at 67 degrees—or what changes I could make, beyond sealing my windows shut in winter, that would improve my heating efficiency. You probably don't either. It's just not instinctual. We've even got a leg up here, because we get bills in the mail every month and at least have a vague idea of how much energy we're using and how our consumption this year compares to last year's. When the military started to care about energy consumption, it didn't have those tools.

Traditionally, there's been only one energy bill for an entire military base such as NAS Jacksonville, and that single bill is seen only by the people in charge of making sure the check gets cut to pay it. This fact was almost as mind-blowing for me as the experience of driving down a tarmac next to a C-14 Hercules. Utility bills are an unavoidable part of everyday life and budgeting for individuals in the civilian world.[8] We know about them from the time we're little. Whether we rent or own, there's still a utility that has to be paid. It's a cost of living and a cost of doing business.

That's not the case in the military, however. There, the knowledge of how much energy families and offices use simply vanishes down a black hole—a direct consequence of that old way of thinking, where energy use was just a fact. Consumption had to happen, so the government would pay for it. Even today, when the navy builds LEED aircraft hangars and the Department of Defense worries about climate change, most military bases are still places where nobody can tell you how much energy an individual building uses. Usually, there's not even a meter attached.

In fact, until the privatization of on-base housing, many soldiers didn't even get a utility bill at home. Joe Sikes, the director for facilities energy and privatization with the DOD, told me stories about people who ran the air-conditioning with their windows wide open. Or, maybe you've heard the one about the three-star general whose nineteenth-century, high-ceilinged house was privatized. Suddenly he discovered that his energy bill was higher than his entire housing allowance. These people couldn't see the energy they used, so they didn't think about it. After privatization, though, the situation changed. Homes were metered, families started to receive monthly bills, and, almost overnight, Sikes said, there was a 10 to 15 percent reduction in energy use as people pruned away their more nonsensical habits and settled on lives where they got the services they really wanted for less energy at less cost.

Back at Jacksonville NAS, only a few people live on base, but the powers that be still think plenty of changes can be made with a little awareness. Mike Blair, the petty officer who drove my tour van, is right in the middle of this effort. He's in charge of a program called Building Energy Monitors (BEM). Blair recruits young officers and civilian workers, at least one person for each of the 117 commands on base, and trains them to remind their coworkers about simple-to-do but easy-to-forget efficiency measures—shutting off computers and printers over the weekend, for instance, or opening the blinds and working by daylight, instead of by electric lights.[9] Every day, he told me, sailors show up at work thinking about three priorities: safety, security, and basic environmental issues such as recycling. It's built into their training and drilled into their heads, so they really can't *help* but remember. The BEM program aims to make energy the fourth priority that sailors always think about.

The hangars and training facilities at Jacksonville are divided so that each building or each chunk of a large building is mostly populated by sailors of the same command. So, in a way, BEM kind of functions like a living electric meter or utility statement for their buildings, reminding people that services come at a cost and that there are ways to get the same amount of useful work accomplished for less expense. I saw this in action at a place called Building 700. Unlike Hangar 511, there's nothing to make Building 700 look special from the outside. It's simply a two-story, concrete-block rectangle with a few windows breaking up the gray expanse, connected by a covered breezeway to the similar-size, metal-clad Building 701 next door. Inside, Building 700 had flat white walls and linoleum floors, tiled mostly in white, with some red-and-blue dot matrix patterns scattered about. It sort of reminded me of walking around a cheaply built new high school, which made sense, to a certain extent. This was, after all, a teaching command, where new sailors came to learn skills such as truck driving or—more exciting—how to operate a crane on the deck of an aircraft carrier. There were offices for the teachers, some desk-filled classrooms, and a few mini-hangars for hands-on training. This was where I spotted the first real difference in Building 700, walking down a hall, past doors that led to the empty hangars. Every one was dark. The BEM for Building 700, Petty Officer AS2 Williams, seemed simultaneously proud and relieved by this. As recently as a year ago, he told me, the lights in here would have been left on 24-7.

Instead, Building 700 has become the model for how a successful BEM program can work. In September 2009, when the BEM program began, Building 700 consumed almost 200 megawatt hours of electricity. In 2011, the most the building consumed in a single month was 138 megawatt hours. In real dollars, BEM is saving this one command more than $6,000 a year. Part of that success has to do with the energy program fitting particularly well into the education mission of this command. "What You Can Do to Save Energy" is a lesson that has worked its way into the basic orientation classes they teach all new sailors. "How Well We Are Succeeding at Saving Energy" is a benchmark the command's head honcho includes in regular briefing reports, known as quarters.

Energy efficiency had even wormed its way into the infinite loop of sibling-style ribbing that seems to rise up out of the ether any time at least two sailors are gathered together for longer than ten minutes. "You better turn off that computer, or Williams will come and get you," they tell one another. If a sailor sees his buddy hard at work, he might shut off the lights on his friend, as a friendly way of saying hello. It's part of the camaraderie, and it works because the monitors aren't big brass tossing around orders, they're only guys with a mandate to educate. The fact that Williams managed to convince the denizens of Building 700 to trade in a bunch of individual coffee makers, hoarded at desks, for a shared one in a common room, speaks volumes.

Walking through Building 700, I passed dozens of rooms, some with people in them, others without. Only two—both of which were occupied—had the lights on. That's a big deal. Yeah, these guys knew I was coming, but I've been to a lot of Green buildings where my arrival was known well ahead of time. This was the first one where I'd seen such a pervasive awareness of whether the electricity being used was actually necessary.

Williams told me that he'd seen sailors change their habits once they realized how big an impact one person's little choices can make. Add that together with the miniscule steps taken by other people, and you eventually have a mighty long stride. That's the human factor of efficiency, and you can't discount it. In fact, the lessons about energy efficiency that Williams learned after he signed on to be a BEM led him to make changes at home—for example, swapping out all of the incandescent lightbulbs in his house for compact fluorescents. Those little acts, such as turning off the lights in Building 700, matter. At least, that's the theory.

See, there's a difference between one person choosing to turn off a light in his house and what's going on in Building 700. The energy-efficiency successes that have happened at NAS Jacksonville are hardly an example of spontaneous individual decision-making, prompted by an all-sailor book club reading of *100 Things You Can Do at Home to Save the Earth*. Some changes, such as the alterations to Hangar 511, are clearly top-down decisions. Yet even the apparent bottom-up change at Building 700 comes with an awful lot of top-down encouragement. In many ways, these results have happened only because Jacksonville's commanding officer and the DOD above him decided to make energy a policy priority. Without that, Jacksonville NAS might still be full of people who opened the windows when the air-conditioning got too cool.

Think about it this way: Say it's winter, and there's snow. Not just a sugar frosting, but a serious, knee-deep, civilization-squelching snowfall. This happens in Minneapolis a couple of times a season, and it's no big deal. Half of the time, plows and sand trucks are out patrolling before the blizzard even starts. Two days after it stops, the sidewalks up and down my block will be clear. There's a whole organizational structure—city plans and contractors, citizen awareness, even enforcement. Technically, if I get lazy and don't shovel my stretch of public sidewalk, I could be fined.

Now imagine that same scenario, but this time in Birmingham, Alabama, where I lived for two years after college. It would be chaos, the end of the world, y'all. There's no system in place to deal with snow there. People clear bread and milk out of the grocery stores whenever there's a chance of flurries. Without the structure, with only individual decisions, clearing a city of two feet of snow would be a lot harder, would take a lot longer, and might not even get done at all in some places.

Basically, individual decisions about energy efficiency are great if there's nothing pressing going on, but if saving energy is about more than simply trying to cut a couple of dollars out of the electric bill—and it is—then individual decisions don't really matter. At least, they don't matter in comparison to the kind of systemic changes that drive more people to act in unison, in a shorter amount of time. You can't save the planet. Only policy can.

CHAPTER TEN

....

THE DEFAULT OPTION

A curious thing happened at a 2009 conference thrown by the American Council for Energy Efficient Economy (ACEEE). The topic: "Behavior, Energy and Climate Change." I wasn't at that particular conference, but I've been to other ACEEE events, and I know the score. You spend a couple of days shuffling from one segment of a partitioned hotel ballroom to another. There's a lot of PowerPoint, a lot of discussion about data analysis. It's all very wonky in a way I happen to love.

For most of the conference, you're segregated with the people who are particularly interested in the same subset of information you're interested in, which only adds to gleeful geekery. At some point, though, they drag everybody together into one room, plop you into a sea of circular tables, and ask you what you'd like to eat for dinner. The question goes something like this, "Did anyone at this table request the vegetarian option?" And here we separate the sheep from the carnivorous wolves.

Some people instantly go with the veggies. Others show little hesitation about sticking with the meat. The rest of us pause, a little guiltily, and peek over our shoulders at the next table as if we're cheating off somebody's algebra homework. We examine what our neighbors are eating. We sniff the air and try to guess which entrée is the one that smells so good. Our answers are as capricious as the spinning wheel of catering fortune.

This matters. Food, like the comfort of heat or the convenience of light, is a service provided by energy. It takes a lot less energy to grow plants and feed them to us than it takes to grow plants, feed them to a cow, and *then* feed the cow to us.[1] As it usually stands, an ACEEE dinner might be very energy efficient or not particularly efficient at all—mostly determined by chance.

At the 2009 Behavior and Energy Summit, they did mealtimes a bit differently. Instead of offering a normal meal for normal people and something else for those strange plant eaters, they turned the vegetarian option into the default—essentially telling conference goers, "If you want meat, you'll have to ask for it." Again, the less people had to actively decide to be efficient, the more efficient they were. At a previous ACEEE meeting—themed around the same topic and thus likely attended by roughly the same group of people—more than 80 percent had accepted the meat as it figuratively fell into their laps. In 2009, however, when vegetables became the norm, the numbers did a flip-flop, with more than 80 percent now happily eating the vegetarian option.[2]

Change doesn't happen on an individual basis, and it doesn't have to be a hardship. Nor does it have to be something shoved down our throats—so to speak. At the Behavior and Energy Summit, the people who wanted meat could still choose to ask for it. Instead, change can be something that simply happens—*if* you tweak the norm enough so that saving energy becomes the laid-back, easy thing to do. Right now, though, we still live in a country where the easy thing to do is usually *not* the energy-efficient thing to do.

On one of those hot summer days, similar to what I experienced in Florida, when electric wires droop and asphalt parking lots grow sticky, you can walk into air-conditioned office buildings all across the United States and find an odd sight—people sitting at their desks, wrapped up in cardigans or nestled into pullover sweaters. In these same buildings, you'll find big picture windows, often stretching from the floor to the ceiling. In fact, the bigger the building, the more likely that all of the walls are glass. The views would be fabulous, if most of those windows weren't also hidden behind Venetian blinds. Fully open, they let in so much sun that nobody can read a computer screen. Instead, the blinds are closed, and the fluorescent lights are humming. Those lights stay on long after the workers have gone home. Driving down the highway at night, it looks as if we're a nation of particularly productive insomniacs. In reality, we simply have a habit of assuming somebody else is in charge of turning electrical devices off, not to mention that we work in a bunch of buildings where most people don't even have access to light switches.

All of these contradictions of daily life are evidence of a simple truth: we don't generally design office buildings around energy efficiency. Architects make something that looks cool, building owners edit the design until it's cheap to build, and engineers look at the final plan and pick systems to fit. Traditionally, there's not been anyone who is in charge of reducing energy waste. Up-front costs and aesthetics are what we care about. Providing more comfort for less energy use—and, by extension, lowering the long-term costs of the building—is simply not the first priority on most people's minds.

As I mentioned earlier, we are doing a much better job of making buildings energy efficient today than we did thirty years ago. The dark days of energy use in American buildings began somewhere around the early 1950s—touched off by the combination of increasingly cheap electricity and widely affordable luxuries, such as air-conditioning. People looked around and realized that they no longer had to rely on the building itself to keep them warm or cool or to provide light. Technology could manage those tasks just fine, freeing up the building structure to be anything our hearts desired.

If Americans wanted to work out of a fifty-foot-tall, air-conditioned brontosaurus, the building industry could make it happen. If we dreamed of toasty warm winters in an all-glass house, it could be done.

That mentality lasted pretty much right up until the energy crisis of the late 1970s. This jump in energy costs and the fear that it might happen again were major factors in the motivation behind that 31 percent reduction in building energy use we saw between 1978 and 2005. Today, we do think about building design differently from how we thought about it back then. Insulation is thicker. Respect is paid to the fact that we never did get around to mastering a Jetsonian source of free electricity. You can think of these changes as our defensive game. The trouble is, we've never worked too hard at putting together a good offense, and the bench is still packed with a bunch of squeaky-kneed oldsters who are dragging us down. The military knows all about that. Places such as Naval Air Station Jacksonville were largely constructed during the 1950s, the 1960s, and the 1970s. Folks there tell stories about buildings with no insulation at all and aircraft hangars so leaky, you could stick your fingers through the walls and wiggle.

This is why it's important to change the systems we use and the environments we live in, rather than relying only on personal choices to reduce energy use. If there's a mechanic who spends her day inside a metal box in Florida, where any injection of cool air leaks right out again through the walls, expecting her to voluntarily use less air-conditioning is a lot like hoping the turkey will baste itself. Very few of us are that masochistic. Are the occupants of that all-glass office building really going to shut off the overhead fluorescents, open the blinds, and work by the light of the sun if doing that means they have to spend the day periodically wrestling their computer monitors out of the line of glare?

A big part of changing our approach to energy is making it easy. In practice, that means focusing less on what people can remember to do and creating environments where the green option is the default. It also means treating energy savings as a benefit, not a punishment. I once talked to maintenance staff at a Midwestern university where the powers that be had tried to cut electric consumption in the winter by going from office to office and confiscating small personal space heaters. The Space Heater Police did not care if your toes were cold, but they did effectively demonstrate the *wrong* way to remove personal choice from the equation.

So, how do we do it right? Instead of worrying about how to change people, you change the world around them. The navy did that when it built its LEED-rated aircraft hangar with improved insulation and added a paint job that made artificial lighting less necessary. It's the same thing with Passive Houses. Bernice Dallas doesn't have to huddle in the cold, nor does she have to remember a long list of complicated protocols for saving energy. Her house itself does the heavy lifting. She simply lives in it. Think back to that hypothetical office building where the lights stay on all night. Memory and responsibility are constant, nagging authority figures. You can shake your finger at somebody and hope the guilt and the shame will get results, or you can create a world where making the right choice comes naturally. Instead of waiting for employees to get the hint and flip a light switch, a computer can do it for them. All you have to do is make the room smart enough to know when it's been left alone, and you can get all of the benefits of Jacksonville's Building Energy Manager system, without the work.

Not only do you get energy efficiency with automation, you also get some mitigation of the direct rebound effect—that tendency to use energy precisely *because* we've saved energy. This works, because if you control the system, then the decision to consume more is partly taken out of human hands. It becomes harder to say "We've done a good job shutting off the lights this month, so we can afford to crank the heat up a notch." Instead, efficiency is constructed as part of the building and wired into its walls. Counteracting it now takes more effort than simply sitting back and letting it happen. Relax. Let go— and let engineering.

So, what does it look like when this perspective plays out in the real world?

The headquarters of Great River Energy is a pretty good example. This cooperative utility—a for-profit company that's partly owned by the same electric cooperatives that it serves—generates and supplies electricity for most of rural Minnesota. In 2008, it built a new headquarters in one of Minneapolis's farther-flung suburbs, between an upscale strip mall and a couple of brambles of large beige houses. The building is made up of three elongated rectangles, staggered along one another so that most of the length of each is exposed. The long sides look as if they're all glass, facing north and south.[3] On the short ends, turned toward the setting and the rising sun, the walls are almost completely solid, with only a few small windows cut into the facade. Right away, this basic design saves energy.

The building's shape ensures that lots of light gets in, but it's biased toward *useful* light. If Great River Energy had built a big square, a good portion of the offices would have been far from the windows—too dark to work in by only natural light. Meanwhile, plenty of other offices would have had bright, uncomfortably hot glare in the morning and the afternoon. By altering the shape of the building and the direction it faces, the architects were able to block out a lot of AC-inducing heat, while getting more *comfortable* light to more places.

These wise structural changes are backed up by smart wiring. Employees of Great River Energy don't have to remember to turn off the electric lights when they're getting plenty of daylight, and they don't have to go through the hassle of turning lights on again when the sun goes down.[4] Instead, sensors keep tabs on where people are and how much daylight is bouncing around the building. During work hours, those computers make the humans comfortable. Humming servers switch on lights in the morning when workers arrive and shut them off as daylight fills the offices. In the afternoon, mechanized rotors draw blinds in just the right places to block glare. Lamps switch on, by themselves, as darkness falls, and they turn off again as the last lingering workers head home. The whole building is attended to by a friendly robot butler. If you don't think we're living in the capital-F Future, perhaps this would be a good time to reevaluate your perspective.

It makes a difference, having Robo-Jeeves on hand. The Great River Energy headquarters uses 40 percent less electricity for lighting than a building its size would usually consume.[5] Lighting accounts for a quarter of the total energy use in a commercial building such as this, so that's a big deal on its own.[6] Then you can add the fact that electric lights produce heat. The less time you have them on, the less hard the air conditioner needs to work. A more efficient lighting system makes other devices work more efficiently as well. That building isn't only saving energy. It's getting all of the benefits of using energy while saving energy.

I'm a little hung up on buildings, I know. It's just that they're responsible for so much more of our national emissions than people think and are such a good example of how systems that were designed when energy was cheap aren't going to age well. In 2009, remember, we used 21 quadrillion BTUs of energy on residential buildings and 18 quadrillion BTUs on commercial buildings. Together, that's 39 quadrillion BTUs, far more energy than we used on either transportation *or* manufacturing.

"Wow" moments like that are why I got interested in energy issues to begin with, but this idea of creating a world where efficiency is the default, not a choice, goes beyond buildings. You can engineer socially, as well as physically. Think about the ACEEE dinner I told you about at the beginning of this chapter. Just as in that example, people will save more energy if saving energy is the default. Again as in that example, making energy efficiency the default doesn't mean completely obliterating human choice.

For instance, if done right, an altered environment and a robot butler can do a surprisingly good job of making people feel as if they have *more* control, not less. That's because, done right, these buildings are smart enough to understand that human beings are individuals, rather than a hive mind. We don't all have the same pant size. We don't even all wear pants. So it doesn't really make much sense to heat and cool and light a building full of hundreds of people as though they all want the same working environment. Instead, buildings with automated efficiency often come with lots of opportunities for people to personalize the experience a bit.

Let's go back to Great River Energy. Imagine an employee sitting at her desk, working very hard to focus on the memos she has to read before she goes home. An automated sensor has decided that enough daylight is getting into her cubicle space, and electric lights aren't needed. Now, maybe that works fine for most of the people in the office, but it only makes this particular employee feel as if she needs a new contact lens prescription. Luckily, she's not stuck with what works for most people. Instead, she gets to personalize and make her space comfortable for her. All that it takes is a desk lamp. Lit by LEDs, the lamp brightens up the immediate area while drawing very little electricity, itself.[7] The worker gets light where she needs it, but the building doesn't have to burn energy to light up everything.

This kind of setup—lots of built-in daylight, backed up by automated overhead lights and personalized with little LED desk lamps—is becoming popular with energy-conscious designers. I've even talked to some building engineers who've taken the system home, rigging up their houses with motion and light sensors. This is still a fairly expensive project to undertake on a residential scale, and the electricity is often cheaper when you're buying it for your house, so it's harder to pay off the investment. For an office, though—where lighting is often the biggest single source of energy use—it's a relatively cheap way to save a lot of energy. There's also some evidence that the combination of more natural light and personal control makes for happier and more productive employees.[8]

Automate efficiency, and you get reliably lower energy use, cash savings, and opportunities for personalized comfort. Yet all of the automation in the world won't eliminate our opportunities to choose to use more energy. The rebound effect is still with us. Sure, when Great River Energy installs a more efficient lightbulb, the robot butler is there to make sure that the bulb doesn't get left on more often than its predecessor. Likewise, a convention-hall dinner that's default vegetarian will save energy and money but isn't likely to result in ACEEE serving its conventioneers a fourth meal of the day.

That's all about the *direct* rebound effect, however. Remember, I mentioned earlier that the rebound effect can also operate in ways that aren't as obvious. Outside the confines of a single office building, after the conference has ended, there are still powerful forces at work. Great River Energy is an electric cooperative that supplies electricity to other utility cooperatives. More than 70 percent of the electricity GRE generated in 2010 came from coal.[9] When energy efficiency improves its bottom line, some of that cash will likely trickle down to the member-owners of the co-ops GRE supplies power to, and some will be used for improvements. What will the members buy with their shares? Maybe they'll upgrade their cable and get a second DVR that sits all day, plugged in, quietly sucking down as much 390 kilowatt-hours of electricity every year—as much as a lot of full-size refrigerators.[10] How will Great River Energy supply that increased demand? These are the indirect rebound effects that can't be ignored.

It's not that the people who make these choices are bad. It's not even, exactly, an issue of good people making bad choices. What this is about, according to the researchers who study efficiency and the rebound effect, is information. I bet you didn't know that a DVR box used that much electricity, even when it looks as if it's turned off. I sure didn't, until I saw the research. People don't make a choice between "undermine the efficiency and emissions benefits produced by my utility company" and "go without a DVR." They simply decide how they'd prefer to watch TV and don't have the information they need to make an energy-efficient choice even if they wanted to.

I drank my first cappuccino sometime around 1994. It was creamy and luscious, like a hot, steaming milkshake. I bought it at the gas station, over by the soda fountain, near the plastic benches where old farmers sucked down Styrofoam cups of black Folgers and played video Keno. Another year went by, at least, before I figured out that there was a significant difference between my cappuccino and the stuff they were drinking on *Friends*.

At the time, I was as unfamiliar with environmentalism as I was with serious caffeine dependency. We talked about conservation at school—but more in the sense of, "Hey, maybe we *shouldn't* kill off an entire species just 'cause." My family had gone through phases where we recycled pop cans, but that was for the money you got from the scrap metal place, and it involved the laborious process of individually smashing each can with a sledgehammer and then hauling the bounty of half a year several miles by pickup truck. I sat in the back to make sure the bags didn't blow away.

Where I lived, in central Kansas, that experience felt like the norm, so it's a little mind-blowing to remember how much that norm changed within less than a decade. By 1999, when I graduated from high school, I worked in a real coffee shop, and had friends who worked in the *other* real coffee shop across town. In some places, Walmart had already set up recycling centers, where you could drop off aluminum, glass, plastic, and paper—not because you got paid, but because you were actually concerned about how much trash you produced. In the case of recycling, what started as an economic exercise later became easier, a cultural norm and something like the default option. In both cases, we'd learned to care about issues we'd kind of rolled our eyes at five years earlier.

Here's another example. Around the same time I started to experiment with crappuccinos, soldiers at the army's Fort Hood in Texas—one of the largest U.S. military installations in the world—held their first Earth Day Festival. Actually, it's a festival now. In the beginning, it was really more of an Earth Day table, set up near the checkout lines at the post's PX—sort of an all-purpose proto-Sam's Club, where service people can buy everything from groceries to stereos at a discounted military rate. I can imagine that little would-be festival, sitting forlornly in front of a towering precipice of toilet paper or something. The attractions consisted of, in no particular order: one volunteer, one small stack of laminated pamphlets, and one taxidermied bobcat.

In 2010, the Fort Hood Earth Day Festival was held under a tent, stretched out over the field at the post's football stadium. Fourth- and fifth-graders from all of the nearby schools were there, as part of their classes. The event drew thousands of people. Either that bobcat was more entertaining that you might guess, or a serious shift had happened, altering the way Americans think about the environment. Which is to say, we now actually think about it.

You can see the numbers behind this shift if you look at the Environmental Protection Agency graphs that plot out the growth in municipal solid waste recycling during the last five decades. Prior to 1985, both the amount of waste recycled and the total percentage of waste recycled were pretty stagnate. In 1960, 5.6 million tons of trash were recycled in the United States—a mere 6.4 percent of the trash we produced. By 1985, that number had crept up a bit, to 16.7 million tons, or about 10 percent of our total trash.

After 1985, however, it's clear that something had changed. In only the next five years, recycling increased more than it had during the previous twenty-five. By 2000, more than 28 percent of our trash was being recycled—69.5 million tons' worth of junk that would have otherwise ended up in landfills.[11]

I think this cultural shift—America's embrace of recycling and the basics of environmentalism—is, at its heart, really about access to information. Not only the information that different behaviors and products existed, but also the information about how our neighbors and friends were participating in those new activities. Between 1985 and 2000, messages about recycling found their way into schools and TV shows, laying out the facts about trash and wanton pollution in front of the public in a much more saturated, mainstream way than had ever happened before. The spread of the Internet made it possible to get a better view of what real people were doing about threats to the planet, far from our hometowns or even our home states. Along the way, the information seeped over from educational settings into cultural ones. By the time I graduated from high school, I knew enough people who recycled that I had started to ask my friends where I should put the empty cans of soda I drank at their house. It was no longer a given that the can would go into the trash.

My behavior was shaped first by new knowledge, then by the influence of my peers, and finally by the ability to act on that knowledge and influence in a relatively easy way. The education made me realize recycling was important. The actions of early adopters made me think of recycling as something that was possible and maybe even desirable—I started to do it occasionally and started to think that I ought to do it more. Moving to a city with a biweekly curbside recycling program made recycling a part of my life.

Information and the ability to act on that information can make a difference in how we use energy, too. As I researched energy efficiency, how it's being promoted today, and how we could make energy-efficient behaviors more prevalent, I picked up a few important lessons. When I look at what I've learned, I see everything pointing back to a need for information. Even when the vegetarian dish is the default entrée, there are a lot of people (myself included) who would still choose the meat if they hadn't already gotten the idea that there was a downside to that.

Americans, as a whole, use so much energy that our individual contributions become about as important as a single raindrop in

Lake Superior. Even the U.S. military, the single biggest energy consumer in the country, accounts for only 1 percent of our total energy
consumption. If the entire Department of Defense ceased to function tomorrow, we still wouldn't even be close to solving our issues
with energy use and energy waste.

Because of that, it is true that the little personal acts we do to
save the planet don't really do much to save the planet. Side-by-
side, a single compact fluorescent light bulb can use about
75 percent less energy than one of the old incandescent bulbs you
grew up using.[12] If you make the swap, it seems as if you've made
a big difference, but zoom out, and that single decision no longer
looks so important. The ACEEE estimates that lighting accounts
for only somewhere between 5 and 10 percent of all household
energy use.[13] One little lightbulb swap won't make much of a difference by itself.

Yet the individual decisions we make don't necessarily happen
inside a vacuum. If I turn the lights off in my home office during the
day, I've saved some energy, but I haven't made much of an impact
on the world. At the Naval Air Station, however, the results are a bit
different. When Building Energy Monitors turn the lights off in *their*
offices—and encourage the people they work with to do the same—
they can prompt an entire office building to use less energy. On
one hand, our individual decisions don't matter, in so much as they
reduce energy use on a person-to-person basis. On the other hand,
our individual decisions do matter, in that they can help influence
the behavior of our friends and coworkers.

That's an important distinction. It means that if you feel smug
about your personal energy decisions, you're doing it wrong.
Significant levels of change—what we've seen in the Department
of Defense, what we've seen since the 1970s in the way residential
buildings use energy, and what we saw in the 1990s as Americans
embraced recycling—do not happen because of an individual's personal choices. Those changes happen because large groups of people
influence one another. Information, being able to notice that other
people in your community are trying out new ways of living that might
be appealing to you, is a major part of making those community-wide
changes work.

The second principle I learned is that top-down strategies are a really good way to foster fast changes on a community-wide scale. That's because the environments we currently live in and the systems our world is shaped around aren't necessarily conducive to encouraging the kind of energy changes we need to make. In a traditional building, using less energy might mean being a little cold and uncomfortable, or it might mean not being able to do your job very well. In that situation, you probably wouldn't make the choice to reduce energy use, even if you saw your peers making that choice, because what you saw wouldn't look that appealing. Alter the environment, though—build a Passive House or a LEED-certified aircraft hangar—and it's a lot easier for individuals to buy into community-wide change. Information doesn't have to be what you read in a paper or are told by a friend. In these cases, the buildings themselves worked as sources of information, by effectively telling people that they could use less energy without making their lives harder.

Having multiple sources of information—direct education, the influence of your peers, the implicit lessons you pick up from a well-designed building—is a big deal. That's because of the third principle I learned: energy isn't obvious. We live with this stuff, we use it every day, but it is not intuitive. Even when your television is off, it and your cable box are still buzzing away, drawing as much electricity as a refrigerator. Buildings themselves work as systems, and it isn't always easy to see what effect a single change will have on the whole unit. Build long and rectangular, with windows facing north and south, and you can use more daylight. Use more daylight, and you need less air-conditioning.

These connections are not easy to notice without help, and that's before we even start talking about money—how to get the most energy reduction for the least layout of cash—or the rebound effect. Once you consider all of the different factors that are involved, the ostensibly common-sense world of energy efficiency takes on the comic complexity of Maxwell Smart's daily commute. Every door reveals another door. The same path might not work for two different people. You can blow through a wad of money and not save as much energy as a neighbor who spent less. You could reduce energy use in one aspect of your life but actually increase your overall carbon footprint. In many ways, we're still every bit as clueless about energy as those soldiers who used to open a window when the air-conditioning got a bit too chilly.

You can change the cycle, though: information, usually about economics, prompts individuals to make decisions about changing their own behavior. Individual decisions influence other people and lead to community-wide cultural change. Cultural changes prompt the people in charge to start taking decisive action—changing infrastructure and environments in ways that make it easier for individuals to decide to change their own behavior, which alters the culture. This is the song that never ends.

From where I sit, all of these lessons add up to one important message: if we want to reduce the amount of energy Americans use and the amount that they waste, we need to make information about energy a lot more obvious and easily accessible. It needs to be embedded into our lives, so that even if we don't know the specific numbers, we can at least get a relative approximation of how much energy we use and how that compares to other people.

Although today's utility bills tell you a lot about what is normal in your household, they are completely mum on the subject of what is normal at a societal level. Frankly, that information is pretty well hidden wherever you turn. Dig around on government websites and you can find national or state averages, but they seem about as abstract as a natural disaster halfway around the world. It's hard to think about those data as anything but numbers. A neighborhood average would be more useful and would have more of an emotional impact, but utility bills are seldom a topic of conversation at block parties and backyard barbecues, because it is rude to bore your guests.

Some utilities are experimenting with adding that information to the bill. Instead of comparing yourself to yourself, the new bills stack up your energy use against that of people who live nearby, in similar-size houses. There are no more fancy purple ribbons handed out to all of the kids who participate. Now, there's a trophy at stake, and that makes it interesting. Because if there's one activity we Americans enjoy, it's a good, heated competition.

In fact, Opower, one of the companies behind these enhanced billing experiments, says it has found that Americans respond better to competitive messages than they do to almost any other way of pushing household energy reduction. It works better than talking about the money we could save or reminding us about the sad, dying polar bears. Just tell us whether we're doing better or worse than the guy down the road, and we hop into action. Opower programs have reduced energy use by an average of 1.8 percent. When Opower programs are targeted toward the homes that consume the most energy to begin with, customers reduce their energy use by an average of 6.5 percent.[14]

There seems to be a couple of reasons the Opower approach is succeeding. First off, it's not really focused on conservation, and it's only marginally concerned with the idea of doing more with less. Instead, what Opower really wants is to stop the constant hemorrhage of pointless waste. You may not leave the windows open while your air conditioner is running, but, chances are, some of your behavior would look just as silly to you in retrospect, once you become aware of it.

Second, getting results is about more than appealing to a competitive nature—you have to offer some coaching as well. So, OPower has crunched the numbers on what kind of calls to action ought to follow the neighbor-to-neighbor comparison. Limited-time offers work well, for instance. A utility or a state government might offer a rebate on any purchase of insulation that happens within the next few months. Yet a more successful strategy is simply taking the overwhelming and reducing it to a moderate whelm.

"You have to give people insights, not data," says Ogi Kavazovic, the vice president of marketing and strategy with Opower. "If you take a list of two hundred energy-saving options and narrow it down to three that are relevant, that's much more actionable." Opower uses information from people's utility bills to personalize the energy saving tips it recommends. For instance, if somebody has abnormally high summer energy usage, it could be because they have a swimming pool with an electric filter system. So Opower might include information about how to run that system more efficiently right in the person's electricity bill. If a family consistently uses a lot of electricity at night or during the middle of the day, they'd be pointed toward a new thermostat that could be scheduled to kick off and on with their daily routine.

To be fair, many utility companies hand out energy-saving tips, but without personalization, those helpful fliers seldom reach beyond the obvious. More important, when people make the decision to act on that advice, their choice is kind of like a little desert island, sitting all alone in a vast and empty sea. Nobody knows about the change except the homeowner and his or her utility company. There's a benefit, but it's small. Whatever happens here, it doesn't have much effect on anyone else. The point of programs such as Opower is to turn that lonely island into a densely populated archipelago. If the advice comes along with information about what other people are doing and what impact their choices have had, then an individual choice becomes a lot more important. Now it's part of a social system. It can influence other individual choices. It can help change what people think of as "the normal thing to do." Individual choices can be powerful, if they're linked together by information.

Information and community-wide change can make a difference, but there's still a big part of the energy problem that we haven't solved. I've mentioned the Jevons paradox and the rebound effect. Let's say we do reduce household energy use by 6 percent. That's great, but we are also likely to take some of the money we've saved on household energy and spend it on other products and services. It takes energy to produce these goods and services and energy to use them. So, in the end, our net energy reduction is really something less than 6 percent. If a Jevons paradox happens, it means energy efficiency led us to actually use more energy than we had before. For instance, if we had a gross energy reduction of 6 percent, but a Jevons Paradox happened, our net overall energy use might actually rise by 5 percent. A rebound effect is the same but smaller. So, if a rebound effect happened, that would mean we still reduced our overall energy use but just not by as much as we thought we would—3 percent, for instance, instead of 6 percent.

This pair of economic complications is always with us, and they aren't all bad. In fact, they're a big part of why the United States has been able to become wealthier. A hundred years ago, it took a lot more energy to do a lot less work. Now we can make products, provide services, and build wealth for less energy and less cost. Even while they help pad our pocketbooks, however, the Jevons paradox and the rebound effect do make it harder to use energy efficiency to reduce our dependence on fossil fuels and cut our carbon emissions. The trouble is, we don't really know *how much* harder.

Researchers have been studying the way the Jevons paradox and the rebound effect play out in the real world for only a couple of decades. There's not a lot of empirical data. The experts frequently disagree. It's relatively easy to study what happens to the Jevons Paradox and the rebound effect within one sector of energy use— what we call direct effects—or between a couple of related sectors, indirect effects. Yet it's a lot harder to know, definitively, how these forces affect nations, let alone the planet. In order for energy efficiency to really matter, it has to happen on the big-picture scale, with whole communities participating, all around the country, but that's exactly the same scale where our knowledge of the rebound effect and the Jevons paradox breaks down.

You've heard about the Chaos Butterfly—that insectoid Bond villain who lives in Brazil and torments the world by flapping his wings and causing hurricanes. Can you imagine trying to trace and quantify the Chaos Butterfly's economic impact? Economywide rebound is like that. The state of New Jersey decides that all government buildings must use compact fluorescent lightbulbs. Later that year, we discover that carbon emissions for the United States have slightly increased. Quick now, how much of that increase can be blamed on the indirect rebound from energy-efficiency mandates in New Jersey? You see the problem. When we start talking about economy-wide effects, there are just too many variables. Too many things change in too many places, all at once. Much as they'd like to, even the people who study this stuff for a living say they can't simply walk in, all firm and authoritative, and declare that X is causing Y. Yet that doesn't mean we get to blow off any concern about what X might be up to. We know that economy-wide effects happen. Not only does it make sense, but you can see them—or, at least, their shadow—by looking at historical data.

California is one state that's made energy efficiency a serious priority. During the last thirty years or so, the California Energy Commission has led the rest of the country in implementing energy efficiency programs. The state's energy use trends show evidence of energy-efficiency success and economy-wide rebound effects and how tracking the success of energy efficiency programs can be far more complicated than we give it credit for.

As of 2009, California ranked forty-seventh in the United States in energy use per capita, but number 8 in GDP per capita—further evidence that economic success and uncontrolled energy use aren't necessarily dependent on each other.[15]

Since the 1970s, Californians have kept their energy use low. They actually use about 22 percent less energy, per capita, than they did in 1974.[16] Economy-wide, however, energy use has increased. Between 1974 and 2009, California's total energy use went up by 37 percent.[17]

This gets complicated, because experts don't agree on how much of California's per capita energy use reduction can actually be attributed to its energy efficiency programs. There are other reasons energy use could have declined. For instance, California has a larger number of people living in each household than the American average, and the types of industries that operate in California could already be expected to use less energy than an American average of industrial facilities. Factors like that aren't directly tied to California's energy efficiency policies, and it's difficult to tease apart where the policy effects end and the other factors begin.[18]

People in California did save some energy through energy efficiency measures, however, but they also got wealthier, produced more, and attracted more people to their state. There's certainly an economic benefit to all of the energy efficiency California has picked up and an environmental benefit, too—if California had kept up with the growth rate of per-capita energy use in the rest of the country, its total energy use and total emissions would be much higher. Yet that wasn't enough to make *total* energy use go down. You can see how measuring economywide effects gets very complicated very quickly.

The same trends show up in national numbers. Starting with the energy crisis of the late 1970s, everything in this country, from factories to farms to family homes, started to become more efficient—albeit not as efficient, as quickly, as in California. As that's happened, you can see our economic growth separate, at least somewhat, from the growth of energy use. Prior to the 1970s, energy use and the GDP grew at pretty much the same rate. Today, GDP grows about 2.5 percent faster than energy use.[19] We're seeing efficiency at work. Our country got more efficient, and now energy use is increasing at a slower pace than it used to, but it is still increasing.

So, how do you deal with that? Is it possible to put energy efficiency to use and get the economic benefits of rebound effects, but without having the environmental effects blunted by those same forces? The economists who study rebound told me it could be, and they all came back to the same possible solution: give people better information.

On a small scale, information is the key to making sure that energy-efficient behaviors take root. Information can change culture in ways that lead to significant reductions in energy use. It also works better if that information is embedded into the way we live, rather than something we have to memorize and remember every time we make an energy decision. It turns out that the same basic ideas might work on the level of whole economies, too. To counteract the rebound that happens across a state or our entire country, you have to supply information that is every bit as far-reaching. There has to be a way to tell people, with every decision they make, how much energy they are using and (more important) what the long-term effects of that choice will be. Essentially, you have to take the invisible world of energy and hook it up to a big flashing neon sign.

How do you make the impact of energy use that obvious? Here's what the economists I spoke with suggested: put a price on fossil fuels that reflects all of the economic factors we don't currently consider when we use them.[20] However you do it, that price would become a very important source of information, helping us understand our energy use in ways that most of us don't have the time or patience for right now.

Information in the form of a carbon price is really the only tactic likely to ensure that the rebound effect is working for us, rather than against us, economists say, although it's much less clear how we should go about establishing that price, and implementing it. All of the possible alternatives—carbon taxes, cap, and trade—have downsides. They could be unwieldy to implement. They could also end up being too broadly applied, not taking into account important distinctions between energy sources and types of use.[21] This is tricky. It's easy to screw up. Yet it could be exactly what we need.

For example, a carbon tax could be very effective. That's because with a tax you might be able to better balance the trade-offs between economic growth and increased fossil fuel use. One way to do that would be to tie the tax on carbon directly to yearly, economy-wide increases in energy efficiency, says Horace Herring, a visiting research fellow at the Energy and Environment Research Unit in the Faculty of Technology at the UK's Open University. We get 3 percent more efficient, and the cost of carbon goes up 3 percent, too. The tax money could go toward getting us off fossil fuels by increasing research and development of cheaper low- and no-carbon energy that gets made. Alternately, the tax money could also be used to help mitigate the social effects of rising fossil fuel prices, says John "Skip" Laitner, the director of economic and social analysis for the ACEEE. It could be funneled into programs that make sure certain nobody is priced out of necessary services such as heating and lighting, or it could be used to build up infrastructure that makes energy-efficient choices easier.

Ultimately, a carbon tax is no different from a cigarette tax. When states raise the cost of cigarettes through taxes, smoking rates go down.[22] People have more disposable income that they can spend on products other than cigarettes, and the nation, as a whole, benefits over time from fewer long-term smokers affecting the cost of health care. If you think back to chapter 2, you'll also remember that previous cap-and-trade systems have successfully made it cheaper for us to stop producing other harmful pollutants than analysts had previously estimated.

Energy-efficient technology makes it possible for a factory to churn out just as many widgets for less energy. Yet if the cost of fossil fuels is rising along with the growth of efficiency, there's an incentive for the factory owners to spend the money that they've saved on something other than fossil fuels. For instance, instead of buying more coal-generated electricity, they might invest in low-carbon energy produced on site. With a price on carbon, the rebound wouldn't totally vanish, and that's a good thing. We want those economic benefits. A price on carbon, however, would force the rebound toward products and behaviors that didn't damage the environment or keep us hooked on fossil fuels.

At the same time, a carbon price could also set off that cycle of cultural change. Everyone's choices become connected—not because we're being explicitly told what our neighbors are doing, but because we know everyone's decisions are motivated, at least in part, by the same information. It's actually less like getting an Opower enhanced energy bill and more like the military adding metering, for the very first time, to soldiers' homes and offices. The carbon price ensures that we all notice that there's a problem. We respond to that information by changing our lives and making choices we wouldn't have made before. Those individual choices then matter, because they're something we do together, creating a new normal. Eventually, we look back on the old ways—when we wasted fossil fuels without even noticing and carelessly produced emissions for benefits we barely cared about—and we laugh. What kind of idiots would open a window and leave on the air conditioner?

There are other benefits, too. For one, a carbon price would neatly separate the goods and services we like from those that hurt us. Energy, after all, isn't inherently bad. Energy has built us a more comfortable, more convenient world than the one our grandparents or great-grandparents were born into. The problem is not the fact that we use energy, per se. Instead, the problems are related to the *type* of energy we use the most. Our problem is fossil-fuel dependency. Our problem is climate change. When we make decisions about when and how to use energy, we need to know how our daily lives contribute to those looming threats. Left alone, the costs of emissions and fossil fuels will rack up anyway. We'll pay good money to adapt to climate change and to help save people at home and abroad from flooding, fires, droughts, and other effects. As fossil fuels become harder to collect and process, the price will keep going up. Without the development of viable alternatives, our descendants will be stuck paying some very large bills.

Using a carbon price as our source of information would also ensure that energy information becomes extremely portable—with us wherever we go, no matter what we're doing. Knowing something about the interaction of energy, emissions, and your daily life is a privilege, reserved for people who have the free time to study it—or who, like me, get paid to do the research. Most people have too much going on in their lives. Even if they're concerned about the downsides of fossil fuel use, it's unreasonable to expect them to work out the emissions implications of everything they do, every day, and always make the "right" choice. I don't do that, and I don't know anyone who does—no matter how dedicated he or she is to sustainable living.

Right now, gaining access to and making sense of energy in our lives are a lot like trying to take a cross-country road trip with only a stained, outdated atlas as our guide. A price on carbon would tell us what we want to know instantly, with up-to-the-minute accuracy—like trading out that beat-up Rand McNally for an iPhone. A price on carbon makes our daily energy choices easy. All you have to do is be cheap. If you're trying to decide between two products or two ways to lower your utility bill, the less expensive option is probably the one that used fewer fossil fuels and produced fewer emissions. People don't have to become energy experts; they simply have to pay attention to the good deals. You're capitalizing on the power of information and also on the power of automation. Like the conference attendees who temporarily went vegetarian because it was the default dinner, we'll all make decisions that are good for the planet and good for our own futures because those will be the easy decisions to make.

Today, we talk about energy efficiency as if it's something that happens from the bottom up. I want to do 101 small things and save the planet. Yet in the places where energy efficiency really works, it appears, at first glance, as if it relies on the people in charge setting the scene. Ultimately, though, neither direction is the best way to create an energy-efficient society. Instead, bottom-up and top-down will have to meet in the middle. We have to use information to link individual choices together so that they can take on a real, culture-changing significance. As Americans decide what the new normal should be, they need the lawmakers to back them up with policy that makes it easier and more convenient to live an efficient lifestyle. It's a partnership, one that starts with a clear, obvious, and easy-to-understand source of information.

Americans care about energy, and we're willing and able to use less of it. There are ways to make our individual decisions matter, linking us into networks that reduce energy use on a grand scale. Meanwhile, carbon prices can be that big blinking neon sign, offering information that pushes us away from fossil fuels and toward efficiency. Carbon prices would encourage us to get our energy from low-carbon sources—wind, water, the sun, and more. Yet we can't simply leave it at that. Here's the thing: just as individual decisions about energy efficiency matter only if they're part of a larger movement, alternative energy can work only if it's part of something bigger, too.

CHAPTER ELEVEN

···

HOME FIRES

Energy production is something that happens to other people. We don't see it. We don't think about it. We just trust that the magic elves who live in our walls will make the lights shine and keep the furnace toasty. Yet there are changes afoot. Slowly, very slowly, the United States is shifting from being a place that gets its energy from giant, anonymous monoliths in the middle of nowhere to a place that also gets its energy from the farm fields in our county, the factories where we work, the dumps where we send our trash, the rivers that run through our hometowns, the hilltops where we built our universities, and even the rooftop of the house next door.

Before you can understand where energy generation is going, you have to know where it comes from today. I like to talk about the electric system in this country. Partly, that's because the generation of electricity and the way we use it in our homes and offices make a larger impact on the environment than most people realize. Yet I also simply think it's interesting. Electricity is an intimate part of our daily lives that is simultaneously very distant from our thoughts. It's different from the energy we use for transportation. Oil gets refined before we use it, but in general, it comes to us in much the same form as when it was pulled out of the ground. It's hard to psychologically separate yourself from oil when you regularly spill gasoline on your shoes at the local service station. With electricity, on the other hand, all that we see are the services. Lights come on, computers hum. We use this form of energy every day, but only a very few of us have ever held an actual lump of coal in our hands.

To make sense of energy *generation*, though, I have to zoom this picture back out just a bit, back to that 94.6 quadrillion BTUs of energy we used in 2009. That number encompasses all of the tasks we use energy to perform and all of the sources we get energy from. Wrapped up in that 94.6 quadrillion BTUs is every single megawatt-hour of electricity that coursed through the grid, every mile driven by every vehicle, every factory furnace and diesel generator, and even every barrel of oil that was used to make some other product, such as fertilizer or plastic wrap. Sixty years ago, the amount of energy Americans used would have lined up nigh-on perfectly with the amount we produced, but that isn't the case today. As we talk about how energy is made in the United States and how it might be made differently in the future, it's important to keep in mind that we mean only the energy that *is* made in the United States.[1] Of the 94.6 quadrillion BTUs we use, 30 quadrillion of that was imported.[2]

Today, almost all of the energy we use—whether domestic or imported—comes from fossil fuels. In fact, that's been true for a very long time. The United States was founded on wood power. Back in 1775 and for a hundred years afterward, the forest was our derrick, the ax our refinery. We burned logs to cook, to stay warm, to have light, and to make steam. In 1885, however, that changed. That year, coal overtook wood as our predominant energy source. Ever since, fossil fuels have been our number-one source of energy—and our number two and our number three. If you look at a graph of our energy use over time, the twentieth century looks like a mountain range, set against the plain of earlier generations. Petroleum is a craggy Everest, looming above everything else. Natural gas is a smaller mountain. Coal is a steeply rolling foothill. Comparatively, no other energy sources even warrant their own geological analogy.[3] That's for the consumption of energy, but the trends hold true for the production of energy as well. Of the 75 quadrillion BTUs we produced in 2010, fossil fuels accounted for almost 59 quadrillion.[4]

Despite their differences, though, all of our energy sources—from petroleum to wind power—share something in common. It has to do with the way we turn a source of energy into usable energy.

Today, all of our significant sources of energy tend to be used as part of what's called a "centralized generation" system, which is what happens when we make energy in big batches and then ship it far away to where it will actually be used. This is how petroleum is refined and transported around the country today. It's also primarily how electricity is produced—even the stuff that comes from the wind and the sun.[5] Large energy farms turn environmental resources into electricity, then transmission lines move that electricity to far-off places. This is how almost all of the energy in the United States is made. (In fact, this is pretty much how almost everything in the United States is made.) If you look around, though, you can see that reality starting to change. Across the country, we are starting to shift toward a mixture: centralized generation, plus decentralized generation—taking advantage of resources where we find them, to make energy that's used relatively close to the source.

In the world of electric generation, decentralized energy really isn't as weird as it sounds. In fact, centralized energy is the odd duck— a creation of the mid-twentieth century. Even the first attempts at centralized electricity generation were really examples of what we'd call decentralized energy today. Remember the electric power plant that opened in Appleton, Wisconsin, in 1882? That original Appleton plant was ten scant blocks from the city's downtown, and it was closely tied into a larger local industrial system, electrifying two paper mills and even initially using the same water turbines as one of the mills. For all of the changes our electrical system has seen since the nineteenth century, decentralized generation still exists, and what's out there still looks an awful lot like the plant at Appleton. That's because of a key lesson about energy I mentioned earlier: energy is governed by economics and incentives. Nobody planned for us to have a mostly centralized system of energy. It simply grew that way. The small amount of decentralized generation we have today also grew for the same reasons: money and other outside incentives.

Decentralized generation happens today in factories, in business parks, and on university campuses. Usually, in those contexts, it involves using natural gas to produce steam for heating and getting a side order of electricity as an added bonus. There's also decentralized generation happening in places such as hospitals and computer server farms, in the form of diesel-powered generators that switch on any time the primary source of power becomes unreliable. These decentralized generators keep crucial electrical services up and running when times get tough.

Right now, decentralized electric generation makes up about 19 percent of the total electric capacity in the United States.[6] Most of that is coming from those emergency or standby generators, which run only if there's a problem on the main grid. If you look solely at the capacity that operates on an everyday basis, only 4.5 percent of the total U.S. electric generation is distributed. That's tiny. Piddling, even. There are a lot of opportunities for expansion, however, and some good reasons a mixed, centralized-plus-decentralized system of generation makes sense. Some of that growth will involve natural gas–powered generators, but distributed generation is also an important part of putting a wide range of renewables to work, which includes hydro, solar, and biofuels.

Yet before we get too excited, we first have to take a second look at a basic concept from Introduction to Economics 101. It's time to rethink economies of scale.

The United States didn't embrace colossal coal-fired generators capable of supplying electricity to seven states at once simply because we liked the ambiance of great big cooling towers. We did it because it made economic sense.

During the course of the twentieth century, utilities found that the up-front costs of building bigger power plants were dwarfed by the bigger profits those big plants could produce. Infrastructure is always expensive. This was a way to make it a little cheaper. Compared to a bunch of small generators, one large system needed fewer skilled managers, could buy coal at a bulk rate and get it to the site with fewer complications, and served more customers. The rate of production went up; the cost per unit of production went down. That's the basic math behind the "economy of scale." That equation continued to work until—depending on whom you ask—somewhere between the late 1960s and the early 1980s. It's not clear exactly when the trend shifted. It is clear, though, that during the last thirty years, electric power plants have no longer grown in size and scale with every successive generation. It's not that the economies of scale that worked for our grandparents suddenly stopped working for us. It's just that like almost everything in our lives, they got a bit more complicated.

During the last few decades, American enthusiasm for all things great and big met the killjoys in the engineering department. It's true that bigger is better—you really can make generators bigger, while simultaneously making them more efficient and easier to operate with fewer people. Yet that works only up to a point. Eventually, growing larger starts to become a lot more expensive. Your profits stop going up and start to shrink. If you push past that point and keep on making ever larger power plants, you'll finally hit a wall where the size will become technologically unfeasible. Too big really can be as bad as too small.

That fact alone isn't enough to make the trend toward centralized generation reverse itself. The sweet spot—that line in the sand before "big enough" becomes "too big"—still leaves you with a power plant that's pretty damn massive. There are many coal-fired power plants with capacities above 500 megawatts—enough power for 375,000 homes.[7] The *smallest* nuclear power plant in the United States has a capacity of 476 megawatts, and, trust me, it gets by just fine. The really important changes didn't happen in the physical world but in the legal and cultural ones. Economics made power plants big, but social incentives, in the form of environmental protections and NIMBYism (Not in My Backyard), are now constraining "big power" until it makes less economic sense.

For most of U.S. history, there wasn't a good way for an average person to make his or her voice heard on the subject of infrastructure development. If a utility company wanted to build a power plant on your land, you could always refuse to sell to the company, but the land could still be had via eminent domain.

If you didn't actually own the land, well, you were pretty much out of luck. "Most energy projects required approval of the Federal Power Commission and various safety commissions," says Michael Gerrard, a professor of environmental law at Columbia Law School. "There were proceedings you could engage in, but they were very expensive and involved arcane technical issues. It was rare for citizens to have the wherewithal to participate, and even if they could, the grounds were limited and technical." Then came Storm King.

After World War II, the United States developed a very different, much more intimate relationship with electricity than it had previously enjoyed. More people had access to home electricity. There were more electrically powered doodads, and more people could afford to buy them. It was kind of the high point of America's love affair with convenience, and electrified everything was a symbol of that—as sure as a diamond ring is a symbol of marriage. During the course of the 1950s and the 1960s, demand for electricity skyrocketed. Americans started to watch television. They traded clothes pins for electric dryers. They shut their windows in the summer and turned on the home air conditioners. The electric infrastructure that had existed before the war couldn't keep up with the growth. New power plants had to be built.

For the residents of New York City, a place with limited space for large industrial construction projects, the new power plants would have to be built miles away, in the semirural reaches north of the city. Utility company Consolidated Edison chose Storm King Mountain, in the Hudson River Valley, as the location of a new, massive centralized electric plant. At first, pretty much everyone approved of the decision. New Yorkers liked it, because it meant more access to electricity for them. The people who lived near Storm King Mountain liked it, because the power plant came with a lot of promised jobs. Yet not everyone was enthusiastic.

At the same time that U.S. demand for electricity was growing, so was American interest in suburban living. Places that had once been small towns became commuter hubs where busy executives could spend their evenings and weekends in rural repose, and where their families could grow up surrounded by pristine nature. From this perspective, a power plant didn't look beneficial. It looked like a parking lot in paradise. One family that lived nearby—a Wall Street lawyer and his wife—decided to take action to try to prevent the proposed industrial site from leaving a stain on the Hudson River Valley's aesthetics. They formed the Scenic Hudson Preservation Conference and slowly convinced their neighbors that the power plant should be stopped.

This all sounds fairly routine today, but it was a big deal back then. Until 1965, nobody had ever managed to block the development of an infrastructure project solely because of the project's impact on something such as local beauty or historic value. That year, the Scenic Hudson Preservation Conference became the first, successfully convincing federal judges that noneconomic issues were still reasonable grounds to sue for stopping energy infrastructure development. The decision opened up a whole new world.

Within five years, Americans would see another big high-profile case where public pressure and protest—this time sans courts— halted a major urban development project. The Lower Manhattan Expressway would have cut across New York City and razed thousands of homes and hundreds of businesses in Greenwich Village, Little Italy, and Chinatown. Instead, the plan was shuffled off to the Island of Forgotten Engineering.

Around the same time, the federal government established the National Environmental Policy Act, which required any large project to prepare impact statements and environmental assessments and basically prove that it wasn't going to be an undue burden on the natural world. Taken all together, these assertions of citizens' rights and the importance of environmental protection added up to a very different business environment for utility companies. Although, it's essentially calling for infrastructure to be invisible, located far from the places where people live, the kind of activism that we know as NIMBY ironically creates economic pressures that make *decentralized* generation a more appealing option.

Building a big power plant ain't what it used to be, say both scientists and energy industry experts.[8] The site you pick might be expensive to obtain, but even if the owners will let you have it, you still have to work your way through years of slow-moving environmental checklists, costing you more money. Community resistance can delay or change plans at any point. All the while, you're stuck paying interest on millions of dollars' worth of loans you've secured, and you still have to spend even more money to deal with the excess electricity demand that caused you to need the new power plant in the first place. This can go on for years. It only gets worse when you start talking about doing anything with the electricity your new plant generates.

Centralized generation plants aren't located very close to the customers they serve. Transporting that electricity where it needs to go means traipsing your way across multiple counties and states, sometimes over protected lands, and through the paths of hundreds of private landowners. The logistics of constructing power lines are so complicated that several sources told me it's often actually easier and cheaper to build the power plant than it is to build the transmission lines that the plant feeds. These problems are a millstone for coal- and gas-powered generators, but they also cause problems for nuclear plants, large-scale hydroelectric generators, and wind farms.

All of these indirect costs add up to an opportunity for smaller generation systems sited closer to the communities that use them, NIMBY be damned.[9] If you can build a 100- or 200-megawatt power plant faster, for less money, and need fewer miles of transmission lines to boot, you've got yourself a pretty good deal, even if the economy of scale isn't as powerful. A power plant that size would still count as centralized generation to most people, but the same basic cost-saving and speed-increasing measures apply to truly decentralized power as well.

When we talk about the decentralized generation that already exists today, we generally mean cogeneration power plants. Similar in concept to that first, early power plant in Appleton, Wisconsin, cogeneration plants are large enough to serve the electricity needs of thousands of people, but small enough that they can be built within sight of their customers. That's important. The location allows cogeneration plants to work better and perform tasks that larger power plants can't do.

I've explained how electricity is generated—it's really just about finding a way to get very large magnets spinning inside rings of coiled conductive wire. Most of the time, that mission is accomplished by producing heat, which turns water into steam, which forces the blades of a turbine to move, which spin a shaft, which moves the magnets, which generate the electricity. Whether the plant uses coal, natural gas, or nuclear power, the defining factor is how you make the heat, not the electricity itself. Now, if you know anything about what happens when you convert one form of energy into another, you can already see the problem here. At every step of that process, some of the energy doesn't do what you want it to do. Effectively, that energy gets lost. It doesn't simply vanish. That's not how energy works. Yet it is "lost" in the sense that you used resources to produce it, and now you can't get any work out of it. To varying degrees, every electric generator out there has to use a lot more energy than the system really needs to produce the amount of usable electricity we get out of it.

All told, these conversion losses amount to 24.6 quadrillion BTUs. To put it another way, 66 percent of the energy we put into electricity generation never gets used by anyone.[10]

Cogeneration helps to fix that problem. It works because the "lost" energy has really just turned into heat. A cogeneration power plant captures that heat and puts it to good use, most often using it to make steam. Standing alone, a combined cycle natural gas power plant can have an efficiency as high as 55 percent —that is, of the energy that is put in, 55 percent comes out as useful electricity. That's only with the newest technology, however, and on the most ideal days, under perfect conditions, says Tim Roughan, the director of distributed resources with National Grid. Other times, those power plants can be a lot less efficient and lose a lot more energy. Cogeneration facilities, on the other hand, produce steam for heat, then capture the lost energy and use it to make electricity. The can be around 60 percent efficient, averaged out over an entire year.[11] Cogeneration can give you the same services for less fossil fuels burned, saving money and emissions.[12] Yet it works only if your power plant is small enough that it can be located right next to something—a university, maybe, or a factory—that needs to use a lot of steam on a regular basis anyway. That constraint pushes cogeneration toward the small side. Depending on the type of generator system you use and where you're using it, a cogeneration plant can save energy and money at capacities as tiny as 50 kilowatts.[13]

Cogeneration is primarily attractive because of its economic benefits. In fact, the money saved through increased efficiency is the
main reason cogeneration is fairly common today, while other forms
of distributed generation are not. Yet there are priorities we value
beyond the immediate state of our pocketbooks.

Take security, for instance. You might fear natural disasters, terrorism, or simple accidental power failures, but no matter what event
temporarily takes the power grid down, lives and livelihoods end
up being on the line just the same. From hospital ventilators to city
governments and emergency response teams to all of the data from
businesses and banks stored like so many Arks of the Covenant in
vast warehouses of computer servers—a loss of power has consequences. When power is almost totally centralized, it's a lot easier
for one relatively small problem to explode into a multistate catas-
trophe. Adding decentralized nodes—and, along with them, more
redundant-in-a-good-way points of connection between generation
stations and customers—makes it a lot easier to wall off a failure
point and keep more electricity flowing to more places. This only
gets more important as our lives become more electrified. There's
a cost up front, and we don't necessarily make our money back any
time soon. If we spend the money now, however, in a controlled way,
we can avoid having to throw around cash in a panic later.

That same basic idea—that maybe it's better to spend money solving problems *before* they blossom into disasters—can also apply to climate change and renewable generation. I've never found an expert
consensus on how important decentralized generation will be to the
spread of renewables, but many scientists see the two concepts as
interconnected, at least on some level.

There are several places where renewable power and decentralized
power cross paths. First off, think back to what we already learned
about "peaking load"—basically, the days and the times of day when
demand for electricity is at its highest. The daily peak load happens
in the late afternoon, and the seasonal peak load occurs in the summer. Late afternoons in the summer are the peak's peak—when the
grid is stretched thin and rolling blackouts are most common. Grid

controllers try to predict what the peak will be—how high electricity demand will rise. Utility companies need to have the capacity available to meet the spikes in demand—even if those generators aren't really needed much of the rest of the time. Yet there's always a risk that the peak will go higher than they counted on.

The peaks aren't consistent from place to place, either. Minnesota's summer peak, for instance, is lower than Texas's, simply by virtue of the fact that Minnesota is often a pleasant 75 degrees Fahrenheit on days when Texas is approximately the same temperature as the surface of the sun. People in Minnesota need to use less energy to stay comfortable in the summer than do people in hotter climates, but that's not where the variability ends. Weather patterns don't observe state boundaries. It might be 75 degrees in Minneapolis and, on the same day, 65 degrees in Duluth. There's also the heat island effect to take into account. It's warmer in the city than it is outside it. Downtown Minneapolis might be 75 degrees, while its outer-ring suburbs hover around 70 degrees.

Peak load, especially summer afternoon peak load, is like a pop quiz. Grid controllers are well-prepared, responsible students. They've been paying attention in class, so they can be pretty sure they'll do well, but it's still a stressful event. It's not only the generation that matters. Peak load is also rough on transmission lines. That's because power lines can take only so much heat. You might have noticed that, normally, taut wires droop a bit on particularly toasty days. Part of that droop is caused by the air temperature, and part is caused by the increased heat of peak load electricity coursing through the system. Droop happens, and when it does, power lines are more likely to touch something—a tree branch, for instance— that blocks the flow of electrons and causes a power outage.

Here's where distributed generation comes in. If you can provide more peaking power, located closer to the places that actually need it, you can avoid making major investments in big power plants that you don't fully use for most of the year, and you can get the electricity where it needs to go without stressing quite so much of the transmission system. And the renewable generation? It turns out that solar electricity is most plentiful in the parts of the country, the times of year, and the times of the day when peak loads are also at their peakiest. Using distributed solar to meet peak loads is probably the most cost-effective way to harness the sun's energy today.

The second place where distributed generation and renewable generation cross paths is transmission. Transmission is transmission is transmission. It doesn't get much easier or cheaper to build multistate power lines just because there's a field of solar panels at one end, instead of a coal plant. Centralized renewable generation benefits from the same economies of scale that fossil fuels do, but it's also at the mercy of the same transmission problems. In addition, centralized renewable generation is likely to be, in many cases, even farther from customers than the fossil fuel version, says Mark Petri, the technology development director within Argonne National Laboratory's Energy Sciences and Engineering Directorate—all thanks to the way the quality of renewable resources varies by geography and the fact that a centralized renewable power plant needs a lot more land to produce the same megawatt capacity as a competing fossil fuel plant.

When I talked about how the grid works, I mentioned that the stated capacity of a wind farm is not the same as the amount of electricity that wind farm actually produces on a regular basis. Grid controllers call the difference between capacity and actual reliable output the "capacity factor," and the capacity factor of wind and solar power is particularly low. With a wind turbine, you can expect to have reliable access to only 34 percent of its stated capacity. Solar photovoltaic panels are even worse. A panel that is mounted so that it can move, following the sun across the sky and collecting solar energy for a larger portion of the day, might capture 25 percent of its stated capacity. Stationary solar panels, however, the kind that most people install on their roofs, don't get much better than 18 percent.[14] Meanwhile, coal, natural gas, and nuclear power all have capacity factors of 85 percent or higher, and hydroelectric dams operate at 52 percent. Capacity factors incorporate several variables, including the minute-by-minute changeability of the resource—the same issue that makes wind and solar fit poorly into our current grid.

Capacity factors mean that if you want 100 megawatts of electricity available, you need a lot more wind turbines or solar panels than the number that would give you a 100-megawatt capacity.[15] Once you have enough, they're going to take up a lot of land. The

500-megawatt-capacity Roscoe Wind Farm in Texas covers a hundred thousand acres—an area about the same size as all of Corpus Christi.[16] There are not a lot of places where that much land is available near areas that are densely populated enough to need 170 megawatts of power, let alone the full 500. Add to that the fact that a lot of the best wind resources are in the middle of nowhere to begin with—the plains of South Dakota, western Kansas and Oklahoma, or maritime Alaska—and you've stacked up some serious transmission issues.

Decentralized generation can get you renewable power, without the transmission. Sure, it can't be nearly as big—and with the capacity factor, that does mean small. Yet what you lose in volume, you make up in easy access to electricity customers and vastly cheaper transmission infrastructure. We already make these trade-offs when we choose not to build a huge wind farm in gusty-but-isolated Montana, in favor of a smaller cluster of wind turbines in less windy Illinois, significantly closer to Chicago.

Finally, decentralized generation just plain fits with how renewable resources work. Remember those trade maps of the United States from grade school social studies textbooks—the ones that peppered the country with little icons of smiling pigs, waving wheat, and smokestack-y textile mills in order to illustrate how various states made and sold different products? Someday, kids might be looking at energy maps laid out the same way, with little suns hovering over New Mexico, chipmunk-cheeked cartoon clouds blowing air over West Texas, and plots of prairie grass dotting southern Minnesota. There are great reasons for using renewable generation on a centralized scale, but at a fundamental level, this is about forms of energy that are available in some places and less available—if not completely absent—in others. Biofuels, especially, if they turn out to be something we can sustainably produce only in limited quantities or from waste products, become hyper-localized. Decentralizing generation makes local energy a feature, rather than a liability.

The big trick in coming years will be finding the right balance between economies of scale and economies of local. Again, one solution won't fit everybody. The scale of generation that works best depends on the source of energy and how you're using it and what goals you have beyond simply turning on a light.

....

CHAPTER TWELVE

BIGGER LITTLE

One bright and blustery morning in May 2009, I left my home in Minneapolis and headed into unfamiliar territory. For three years, I'd lived in archetypal Minnesota—a land of lakes and deep dark forests, guys in flannel swilling beer, and mosquitoes swilling guys in flannel. Now I was on my way to a corner of the state far removed from that eternal hunting camp atmosphere. As I drove southwest from Minneapolis, the trees got thicker, the hills got taller, and then suddenly both vanished.

The edge of the prairie is a sharp, clear line, extending diagonally across Minnesota from Fargo in the northwest to Rochester in the southeast. On one side, the state stretches up to Canada, all Paul Bunyan, Pabst, and parkas. In the opposite direction, touching Iowa and the Dakotas, is a triangle of mostly treeless flatland that feels like a graft made from the skin of some other state. In the middle of that prairie transplant sits Madelia, a town of a little more than twenty-three hundred people that is surrounded on all sides by miles upon miles of brown soil, tilled into neat rows. If you flew there in an airplane, Madelia would look like a button, sewn into the middle of a patchwork quilt—each farm divided into fields shaped like squares and circles, bordered by pale yellow gravel roads and by the narrow strips of bright green grass that grow alongside creeks and drainage ditches.

Madelia is a farm town. It has always been a farm town. It rose out of the prairie 150 years ago in response to the people who flocked to this part of the United States in search of a chance to own their own land and grow crops on it. What those people couldn't make themselves, they bought in Madelia. When their kids needed an education, Madelia opened a school. When the prairie felt a little too big and empty, Madelia offered a respite from solitude. Sixty or seventy years ago, there might have been a couple hundred small farms orbiting a town Madelia's size. On a Saturday night, those farm families could double the population and light up the sleepy downtown with crowds desperate for a weekly brush with social interaction. Folks got their hair done, went to dances, and gossiped. They sipped some whiskey, saw a movie, and did some gambling. On Sunday, they completed the cycle with church.

Even today, after the farms have consolidated and Madelia has become more of a bedroom community for people who work and shop someplace else, farming is still a cultural force. In that way, it's not too different from the small towns in Kansas where my family lives. These are places where most of the adults grew up with farmers as their primary role models and with farm life as the ideal. Even if being a farmer is financially out of reach—or not quite what you want to spend your days doing—it's still a part of how you define yourself. A man might have a good job miles away but will spend his weekends managing several dozen acres for his father-in-law, just because he kind of likes the way it makes him feel.

When the residents of a town such as Madelia think about the future of energy, the solutions they come up with are unsurprisingly centered on the land and what it can grow. In Madelia specifically, however, those agrarian solutions look a little different from what you might expect. When Madelians imagine the future of energy, they don't see prairie dotted with big ethanol refineries, where corn grown by hundreds of farmers is processed into fuel that will be sold all around the United States. Instead, they're thinking about something much more local.

Madelia is a small town with a big plan to produce fuel made from local materials for local markets. From the native grasses that easily grow in prairie soil to leftover beaks and pieces from a nearby chicken canning factory, anything that can grow within a twenty-five-mile radius of town is fair game. Turn those local resources into fuel, and maybe you can get some local economic development, while simultaneously preserving the future of farming. That, in a nutshell, is the plan behind the Madelia Model—a grassroots experiment in rural business and environmentalism. Almost a decade in the making, the Madelia Model is only now, in 2011, starting to become something real, something more than just a nice idea. It will be months at least, probably years, before we start to see how well the first tests of the model work, but when the results do start to roll in, they'll be more than simply a verdict on one town's ambition. The lessons learned in Madelia, good and bad, will be part of a national conversation.

As I dug into the stories and the science surrounding alternative energy, I found a common theme popping up over and over. It stretched from rural fields to urban rooftops, from liquid fuel to electricity. For more than a century, we've produced energy in larger and larger quantities, at facilities increasingly removed from where that energy is actually used. During a few generations, energy went from being something that every household handled and consumed on its own to being a mass-produced commodity. Today, energy in the United States is largely the same wherever you live—gasoline is made from the same ingredients, in the same way, whether you fill up your tank in Cleveland or Albuquerque. The process of making energy happens out of sight and largely out of mind—electricity works when you flip a switch, but have you ever seen the place where your electricity is made?

That's the status quo on energy today, and there are very good economic and social reasons for why it got to be that way. Energy is economics. Our infrastructures evolved to be what they are today because of financial and social incentives. The way those systems work now isn't the ideal, but during the last decade, it seems as though the incentives are starting to reverse the trend toward centralization—at least, somewhat. You and I won't be warming up ethanol stills in our backyards, though, and it will probably be years before solar panels are a common sight around your neighborhood. Remember the other lesson about energy: we don't all get what we want, when we want it. Nevertheless, energy seems to be getting smaller and more local, relative to what it was in the twentieth century. Where companies once built power plants to serve millions, maybe they're thinking about serving hundreds of thousands—or even tens of thousands. Where local industries and local resources once didn't matter at all to energy production, they're starting to matter a little. Right now, this shift is happening in niche applications and special markets. It's happening in places that have particularly good access to a valuable resource or some unique reason—beyond simple entrepreneurship—to throw themselves into a risky experiment.

That's where Madelia comes in. It's a place with both a resource *and* a reason. The resource—agriculture—is easy to see. All you have to do is look around. The reason is a little more confusing. It certainly confused me when I first heard about the Madelia Model. Why would a generally conservative town, populated by a lot of generally risk-averse farm families, want to stake a decent amount of time and money on the cutting edge of alternative energy? Yet I only had to visit Madelia once to get it. In fact, on the day I traveled to Madelia, back in May 2009, I ran headlong into the reason before I'd even reached the town itself. Specifically, my moment of enlightenment happened a few miles outside the city limits, on the narrow blacktop of Highway 60, when I came very close to driving my car into a ditch.

The wind had started the day full of bluster, and it was positively furious by the afternoon, while the open, empty fields that flanked the highway offered nothing to slow the wind down. This alone wouldn't have been a big problem. I grew up in Kansas, and I know how to steer a car through a windstorm. The issue was what I could see ahead of me—or, rather, what I couldn't see. Out of nowhere, a gray cloud rose up to hover over the highway, swallowing semitrucks and digesting them into sets of disembodied tail lights. I had barely enough time to realize I wasn't looking at *fog* before I plunged into the thick of it.

The sun disappeared. Gravel pinged against the car windows. I couldn't see anything that wasn't artificially lit. In a panic, I turned on my headlamps just as I drove out the other side of the gritty haze, back into a normal, windy spring day. The "cloud" was made of dirt, and a mile or so up the road, another gray ribbon of it stretched across the horizon. I went through three or four of these dust clouds before I reached the exit for Madelia.

Even in town, though, the dust was not easily vanquished. I parked my car downtown, beneath the prow of a movie theater awning, and stepped out into air so texturized you could almost gnaw on it. Flecks of dust stuck in my sun block. When I opened my mouth, grit came in.

I had traveled to Madelia to meet with Linda Meschke, the woman who had become the driving force behind the Madelia Model, and I'd left my house dressed for the occasion, wearing the tidy business-casual wear of a young reporter. Those dust clouds knocked me down a peg. By the time I'd walked two blocks through downtown Madelia, my skin was turning pink, and my hair was a winded red whirl glued into place under a layer of grime. Meschke didn't seem to mind my sorry state. Instead, she just nodded slowly and said, "It's a little windy out here today."

At that point, I still didn't quite understand what I had seen. Dust clouds such as this, I knew, were related to soil erosion, but it wasn't until I talked to Meschke that I was able to connect the dots between the dust in my hair and the goals of the Madelia Model.

I found out early on in my research that people tended to describe Meschke brain-first. "She really knows her stuff," they'd tell me. "She's a very, very smart woman." They seemed to be a little in awe of her and a little intimidated, as if she were a force of nature—the opposite of a tornado, she blew through town leaving everything more orderly than they it had been before. From the secondhand accounts, I'd expected to meet a big, brassy Delta Burke of a lady. Instead, Meschke turned out to have the quiet, drawling demeanor of the good ol' gal farmer she had been for twenty-five years. She was heavyset with short brown hair, and her tropical-print, button-up shirt was the loudest thing about her, but she really does know how to get the job done—whatever the job in question might be. A former county agriculture inspector, she got involved in rural water-quality issues in 1988. Within a decade, she'd completely revamped the way the counties around Madelia did the work of water protection. Pre-Meschke, the county water programs were all very separate from one another, even if they shared the same watershed. She launched a program that treated the Blue Earth River system—one of Minnesota's dirtiest waterways—as a single unit, helping ideas and money cross county lines. The big-picture approach led to a 9 percent reduction in pollution by 2001.[1]

The cadence of Meschke's voice plodded along, but her hands were restless—fidgeting with themselves, drawing little circles on her notepad. She dealt in the small, deliberate details that got public works projects accomplished—the boring stuff for which bureaucracy was basically invented. Yet she talked in the language of a rabble-rouser, about tossing out the old ways and taking risks on new ideas. It was this part of Meschke's personality that led her to see small-scale local energy as a solution, both to the water-quality problems she'd been fighting for decades and to the threat of soil erosion—which had created the dust storms that plagued my trip to Madelia. Meschke thought that local energy could solve both of those issues, because it could give farmers an opportunity to get paid for growing something other than corn.

Make no mistake, the Madelia Model is about biofuel, but it is *not* about ethanol. This part of the country needs less corn, not more, Meschke told me. Right now, corn and, to a lesser extent, soybeans are pretty much the only crops being grown. Corn takes up more than 45 percent of all available farmland in southern Minnesota, as well as in parts of Nebraska, Indiana, and Illinois—and pretty much every square inch of Iowa.[2] In those same areas, depending on the county, soybeans chalk up anywhere from 15 percent to more than 45 percent of farmland.[3]

From the outside, this system can seem a little illogical, but it's simply specialization. It's no different from a factory making only shoes, instead of a closet full of different clothing products. It's easier to become an expert on two crops, rather than on twenty, and you can grow more for less of an up-front investment. Also, frankly, corn and soybeans pay off. There's a big industrial demand for those plants that broccoli can't match. When demand falls, there are also ample subsidies to guarantee that farmers make at least a certain price for their crops, with government money picking up the market's slack.

The downside is that these two crops, and particularly corn, aren't as great for soil and water quality as they are for farmers' bank accounts. Corn is a greedy plant that needs a surprising amount of attention to grow. Mainly, corn needs fertilizer and lots of it. In 2007, U.S. corn farmers used more than 5 million tons of nitrogenous fertilizer.[4] Yet while corn may have a big appetite for plant food, it's about as efficient at "eating" as a toddler with a bowl of spaghetti. You know the kid will end up wearing as much food as she eats, and a corn field will often use as little as half of the fertilizer it's fed. The rest sits on the soil until it's washed away into the nearest creek by rain or irrigation. Several river systems and thousands of miles away, the Mississippi Delta vomits out water saturated with the nitrogen runoff of every corn farm in the Midwest. In the Gulf of Mexico, the nitrogen becomes a buffet for algae, which—in the sort of natural cycle that completely fails to inspire Disney songwriters—eventually die off in numbers so large that their decomposition consumes every drop of available oxygen, suffocating all aquatic life for miles around. It's the Circle of Death, and it doesn't make a very good musical number.

Water quality isn't the only problem that ties back to this one plant, Meschke told me. Corn grows in tidy little rows—with tidy little root systems tucked underneath. In late May, a cornfield is still a sea of dirt, speckled with green shoots not much bigger than your average bunch of basil. When the wind begins to blow, that topsoil doesn't stand a chance. Since the nineteenth-century dawn of corn farming, some eight vertical inches of Iowa have gone missing.[5] For people who make their living on what they can grow in topsoil, this is very, very bad. The long-term professional danger to Midwestern farmers is no clearer than when one is picking particles of valuable topsoil out of one's skin, hair, and teeth. The dust storms I'd driven through on my way into Madelia were a product of corn farming. My car was caked in the lost future of U.S. agriculture.

Meschke thought she'd found the key to saving America's prairie farmland: Third Crops. That was her term for, basically, anything that isn't corn or soybeans. There was extra credit if it's native and perennial. Her idea wasn't totally unique. Some farmers already use a Third Crop system by rotating fields through corn first, soybeans second, and alfalfa or hay third, which helps keep the soil healthy and reduces the need for fertilizer. Yet Meschke wanted to take this a bit further. First, she promoted planting a wider variety of Third Crops. When a lot of different plants are grown in one region, it becomes less of a Club Med for species-specific pests, which means a decreased need for farmers to buy expensive pesticides. Meschke also wanted farmers to put Third Crops on some land full time, not only in rotation schedules. Land that's severely nutrient-deficient, land that's sloped or has a lot of loose topsoil, and land that sits alongside creeks and drainage ditches could all benefit from the dense, water-and-soil-retaining root systems of perennial plants.

The trouble for Meschke was how to make Third Crops profitable enough that farmers actually wanted to grow them. The perennials native to Minnesota's prairie—mostly, various species of tall grasses—are fairly cheap to grow and are ecologically friendly, because they don't need much fertilizer or irrigation, but they also aren't worth very much. This was where Meschke's interest in water quality and soil health dovetailed into her interest in local energy. There's not really any money to be made in growing Third Crops for topsoil protection or to clean up a polluted stream. Meanwhile, large-scale biofuel production—which currently means corn ethanol—only adds to those ecological problems. You *could* grow native grasses and turn them into fuel. The technology already exists. In fact, there are many different ways to do the job. The problem is that so far, nobody's been able to make any of those methods financially viable on a large scale—the kind of system that would allow big companies in the Midwest to produce barrels and barrels of fuel for use all across the country. To most people, that means cornless biofuel simply isn't ready for the real world yet. Linda Meschke, on the other hand, looked at that same problem and asked, "Why should people at Madelia worry about whether Florida has enough energy?"

Meschke had one key goal here: to get more farmers in the counties around Madelia to grow more Third Crops. To make that happen, she said, the farmers needed a financial incentive. That didn't mean that they needed a national industry, however. A small refinery that could pay farmers for Third Crops, create some jobs for nonfarmers, and produce enough fuel to sell within this one little region of Minnesota would do the trick, Meschke thought. Especially if gasoline prices continued to rise. If that wasn't viable, she said, you could go smaller still. Even the opportunity to make fuel for their own use—a chance to save money, rather than earn it—could be enough to get at least a few more farmers growing Third Crops. Meschke supports local energy because it's on the scale that prairie grass biofuel seems to work at, and because right now it offers the best opportunities to set the Madelia Model into motion.

Yet it's not risk-free. The farms that surround Madelia are large, and they're commodity-oriented, not a home for boutique cabbages. That doesn't mean they're corporate monoliths, though. These farms are family owned, by families who've lived in the region for generations. Sure, they might grow only corn. Over the decades, they might have absorbed acreage that used to house a more populous patchwork of smaller farms, but farming is still a family business and a very risk-averse family business at that. It would take three or four years, Meschke told me, to get a perennial Third Crop, such as prairie grass, established and ready for its first harvest. If a market for the grass failed to materialize, farmers would be left with a very pretty field and a big chunk of debt.

On the other hand, if the Madelia Model succeeded beyond everyone's wildest dreams—if Madelia and the region around it became self-sufficient in fuel—it would drastically change the lives of the people who lived here. Success would change local farming. There would be an economic pressure to start growing new crops that had different needs and different growth cycles. Success would change life in Madelia. There would be new jobs, new businesses, and more consumer choices. Madelia would also be a busier town, with new residents who might be a little better off. Change, like cow pies, happens. How it happened here would depend a lot on whether average Madelians got involved in shaping the future of their community. Their silence on the matter is deafening.

Every fourth Friday at three p.m., Meschke told me, the city holds an open meeting designed to bring Madelia Model planners and the public together. It is a noble plan—and mostly theoretical. The meetings happen, but no more than a dozen people ever turn up.

During our interview, Meschke spoke apathetically about the low civic involvement. It didn't surprise her. It didn't worry her. I got the impression that were she not the driving force behind the Madelia Model and thus inherently interested, Meschke might be skipping the meetings as well. For all of her mesmerizing confidence, she held no illusions about how the grassroots grows. Most people, she said, were just busy with their day-to-day lives. They'd get interested, but only when the Madelia Model finally gave them something tangible to be interested in. "Right now, what do we have to offer?" she said.

I could see her point. The farmers I knew seldom responded well to maybe/possibly/someday. Either you do something and give us the sales pitch when it's ready to go, or you don't do anything, and you shut up about it. (Yoda would have made a great farmer.)

"We've got the choir signed on," Meschke said. "And we've got a tentative congregation watching to see what happens next."

Two years after Meschke told me that, the Madelians finally got to see some action. Ironically, their first glimpse of the future looked an awful lot like the past. In the fall of 2011, researchers from the University of Minnesota planned to drive a pickup truck from St. Paul to the farm country around Madelia. Behind it, on a trailer not much bigger than a small camper, they would tow a system that could turn just about any kind of plant or animal material into fuel. The technology was new, but the concept behind it was more than a century old.

Beginning in the nineteenth century, threshing machines traveled from farm to farm during harvest time. A mechanical system for separating grain from its stalk was too expensive to pick out for yourself from the Sears catalog, so the thresher was a separate portable business. Maybe one guy owned and operated the machinery as his job, or several farmers went in together on a piece of equipment that everyone shared. Either way, farmers paid to have their raw crops turned into something more valuable. The researchers at the University of Minnesota who want to bring a portable biofuel system to Madelia are hoping to repeat that history. Their technology, called microwave pyrolysis, is set to be Madelia's first shot at making local energy.

The system is both simple and delightfully clever. Pyrolysis is all about breaking down plants and other matter into a form better suited to usable commercial energy. Grasses, stalks, manure—any kind of organic material—goes in. That stuff gets heated to a little less than 950 degrees Fahrenheit in an oxygen-free environment, thus releasing a host of volatile gases. Condense the gas, and you get a liquid fuel. There are several ways to heat up biomass, but the university's system is special because it relies on microwaves, stronger versions of the same technology you use to cook popcorn and leftover pizza.

It's a handy method, because it's already proven technology—easy to use and cheap to construct. Microwaves also make the entire biofuel production process simpler. Usually, before any biomass can be turned into fuel, it has to be ground into tiny pieces to make sure every bit can be evenly heated at the same time, but microwaves heat up the center of a solid object just fine. If you're cooking on the stove, it saves time to break a chicken breast into smaller chunks, but if you microwave that breast whole, the center cooks at about the same rate as the outside. The same principal applies here. It takes a lot of time and energy to grind biomass down into itty-bitty pieces. Time is money, and energy doubly so—thus, if you can skip the preprocessing, you have the potential to save some serious cash. In addition, there's more to be saved in shipping costs.

Moving biomass around isn't very efficient. Organic material is generally bulky and not very energy dense. Transporting a ton of prairie grasses uses as much energy and costs as much money as transporting a ton of oil, but you get more energy out of the oil. By using microwaves—a heating technology that's lightweight and can be scaled down to the size of a small camper trailer—the University of Minnesota hit on a way to make pyrolysis portable and bring the fuel factory to the farm. There, each farmer can load up the pyrolysis machine and produce a couple of different products on site. Batch process test runs in the lab took as few as fifteen minutes.

What the farmers get out is useful stuff. Fuel is the main product of microwave pyrolysis. The university's system also produces enough combustible gas that, once started, it can power itself. In general, though, what you're making is a liquid called biogas. It's useable as is, fresh out of the tap, but for best results, it really needs a bit of cleaning up. Any engine will run on fresh biogas, but over time the acidic fuel would tear the engine apart. The university researchers are still working on methods to make biogas compatible with cars, but in the meantime, the stuff can be used in place of home heating oil or sold as a replacement for industrial petroleum.

That's what comes out the business end of the microwave pyrolysis machine, but it's not the only important product to come out of the system. Back up to the head of the production line, and you'll find another output—one that can reduce the quantity of CO_2 in the atmosphere and might be able to boost plant growth, too. When biomass is heated by microwaves, the parts that don't turn into fuel transform into something akin to charcoal. Called biochar, it's a bit different from standard barbecue briquettes, thanks to the oxygen-free environment where pyrolysis happens.

Biochar functions as a maximum-security prison for carbon. Charcoal can trap carbon, too, but not as effectively. Charcoal is chemically made up of carbon joined to lots of oxygen molecules but is primarily ash and has lost most of its carbon to burning. Like sorority girls in a slasher film, the oxygen is easily picked off by bacteria, which speeds up the process of decomposition, breaking the chemical bonds and leaving the carbon that does remain to drift back into the atmosphere.

Subtract the oxygen, however, and the carbon molecules get tough; they form ring structures that don't easily shatter and are more resistant to microbial attack. Lab research suggests that these bonds have the potential to hold fast for anywhere from hundreds to hundreds of thousands of years. That means less carbon in the atmosphere. It's also good news for anyone who'd like to see carbon-neutral or even carbon-negative biofuel production. Of course, that's in a test tube—there aren't many biochar studies being done in the (literal) field, and the real-world research hasn't been conducted for very long.

That's why—despite lots of crossed fingers—we don't yet know whether biochar will make as good a fertilizer as it makes a carbon trap. The key question—"Does biochar-infused soil lead to more crops and better soil fertility?"—is still wide open. Yet some tantalizing data are coming out of those lab tests.[6] It seems that by putting microbial life on slow-mo, biochar also works to trap nitrogen in the soil. Not only does that mean less nitrous oxide—another greenhouse gas—in the atmosphere, it could also mean less nitrogen fertilizer applied to the ground and less excess nitrogen leaching away into the water supply.

This is the Madelia Model in a nutshell: give farmers a reason to grow plants that are better for the land and the water supply than corn is, and then reap the benefits. In go prairie grasses, out come fuel, fertilizer, and economic development. It's not enough fuel and fertilizer to supply the whole country or even the whole state, but that's okay. It doesn't have to do that. The primary goal is to prevent more of the local topsoil from blowing away, not to create a mini-empire of bio-oil production. The Madelia Model only has to work on a local scale.

Of course, whether it can do *that* is still unclear. There are plenty of smart people who think prairie grass biofuel doesn't yet make economic sense, even on a small scale. Maybe especially on a small scale, in fact. There's a reason most of our energy isn't produced the way Meschke wanted to make fuel in Madelia. Small-scale energy has historically been energy that cost more to produce, thus cost more to buy. That might be changing, although it's not clear yet exactly where and when decentralized generation will work. Some experiments will fail, others will succeed. Yet there are good reasons to think that bigger isn't always better, and in many places, far from Madelia, local energy really does make sense.

The East River does not have an especially stellar reputation. If I was aware of it at all growing up in Kansas, it was as a place where the mafia dumped bodies and Cosmo Kramer wallowed in the stench of industrial pollution. As an adult, though, I found it to be a remarkably pleasant place for a stroll, particularly on Roosevelt Island. Here, the breeze off the East River cuts a cooling swath through a grossly sticky August day in New York City, with a smell so cold, salty, and freshly mineral that it's suddenly very easy to reconsider the concept of an East River swim. The island itself is equally counterintuitive—formerly the site of an insane asylum, a tuberculosis quarantine facility, and a city poor house, it was developed in the 1970s using a style of architecture one might charitably call Soviet Utopian, with lots of sheet glass, unpainted concrete, and sharp angles. Yet the ascetic buildings are set among rolling, tree-dotted parkland. The community feels more like a small town—a small town with towering apartment blocks—than a neighborhood in one of the largest cities on Earth. Today, this odd little enclave is where upper-middle-class Manhattanites go to breed. All in all, Roosevelt Island and the East River are nice settings for an alternative energy project that challenges expectations. Under the river, just off the island's eastern shore, there's work afoot—work that will call into question what a hydroelectric plant should look like and how big electricity generation ought to be.

The twentieth century taught us that hydropower is massive, that it consumes. Towns have to be flooded out, valleys drowned, and fish chopped to bits as they pass through the power plant's turbines. Verdant Power is one company that's trying to prove that you can have your hydroelectricity and like it, too—by using a smaller, decentralized installation that has a lot less of an environmental and social impact. However, what Verdant Power is trying to do can't be characterized as a total abandonment of centralized generation, either. Remember, energy is complicated. Reality is seldom zebra-striped, with our choices narrowed down to two diametrically opposed extremes. Yes, the centralization of energy has really been the story of the fossil-fuel-ification of energy. And, yes, modern concerns over environmental impact and land-use rights have made it difficult to centralize power more than we already do, but that doesn't mean we don't get anything good from centralization. It is still cheaper to make energy in bulk than for every household to make its own energy piecemeal, just as it's cheaper, ounce per ounce, to buy one can of tomato sauce the size of your head, rather than a bunch of little fist-size cans.

When I say that Verdant Power is challenging expectations of how big energy generation ought to be, I mean that it is challenging *both* extreme views. The company isn't trying to build a multihundred-megawatt facility that will supply electricity to all five New York City boroughs, but it isn't trying to take Roosevelt Island off the grid, either.

Under the river, between Roosevelt Island and the borough of Queens, Verdant is planning to install a hydroelectric power plant like no other in the country. Instead of using a dam or even an old-fashioned water wheel, this system will turn the motion of water into electricity with the help of what looks like a really out-of-place wind farm. The plans call for sinking a series of triangular platforms, each dotted with several skinny poles, and each pole topped with a rotating fan, similar to the propellers on the wings of a small airplane. As river water flows by the poles, the blades of fans will slowly turn, producing electricity.[7] Thirty of these turbines, grouped into sets of six, will have a generating capacity of 1 megawatt. No one generates power commercially like this today, but from a technical standpoint, it's a pretty simple system and one that Verdant has already shown to be workable. A five-turbine, 175-kilowatt pilot program spun away under the river for nine thousand hours, off and on, between December 2006 and September 2009, providing power to a parking garage and Roosevelt Island's only grocery store.[8] Besides proving the basic idea, the pilot was also meant to investigate how this unique type of hydroelectric generation would affect the local fish.

Yes, there really are fish in the East River. Along with the jokes about pollution and hit men, there's also a widely held assumption that the river is devoid of life. That couldn't be further from the truth, says Jonathan Colby, a hydrodynamic engineer with Verdant Power. There are many species of fish living below the water and diving birds, such as cormorants, that live above. On the day I visited Roosevelt Island, I watched the big jet-black cormorants dive-bomb the river and pop back up with little fish clutched in their bright-yellow beaks. I also watched a man saunter down to the shore and cast a fishing line into the East River, hoping for the same luck the cormorants were enjoying.

This river really was in trouble once, Colby says, but it's improved in a big way, largely because of changes in sewage treatment that were made in the wake of the federal Clean Water Act of 1972. It's just that until recently, no one had documented how the results of that successful clean-up had affected the local fish populations. When Verdant set out to show concerned New Yorkers that its method for generating electricity was both effective *and* safe, it inadvertently ended up running the East River's first wildlife survey in decades. Verdant learned a couple of surprising facts. It turns out that Verdant's water turbines didn't harm a single fish. That had less to do with Verdant, however, and more to do with fish behavior.

To do the study, Verdant monitored the river—both before and after installing the turbines—using a technology called Dual Frequency Identification Sonar, or DIDSON. Although basic sonar tells you that an object is out there in the water, DIDSON can *show* you what the object is—whether a fish or a plastic bag. The images produced by DIDSON look a lot like fetal ultrasound pictures. Suffice to say, the results might appear a little abstract to you or me, but experienced analysts can glean some useful information from this sonar, including the direction the fish are traveling and, in some cases, what kind of fish are out there. Verdant collected two hard drives full of this data every week and sent it off to independent analysts. It's the analysts who confirmed that no fish were harmed, but they also spotted some other really interesting activities going on underwater.

The misleadingly named East River is actually a tidal strait of the Atlantic Ocean, flowing in one direction or the other, depending on the time of day.[9] In between the directional changes, there's a slack tide, when the speed of the current drops significantly. During those periods, the river is too slow for the turbines to spin. Conveniently, that's also when the local fish are most active, taking advantage of the still waters to do their feeding with less of a physical workout. The rest of the time, they mostly just hang out, hiding in rocks along the river's edge. There are migrating fish to worry about as well, but they, too, managed to avoid the blades. For the most part, traveling fish simply swam around the turbines.

"It makes so much sense, though," Colby says, "because bridge piers make signatures in the water. Fish can sense them coming up, and they don't simply run into bridge piers. Literally, our turbines are sending out an acoustic pressure wave that fish can sense up and down the river."

• • •

The way Verdant Power wants to produce electricity is very different from the way that job is done today—in terms of both size and impact on the environment. U.S. hydropower has changed a lot during the course of the last century. In 1882, when the first hydroelectric power plant in the world opened in Appleton, Wisconsin, hydro was a vital part of how work got done in this country. H. J. Rogers may have been the first businessman to use the Fox River to produce electricity, but lots of factories in Appleton already ran on hydropower. Water flowing through the river turned massive water wheels. The wheels transferred that motion through series of cogs and gears, which in turn moved machines. In Rogers's paper mill, the river did the work of beating pulp long before it did the work of lighting the factory. In the early twentieth century, combustion engines took over the physical labor, and hydropower became what we know it as today—a way of making electricity. In 1940, 40 percent of U.S. electricity came from hydroelectric sources.[10]

Today, although hydroelectricity makes up only a small portion of our total electric capacity, it is far and away our number-one source of renewable energy. About 2 percent of our electricity came from the wind in 2009. Solar power accounted for less than 1 percent. Meanwhile, the Energy Information Administration says that hydropower accounted for 7 percent of our electricity.[11] Almost all of that hydrogeneration is centralized, simply because that's how conventional hydroelectricity works. First, you build a dam across a river. Then water builds up behind the dam, forming a lake where there was once a valley. After you have the lake, you can control how much of it you release into the river downstream, using massive gates built into the dam.

The actual power plant is connected to those intake gates. Open the gate, and water flows into a channel. The channel directs the water to a chamber with a massive turbine and keeps the water compressed so that it has enough force to spin the turbine very quickly. The spinning turbine generates electricity. The water finishes its journey through the channel and ends up back in the river. Knowing this, you can see where the environmental concerns about hydroelectric power come from. Water in the lake behind the dam is stagnant, especially compared to river water. Stagnant water carries less oxygen. For a river fish, going from a river to a dammed lake and back into the river again can be a traumatizing—if not outright deadly— experience, akin to somebody throwing a plastic bag over your head for part of your morning commute. The fish that do make it out the other side of the lake then have to survive the water-park ride from hell, traveling down the narrow channel and past the food processor–like blades of the turbine.[12]

Power plants such as these are cheap to operate—the "fuel" is basically free—but, like all energy infrastructures, they're expensive to build.[13] It takes a lot of material and a lot of work to dam a river. Hydroelectric power plants aren't all as big as you might think— only 14 percent of those in the United States are classified as "large hydro," with capacities greater than 30 megawatts. Yet within that category are some massive facilities. The largest—Washington State's Grand Coulee Dam—has a capacity greater than 6,000 megawatts. In fact, the large hydroelectric dams are so big that even though there are many more small-scale facilities, almost all of the hydroelectricity we use comes from that fraction of hydropower that is large scale.[14]

The electricity these systems produce is low-carbon, and, unlike wind and solar power, it isn't considered to be variable. Water levels in a river or a lake do change over time, and that can affect the amount of electricity a hydroelectric plant can produce. Those changes don't happen quickly, however, so hydro doesn't stress the grid on a daily basis. We aren't limited in how much hydroelectric power we can install on the grid, the way we're limited to 20 percent wind and solar, but hydroelectric power *is* limited in other ways.

To make conventional hydroelectric power work, you need the right kind of rivers and a lot of free land. There are only so many places in the United States where you find both features in areas that aren't federally protected. According to the U.S. Geological Survey, there weren't enough good reservoir locations to supply *all* of the energy the United States consumes, to begin with, and, frankly, the best spots are already being used.[15] Most of the 78,000 megawatts of current United States hydro capacity are packed into the Pacific Coast, Montana, and New York State.[16] Meanwhile, other places, like such as Kansas, have almost none. In 2006, though, the Department of Energy (DOE) released a paper that took a second look at the potential for hydro power in the United States. It paid serious attention to places where you could make electricity without building a dam.

The DOE isn't planning quite the same type of project that Verdant is proposing. The technology is different, for instance. Yet the scale is similar and the concept definitely has more in common with what's going on at Roosevelt Island than it does with the Hoover Dam. These reservoirless "small-hydro" projects would involve digging a channel, which would divert only part of the river through a hydroelectric power plant. Water runs through, spinning the generator turbines, and then gushes out the other end of the channel, back into the river.

The small-hydro sites identified by the DOE would all have capacities of less than 30 megawatts, with some less than 1 megawatt. What these new sites lack in size, however, they make up for in numbers. The study found 5,400 sites in forty-nine states where damless hydroelectric power could be developed in a practical way. Taken together, the sites represent as much as 18,000 additional megawatts of electric capacity we could be using but currently are not. It's enough to increase the total U.S. hydroelectric capacity by 50 percent— something that wouldn't be possible to do if we focused only on developing more large hydroelectric dams.[17]

Basically, the DOE has concluded that decentralized generation is the future of hydroelectricity in the United States. Its study shows that the production of electricity can be increased significantly, not by scaling up the size of individual power plants, but by scaling up the *number* of smaller plants—a trick that has its drawbacks but allows us to take advantage of more natural resources in more places. This is one big benefit of decentralizing generation. If the electric generator is large, then the source of energy that powers it has to be correspondingly massive. The Hoover Dam couldn't operate off a small pond. If you shrink the generator, though, suddenly you can put much smaller energy sources to use.

Think about Kansas again. Right now, this state produces almost none of its electricity with water power, and that fact isn't particularly surprising. Kansas is not the most water-saturated state. Although there are rivers and streams, only three rivers are big enough to be legally navigable. I was an adult before I saw my first natural lake.[18] If you think that hydroelectric power has to mean finding a spot where you can build a hydroelectric dam, Kansas isn't going to offer much in the way of water power resources. Yet if you change your perspective on what water power ought to look like, then the Sunflower State goes from being a place that currently has about 1 megawatt of developed hydroelectric capacity to a place with a hydroelectric capacity of 295 megawatts.[19]

All of those potential sites in Kansas that the DOE identified have capacities of less than 30 megawatts, and most of that added capacity—197 megawatts a year—would come from facilities with capacities lower than 10 megawatts. All told, Kansas could increase its hydroelectric generation by 29,541 percent. An extra 295 megawatts of electricity isn't really a lot—in the peak of summer, Kansas's current electricity generation systems have a capacity of more than 12,000 megawatts.[20] Yet in a state where 74 percent of the electric generation comes from coal, even that drop in the bucket means something for CO_2 emissions and for shorter-term air quality as well. Given coal's unfortunate tendency to kill people, an increase in small-scale hydro and a decrease in coal usage would actually save lives. It could be a better compromise between the people who are concerned about access to energy and those who are more worried about the side effects of energy.

There's a very important lesson wrapped up in all of these facts and figures. Decentralizing the way we generate energy doesn't have to mean completely doing away with the grid and forcing each family to make energy for itself. Going off the grid isn't practical for everyone. Access to resources isn't evenly distributed across a city, let alone across the country, but Verdant Power and the DOE small-hydro assessment are prime examples of the benefits of making electricity generation a little smaller than it is now. These projects are still on the bigger side of "little." Even 1 megawatt is a lot of electricity, relatively speaking. The proposed installation in the East River, for instance, would provide electricity for a dense neighborhood, not merely for a single house—and it wouldn't even make that neighborhood self-sufficient. Yet electricity generation of the size that Verdant and the DOE are proposing combines some of the benefits of centralized energy with those of decentralized energy. It also allows cities and regions to take advantage of resources that are currently sitting untapped. If the United States really does start to embrace a more decentralized way of looking at energy production, projects such as these will become a lot more common.

Hydroelectric generation is a place where "bigger-little" decentralized electricity could make a real difference, but the benefits of this sort of decentralization aren't limited to what we can do with water. All across the country, there are pockets of easily accessible resources that are best used on a scale that's smaller than what we've come to know as normal but larger than "every man for himself." The cogeneration power plants I mentioned earlier fit this profile, too. So do a lot of smaller wind power projects. In fact, just about any source of electricity can be developed at the bigger-little level.[21] Liquid biofuel could be developed this way as well. Although the Madelia Model will be tested out on a household scale first, with the University of Minnesota's traveling microwave pyrolysis machine, Linda Meschke eventually hopes to attract a company that would build a larger biofuel refinery in Madelia itself. A project such as this would be miniscule compared to the size of an average ethanol refinery, but it would be big enough that it could sell biofuel locally to people who didn't personally own the resources to make biofuel themselves. Like Verdant Power's underwater windmills and the DOE's proposed damless hydroelectric generators, it would be smaller than centralized but bigger than off the grid.

Another resource that bigger-little energy could help us capture: waste. The United States uses a lot of energy and also wastes a lot. That lesson is true when it comes to power plants, and it's true in some ways that are even less obvious. Right now, we don't get as much benefit out of the products we buy and use as we could. That's why people promote ideas such as recycling and composting—they're both simply ways to turn waste into something useful. It's like meat production. When a cow dies in a slaughterhouse, they don't just cut out the steaks and throw the rest away. The less-photogenic cuts of meat are turned into products such as ground beef, hot dogs, and sausages. The fatty bits and the offal are turned into pet food. Other fat becomes candles and cooking lard and is used by the chemical-processing industry. The skin becomes leather. The bones are dried and ground into a meal that can be used as a fertilizer. In Europe, bone meal is even used as a fuel, something that can be burned to produce electricity.[22] Like our great-grandparents, we don't only eat meat. We make use of a whole animal—everything but the moo.

Yet that's not how we treat all of the products in our lives. Think about everything you throw away. Even if you are the champion recycler and composter on your block, you still have *something* for the trash man to pick up every week. Americans generated 243 million tons of trash in 2009 alone. That averages out to 4.3 pounds of junk from each of us every day.[23] Where does it all go? Mostly, our trash ends up in landfills—places where waste and dirt are layered into a disgusting cake of decomposition. More than 2,300 landfills in the United States are either actively accepting trash or have been recently covered over and are no longer having trash added to them.[24] Every single one of those landfills sets the stage for bacterial production of combustible gas, similar to natural gas. That gas is energy we could be using, energy that is best captured on a bigger-little decentralized scale.

When you bury a big pile of organic material and let it rot, the process of decomposition produces a gas that is roughly equal parts methane and CO_2, along with some water vapor and a nasty mix of various pollutants—substances such as mercury and vinyl chloride. Called landfill gas, it's being made whether we like it or not. Left alone, the gas will work its way out of landfill and into the atmosphere. There, the pollutants can reach people, and the greenhouse gases can do their dirty work. So, we already have good reasons to control what happens to landfill gas. When we do, we create an opportunity to turn a source of local pollution into a source of local energy.[25]

In 1996, the Environmental Protection Agency (EPA) began to require large landfills around the country to prevent landfill gas from being released. That rule left landfill owners with two choices: they could simply burn the gas—a process of chemical change that makes the pollutants less harmful and turns the powerful greenhouse gas methane into less-powerful carbon dioxide and water vapor—or they could burn the gas *and* capture heat from the burn, using that heat as the energy source to power an electric generator. Either way, the gas had to be burned, so the real decision wasn't about *what* to do with landfill gas. Rather, landfill owners had to decide whether they were going to follow federal regulations or whether they would follow federal regulations and make a little extra money in the process. In July 2010, the EPA counted 518 operational landfill gas energy projects, with a combined capacity of more than 1,600 megawatts. And there are enough practical candidates to double both numbers.[26]

Like hydropower, trashpower can't meet all of America's electric needs, and trashpower isn't as environmentally friendly as hydropower. Burning landfill gas produces carbon dioxide and other emissions. In an ideal world, we'd find a better way to deal with our waste and not produce as much landfill gas to begin with. As it is, though, burning landfill gas is better for the environment than simply releasing it. As long as we have to do that, we might as well get some electricity out of it, too. In addition, these sites are inherently distributed. Cities haul your trash away, but until a city has run out of nearby places to dump its trash, it's really not cost-effective to haul it too far.

Trash and water are both energy resources that we've not fully embraced so far, but with the costs of planning and building centralized electricity on the rise, these decentralized—but not too decentralized—resources are starting to look a lot more attractive. You don't need to be an environmentalist to feel that pull. This kind of decentralized power isn't strictly about what's good for Mother Earth. It's also about what's good for your pocketbook as energy prices rise, what's good for your local water supply as the demand for natural gas leads to more fracking, what's good for people who don't want to look at miles and miles of transmission lines, and what's good for people who are worried about increasing our reliance on nuclear power.

Whether we're talking about a spinning turbine under the East River or a New Mexico landfill that doubles as a power plant, projects with capacities between 1 and 100 megawatts can take advantage of economies of scale. They're also less disruptive to build, so it should cost less and take less time to get them up and running. They're closer to the customers they serve, so it's cheaper to site and build transmission lines. This kind of decentralized generation produces enough electricity that it makes sense for some large electricity consumers to build their own power plants. Factories, universities, corporate campuses, even farms—all of these places use a lot of electricity and already need to own backup generators in case of emergencies. If they can make their own electricity, then they can lower their monthly bills now and get improved energy security in the future, while simultaneously reducing demand on the grid.[27] Reduced demand means that utility companies have to build fewer new centralized power plants. In the United States, that tends to equate to fewer new coal-fired power plants.

The lesson you should be learning is this: big-ish can be beautiful. Generation that is decentralized but that can still serve many customers at once gets you lower-cost, lower-hassle infrastructure development in less time. There doesn't seem to be much wrong with decentralized generation on this scale. The key complaint is that they pertain mainly to sources of energy that are more expensive, per kilowatt-hour used by customers, than coal. Yet as Tim Roughan, director of distributed resources for National Grid, a Northeast transmission and distribution company, points out, that might not be such a huge issue in the future, especially if you live in an area where electricity is already more expensive than average. "It is a significant leap in terms of cost incurred," he says. "But the theory, and I think this is valid, is that if you're paying seven cents for your commodity and centralized is getting theirs for five cents, as you look at the infrastructure costs, you can still get a balance if the centralized infrastructure costs are three cents and yours are one cent."

Experts such as Roughan also acknowledge that a big part of the growth of decentralized energy is its appeal to customer choice—that very American sense of being independent and expressing this in decisions you make about the products you buy. When consumers make these choices about energy, they won't always choose a size of generation that promotes independence for communities or institutions. Sometimes they want to feel that power on a more personal level—truly homegrown energy, sized for houses or small businesses. That small-scale, decentralized generation is a much more profound paradigm shift. It has the potential to completely change the way Americans think about energy, and it could give us broad access to the sun—a powerful, largely untapped energy source.

But small-scale decentralization also raises the stakes.

CHAPTER THIRTEEN

GOOD CITIZENS OF THE GRID

Gainesville was everywhere in early 2009. Within a span of three months, this city in a land-locked, sun-soaked area of North Florida had gotten the attention of *U.S. News and World Report*, *Newsweek*, *Washington Monthly*, and dozens of denizens of the Greenie blogosphere. All of those publications carried the same basic message: Gainesville, Florida, was what the future would look like. Here, in a city hall framed by tropical trees heavy with moss, American politicians and a U.S. utility made a choice to try out some very European energy legislation—a system that is best known for bringing more alternative energy to cloudy, decidedly temperate Germany. If the legislation worked, it had the potential to make Gainesville the national model for decentralized solar power. Forget the chicken in every pot. In the future, political success could be measured by a solar panel on every roof.

There's a bit of a disconnect between how different groups used the same words. When I talked to scientists and utility industry experts about decentralized generation, what they pictured was power production on the scale of Verdant Power's hydroelectric turbines beneath the East River or a gas-fired cogeneration plant that produced heat and electricity for a university campus. They thought of biofuels, and imagined a stationary central refinery, much smaller than the facilities that process oil into gasoline for the entire country but large enough to be industrialized. Capacities would be between

1 and 100 megawatts. Economies of scale would still apply. The energy would still have to travel—whether by tanker truck or power line—to reach the people who wanted to use it.

Yet when I talk to my friends and family about decentralized generation, their minds immediately jump to something very different. To them, decentralized generation isn't only a somewhat smaller version of a system that already exists, like a scale model in a toy train set. Instead, they thought of decentralization as the creation of an entirely new, entirely separate system. They imagined a world where they didn't have to pay the electric company every month, because a one-time investment would allow them to make all of the electricity they needed with the help of the sun or the wind. No more rate hikes. No more ugly electric power lines threaded through their lives. That's what my friends and family were excited about. They wanted energy on site, something they could feel that they made by themselves. They loved the idea of the Madelia Model's traveling biofuel machine. Cogeneration plants bored them.

I think that this disconnect boils down to an issue of control. Scientists and utility experts have always been at the helm, guiding energy production. At least, they have been for as long as energy has been a scientific industry, for about a hundred years or so. When the rest of us turned energy production over to this small group, we got some benefits out of the deal. I, for one, enjoy having a boiler that's powered by natural gas and electricity.

In the winter, my thermostat is programmed to make sure that my house is warm before I get up. I spend, at most, twenty minutes a year making sure that happens—just enough time to pay my bills every month and turn the boiler on or off with the season. Contrast that to my paternal grandparents' old house, which was heated with a wood stove. To make sure the house was warm in the morning, my Grandpa had to chop wood every week—after first either cutting down a tree of his own or buying wood from someone else and hauling it home. There was no such thing as waking up to an already-warm house. Whoever got up first, either Grammy or Grandpa, had to bring in chopped wood from the back porch and get the fire going. They had to keep it going throughout the day. There were ashes to haul every day, and a stovepipe to clean.[1] When they moved into a retirement townhouse with central electric heating, my Grammy was ecstatic. By all of the accounts I've read, that's how most of our ancestors responded to the new convenience of centralized energy generation. If the energy is made by someone else, all you have to do is sit back and enjoy the benefits.

Yet you do lose a certain amount of control. If my Grandpa's stove burned through all of the wood he'd put in it, he could go chop some more wood. If I wake up some morning and my gas or electric service isn't operating, then I have to put in a call to the utility and find someplace more comfortable to spend my day. Centralizing generation was a lot like adopting the republic as a form of government, as opposed to a direct democracy. Most of us don't want to sit through all of the meetings, speeches, and negotiations necessary to run a country. We'd much prefer the convenience of electing representatives to do that job for us. Sooner or later, though, we find out that the representatives don't always make the same choices we would have made in their shoes. It doesn't mean the republic is bad. It simply means that there's always a price for convenience, and that price is a loss of direct control. Again, energy is complicated, and there's no way for everybody to get everything he or she wants from it all the time. There will always be downsides. This was one of the downsides of the twentieth century's centralization of energy.

Losing direct control over energy generation—becoming consumers, rather than producers—didn't really bother the first generation of Americans who had the option of trading control for convenience. You can see that just by looking at utility company advertising from the early twentieth century. Take *The Electrical House That Jack Built*. This booklet was published in 1916 as a promotional for the Milwaukee Electric Railway and Light Company and features eighteen pages of *House That Jack Built*–themed doggerel illustrating all of the wonderful ways you can use electricity around your home. Sure, it's a sales pitch, but sales pitches that end up being as successful as the one for electricity eventually was are probably speaking to something deeper than a single company's bottom line.[2]

The booklet really gives you a sense of the honest, wide-eyed amazement and wonder people felt when they thought about comforts and conveniences that we take for granted today. In the new world of electricity, the booklet promised, the toast would never burn, you would no longer need to schedule your week around laundry, and everyone would be healthier and happier. Electricity changed energy production from a difficult in-home process that kept the messy by-products of progress literally in your face into something magical that happened when you threw a switch. The choking smoke was still there, but it wasn't at *your* house. There was still heavy labor involved, but it wasn't done by you or your children.

Yet that trade-off, more convenience for less control, does seem to bother some of us today. When surveys track which forms of renewable energy Americans are most excited about, solar power tends to win the day.[3] Solar power is also the form of renewable energy most associated with small-scale distributed generation. I don't think that's a coincidence. Unlike a hydroelectric dam or a wind farm, solar power can be easily seen as more than just an alternative source of electricity. Instead, it's a way to declare independence, a way to say, "I don't need to be beholden to a utility or anyone else to do the work of energy for me. I can do it on my own." Centralized energy is a symbol of the chains of modern society. The solar panel is your key to freedom.

It's an appealing perspective and a powerful image, but it's also not really the way that decentralized generation is likely to work for most of us. Even when you're talking about outfitting individual houses with solar panels, it's still a system that, ironically, ties you to your neighbors and community more than it liberates you. We can change the future of energy, but we can't build everyone's utopia. With convenience comes a loss of control, a loss of power. Yet what happens when you take that power back? As a wise man once said, "With great power, comes great responsibility."[4]

What's happened in Gainesville, Florida, in the years since it became the solar-powered darling of the media is a great example of that.

Gainesville is bigger than it looks. I spent three days there, feeling as if I were moving around a small college town. It was only later, waiting out a layover on my way back home, that I discovered that the population of the metro area tops out at more than two hundred thousand. Where these people were, I have no idea. It's possible they were simply obscured by the foliage. To someone who spent most of her life in Plains states, the sheer volume of plant life in Gainesville made me feel almost claustrophobic. The residential streets I drove down were like green tunnels. The trees grew thick and close together, arching overhead. Moss and vines seemed to climb over anything that sat still. Even wide avenues near a strip mall appeared constrained, narrowed by dense masses of plants running along the edges. There's a sense that the city was carved out of the jungle—as if mowing the lawn wasn't merely a chore, but a battle in the ongoing war between the will of man and the patience of nature.

It's easy to spot the source of all of that wild growth. Gainesville's climate is an awful lot like that of a greenhouse or a tropical rainforest exhibit at the zoo. The dead of winter here means an average low temperature of 44 degrees Fahrenheit. Summer days are humid, hot, and spiked with sudden downpours that seem to turn on and off like somebody opening a spigot. The University of Florida lures in potential new professors with promises of 255 sunny or partly sunny days in the year. This last bit means that Gainesville isn't only a good place to grow plants, it's also a pretty decent spot for solar power.

Gainesville Regional Utility wanted to harness that resource and give its customers an opportunity to live out their solar power dreams. Since 2006, the utility has been promoting solar power projects that are built on top of households or businesses. Not 100 megawatts, or even 10—the utility is primarily interested in solar systems with capacities under several hundred *kilowatts*. If that sounds like a weird goal for a utility company to have, it's because GRU itself is a little odd. The utility is actually city owned, supplying not only electricity, but also water, gas, and Internet service. Municipal utilities such as this aren't especially rare in the United States—you'll find them all over the country. Yet they do serve a much smaller number of people than the for-profit corporate utility companies most of us are used to. For example, there are five big investor-owned utilities in Florida, while the Florida Municipal Electric Association has thirty-four members, Gainesville included. However, those city-owned utilities supply electricity to only 14 percent of the state's population. Another

10 percent is served by user-owned cooperatives. The rest is covered by the five big companies, which have the ability to expand and grow in ways the inherently local city utility doesn't.

In fact, GRU is so local that until 1972, the town was actually its own walled-off section of the electric grid, separate from the rest of the state, just as the Texas grid is separate from the national grid today. Gainesville joined the larger grid system only when the utility found itself unable to increase electricity supply at a rate that kept up with growing electricity demand. In the years before the city was linked in with the rest of the Florida, the citizens of Gainesville had to live with daily blackouts. This is a town that knows what happens when energy generation is too localized and when the grid doesn't get what it wants.[5]

Given that earlier trouble, why would the utility be interested in encouraging hyper-local generation today? Partly, because it can. Gainesville Regional Utility now buys electricity from other parts of the state but still generates a lot on its own as well. It answers not to a board of investors, but to the city council and, by extension, to its own customers. Because of that, the utility isn't locked into complicated long-term generation contracts, so it can try out new sources of power. When it does, it can be experimental, because decisions are driven as much by city political policy and the desires of its customers as by the need for financial stability.

That flexibility also gives GRU a better chance to plan for the future, says director Ed Regan. He sees local solar power as insurance. Situations are changing in the world of energy. Costs of conventional production are going up, along with costs of building the infrastructure. Climate change and other energy-related concerns could change the rules governing how you can generate electricity. If the utility can get a lot of its customers to produce electricity, using the sun, from panels scattered across rooftops all over town, it will be better prepared to deal with change. Essentially, GRU is building a backup plan to hedge long-term costs.

That plan wouldn't make sense if decentralized generation really were about complete disconnection. If a bunch of customers suddenly went "off the grid," it could help GRU in some ways—for instance, by reducing demand enough that they were able to avoid buying or building new generation. Yet losing customers that way wouldn't help the utility provide renewable energy to a broad swath of society. Nor would it help prepare the utility to compete in the event of rising natural gas prices, renewable energy mandates, or carbon taxes. It certainly wouldn't help the customers who went off the grid, if they found themselves using more electricity than their home system could produce.

When GRU promotes decentralized solar electricity generation, it's not trying to build a system that mimics the way my grandparents heated their home. This isn't about every man for himself. At the same time, though, what the utility envisions in Gainesville is also very different from the status quo, where one company does all of the work and the customers are merely consumers. The future lies somewhere in between those two extremes. It's like farmers' markets. I can shop at a mega-supermarket, if I'm willing to sacrifice a certain amount of choice and control for convenience. I can grow my own food, if I'm willing to forgo convenience and a secure food supply, in exchange for ultimate control. Or, I can go to the farmers' market. There, lots of people who grow food pool the results so that no one has to grow every type of food himself or herself or risk having no food if there's a bad harvest. I can be a farmer, a consumer, or a little bit of both. Either way, I get more control than I have at the supermarket and more convenience than I'd have doing it all on my own. When GRU decided to help its customers produce electricity at home, this is what it had in mind—the grid as a solar power farmers' market.

Making that system work is not easy. Right now, Gainesville—and any other place that sets its sights on generating electricity in this hyper-local way—has two main problems. First, it's expensive to buy a solar electric system, and *how* expensive is a difficult question to answer. Solar power isn't confined to only one device. Many types of solar panels are made using lots of different technologies.[6] This can get a bit confusing, but it's really no different from any of the other products we're more accustomed to buying. If I asked you how much a car costs, for instance, that's not a simple question, either. A Lexus isn't the same as a Kia. The cost of a brand-new, eight-passenger SUV can't be easily compared to the cost of my 1999 two-door Ford Escort. The size, the make, the model, the year, what you want the car to be able to do for you—all of those factors affect the price. All cars are objectively expensive. Most of us wouldn't buy a car on impulse the way we might buy a shirt. *How* expensive varies quite a bit, though. So, when I ask, "How much does a car cost?" I'm going to get a lot of different answers. It's the same with solar panels.

Location also matters tremendously. That's because the true cost of a solar panel is different from the sticker price. Unlike a car, which will only cost you more money in gasoline, maintenance, and taxes, a solar panel does more to earn its keep, financially speaking. There's an up-front cost and maintenance costs, but anyone who owns a solar panel also gets monetary benefits in some way, from the electricity the panel produces.[7] Where you live becomes an issue because how much money you make from your solar panel depends a lot on how much sun you have access to and how high the going kilowatt-hour rate for electricity is in your state. A 2009 study of existing home solar installations in three parts of the United States found that during the course of twenty years, the electricity produced by those systems would likely earn back between 76 percent and 109 percent of what the owners had paid.[8] If you're the person who stands to make a 9 percent profit, you might be a little more keen on solar than the guy who's only going to make back three-quarters of his up-front investment.

In places such as California and Hawaii, where conventional electricity is particularly expensive and solar resources are plentiful, people really can make a profit on their solar panel investments, but the investments are still large. Energy infrastructure is always expensive, even when you're building it at home. Buying and installing a residential solar system can run upward of tens of thousands of dollars. Like a car, it's something few people can afford to buy out of pocket. You lease a car, or you take out a loan. When you buy a solar electric system, you usually seek out some kind of financial help as well. Grants and subsidies can lower the up-front costs a lot. States and the federal government offer these programs because generating renewable electricity helps us meet larger goals—increased electric supply and lowered carbon emissions benefit more than only the people who own the solar panels. Yet there are other ways to handle this.

In fact, Gainesville got famous in 2009 precisely *because* the city adopted a legislative strategy that was meant to make the sticker price of solar power ownership a little less financially draining. It's called a feed-in tariff (FIT), and although the idea is new and unfamiliar to most Americans, it's not really a new idea, per se. More than forty countries have feed-in tariffs. Germany has had one since the early 1990s. There are even other feed-in tariff programs in the United States.[9] Gainesville is simply the first place in this country to run a FIT the way they're usually run in Europe.

Unlike grants or subsidies that give people money to offset the cost of buying and installing solar panels, European-style FITs focus on making sure solar panel owners earn back their investments by selling the electricity they make to a utility company. Essentially, the FIT is just a sales contract—not much different from the kinds of contracts GRU signs with the big centralized generators. Participants in Gainesville's FIT program are guaranteed a set price for every kilowatt-hour's worth of electricity they sell to the utility, for a set number of years. The contract is designed to make sure that solar panel owners recoup their investments and earn a small profit, just as with the contracts GRU has with the big generators.[10] The FIT price, however, is higher than what GRU pays for centralized generation.[11] Gainesville's FIT does raise the cost of electricity for everyone. How much depends on how many solar generators participate.

Because of that, signing up for the tariff isn't one big open free-for-all. People have to apply, and GRU sets limits on how many solar projects—and how much solar generation—it's willing to take on. These programs are run a little differently in every place that has one, but in Gainesville, new FIT contracts are offered once or twice a year in batches. The price paid and the length of the contract will change, depending on the current economic reality. The idea is that this way, the utility can adjust the contracts to reflect how much it actually costs to install a solar system on your roof. As solar panels get cheaper over time, the contracts will offer less money per kilowatt-hour, because participants will be able to make back their investments at the lower rate.

This isn't the only way to pay distributed generators for solar power, nor is it a foolproof plan.[12] Gainesville learned that quickly. Since it began, the program has had to make some big changes, as the utility and the city noticed flaws that needed fixing. For instance, setting the right price for FIT payouts isn't easy to do. Gainesville, along with most of the successful programs overseas, bases the price on an estimate of how much money it would take to pay off the costs of installing a solar system, spread out over the life of the contract—plus a little extra so that the solar panel owners can make a small profit. That's not any different from how we've compensated big-time centralized generation in the United States for decades, but it leaves plenty of room for subjectivity.

In 2010, Barry Jacobson, who runs a business installing solar panel systems in Gainesville, told me that the price GRU originally paid FIT participants was too high. That's because there were already federal, state, and local rebate programs that offset the cost of installation, but the FIT price was calculated without taking those into account. Because of that, Jacobson told me, some participants were making back all of their money before they even *started* to sell electricity to GRU. When the price is that far off, it means that the utility company—and, ultimately, the people paying the higher electric prices—aren't getting the most bang for their buck.[13] It also means that the people who put solar panels up on their roofs have less of an incentive to maintain them for the long haul. There's a decent chance that someone who has already made back his or her investment wouldn't care as much about making sure that the system was working and sending as much electricity to the utility as it could.

Yet FITs *have* been successful. Gainesville's FIT applies only to solar panel systems, but in Germany, which has had a FIT since 1991, any kind of renewable energy generation can sign on. When the tariff began, 3 percent of that country's electricity came from renewable sources. By 2009, the number had jumped to 16 percent, one of the highest renewable-generation rates in the world.[14] The United States' National Renewable Energy Laboratory, which has studied the effects of FITs in Germany and around the world, says the German program contributed to job growth and industry development that wouldn't have happened if that country had tried to encourage renewable energy in a different way.[15] Although the FIT did mean that German electricity customers have paid more per kilowatt-hour for their electricity than they otherwise would have, it hasn't proved to be ridiculously expensive. Through FITs, Germany pays out rates for solar electricity that are eight times higher than the standard going rate for conventionally made electricity, but broken down per household, the FIT added only $3.82 per month to the average German electricity bill in 2007.[16] German citizens got a lot of renewable energy for the price of one fast-food sandwich per household per month. That ain't too bad.

There is still some question about whether the small cost is worth it. If you're opposed to any kind of subsidies for energy generation, then you're likely to be against FITs. Of course, if you take that position, you should also be against the billions of dollars in subsidies that directly and indirectly support oil, coal, and natural gas. None of the energy you consume stands on its own, unaided by public funding. In fact, conventional fuel industries get far more federal dollars than renewable energy does.[17]

Let's say, however, that your city or state adopts a FIT, similar to the one at Gainesville. What happens if the FIT is successful? That's where the other problem with small-scale distributed generation starts to crop up. If you *can* get a lot of small electric generators up and running, then you'll start to have problems with the *local* electric infrastructure. Remember what we learned about the grid and generation bleeding together? There's a grid that moves electricity around the country, from state to state and region to region. That's called the transmission grid, and it's the grid I primarily meant when I was talking about infrastructure. Yet there's also another grid that has to be considered, especially in regard to distributed generation. This is the grid that runs through cities, linking houses and businesses. It's called the distribution grid, and it's meant to be a one-way street, designed for electricity to flow from a power plant or transmission lines to the customers. When that infrastructure was built, no one imagined that electricity might also flow from one customer to another or from a city to the transmission grid. Without changes, the household generation of electricity can upset the delicate balance of the grid.

Earlier, I mentioned the concept of a smart grid—merging the old analog network of wires with digital technology. Some smart grids use intelligent meters that help customers waste less energy and shift when they use energy during the day. That allows customers to take advantage of cheaper off-peak electricity prices, helps utilities avoid having to build new generators, and makes it easier to integrate large-scale wind and solar farms into the grid. Yet the name "smart grid" applies to other concepts as well. In particular, smart grid upgrades are a necessary part of creating an energy farmer's market, where electricity consumers can become electricity producers, too.

Remember, the electric grid is like a channel of water. Consumers draw from it, sources of generation add to it, and, behind the curtain, the wizards try to balance both and keep the depth and the speed constant. All of the strategies we use for pulling off that balancing act are based on the assumption that we know where the inlets and the outlets are and know what they're all doing at any given time. Distributed generation—at least, the kind of distributed generation that operates at a household level—screws up all of that. Right now, the distribution grids within cities aren't set up to tell the wizards where a solar panel is and how well it's operating. Really, they aren't even set up to allow that household solar panel to send electricity to the grid. Electricity is supposed to flow to houses, not away from them.

Think about the channel-of-water analogy. What happens if water is getting dumped into that channel in unpredictable amounts, at unpredictable times, from places where you weren't expecting it? If the current flows only in one direction, what happens if you have a lot of water coming in downstream, but it's really needed upstream? You see the problem. A little bit of hyper-local generation isn't a problem, but the more you add, the less reliable the old system becomes and the more necessary the upgrade. This isn't a problem for Gainesville today. The FIT has increased the amount of electricity the city gets from solar power, but it's not enough to stress the grid—yet.

The technology to fix this problem exists, but it won't come cheap. The changes can't happen if every individual producing distributed electricity thinks of himself or herself as a maverick, rather than participants in a bigger system. Abbas Akhil, a principal member of the technical staff at the Sandia National Laboratory and a longtime researcher of distributed generation, says that if energy consumers are going to become producers, then they must also become "good citizens of the grid"—people who think about electric infrastructure the way that they think about other kinds of shared public resources. If you wouldn't dump your trash in the local park, then you should also be just as conscientious about how you use your local power lines.

One of the upsides to FITs, such as the one that's bringing more solar power to Gainesville, is that they can be used to build good grid citizenship skills. The contract system that accompanies FITs can be used to reward would-be generators who agree to make their electricity a little more controllable. Gainesville doesn't do this yet, but Akhil would like to see U.S. FITs offer a higher price per kilowatt-hour to people who are willing to install some battery storage along with their solar panels, a move that would make the electricity those individuals supply more reliable. Realistically, it would also make that electricity worth more. In Europe, FITs have already been used to give preferential pricing to people who build wind turbines in places that don't already have a lot of existing wind turbines—something that reduces stress on distribution and transmission power lines and helps head off the resentments that are often felt when one region gets stuck with all of the infrastructure construction.

This future—in which electricity is made close to home, as well as far away, and where people who used to be only consumers have become grid citizens—will also change what it means to be an energy utility company. When the first power plants in the United States opened, utilities were the entities that generated electricity and made sure it got to your house. In general, that's probably how most of us think of these companies today. Yet the situation is already very different in many places. Following electric utility deregulation in the 1970s, the jobs of generating electricity, transmitting it over long distances, and distributing it around localized regions have increasingly been done by different entities.

This is happening now, outside of the shift toward alternative energy, but as we generate electricity using more renewable resources—as generation becomes increasingly distributed, to match the locations of inherently local sources of energy—that trend will only accelerate. The day may come when no electric utility generates anything. Instead, it might simply coordinate the movement of electricity between generators and customers. Rather than making and selling electricity, GRU could someday find itself selling the service of making sure that all of the solar panels in town work together in a reliable way, alongside storage systems and midsize power plants.

If there's one lesson you should pick up from this story, it's that alternative energy isn't only about changing what we put in our fuel tanks or how our electricity is made. Alternative energy is going to alter entire business plans and change who we are, what our responsibilities are, and how we think about ourselves. If it helps, though, this transition is nothing new. The United States has already gone through it once before. This country began as a place where energy was individual labor—something most people had to physically be involved with every day, whether they were chopping wood or driving a team of horses. Fossil fuels—oil, coal-fired engines, natural gas—changed all of that. During the course of the twentieth century, energy became a commodity. Most Americans didn't directly labor to produce it. Most of us didn't have to think about it at all, except when we paid the monthly bills.

Now, as where we get our energy from shifts again, what energy is—what it means to us—is changing again, too. Yet we aren't reverting to the nineteenth century. We're creating something new. The future of energy is a world that shares characteristics of both the past and the present. In the future, we will see where the electricity we use is made. It'll be on our roofs, in our rivers, closer to our cities. Because more of us will make electricity, more of us will have to pay attention to how the grid works and how our choices affect it. Third parties will still handle the complicated details of keeping that energy supply reliable. There will still be wizards of the grid. Utility companies will still exist, even if their primary business model is fundamentally different. You and I are still going to enjoy the convenience of not having to chop wood every time we want a warm house. It will be different, and we won't all get what we want, but different and imperfect don't necessarily mean bad.

This can work. This future can happen. Yet it won't simply happen on its own. Standing between us and the future of energy is an awfully big wall. Whether we can scale it will depend on how well we can plan and whether we have the willpower to follow those plans through.

NOTES

Introduction

1. Gallup polls from 2007 and 2008 showed that 63 percent of Americans thought that global warming was a "very" or "somewhat" serious threat. In 2010, that number had fallen to 53 percent. Pew Research Center polls, asking the same question, found that 79 percent of Americans were concerned about the threat of climate change in 2006, while 63 percent were worried in 2010. Pew also found that American belief in the evidence of climate change fell during that time, too—from 79 percent in 2006 to 59 percent in 2010. See Gallup at http://www.gallup.com/poll/147203/Fewer-Americans-Europeans-View-Global-Warming-Threat.aspx; and Pew at http://pewresearch.org/pubs/1780/poll-global-warming-scientists-energy-policies-offshore-drilling-tea-party.

2. A 2010 Pew study found that 64 percent of Republicans supported increased funding for energy research, 73 percent supported higher vehicle fuel efficiency standards, and 55 percent supported spending more on public transportation. See http://pewresearch.org/pubs/1780/poll-global-warming-scientists-energy-policies-offshore-drilling-tea-party. A 2011 Gallup poll found that 75 percent of Republicans supported Congress passing an alternative energy bill. See http://www.gallup.com/poll/145880/Alternative-Energy-Bill-Best-Among-Eight-Proposals.aspx.

3. For instance, this poll was done by the Pew Research Center in October 2010: http://pewresearch.org/pubs/1780/poll-global-warming-scientists-energy-policies-offshore-drilling-tea-party.

4. Gallup poll numbers document changes made between March 2009 and March 2010. These numbers have been largely stable, with very little fluctuation either way, since 2000. See http://www.gallup.com/poll/127292/Green-Behaviors-Common-Not-Increasing.aspx.

5. Energy Information Administration, "Primary Energy Consumption per Real Dollar of Gross Domestic Product, 1973–2010," http://www.eia.gov/totalenergy/data/monthly/pdf/sec1_16.pdf and "Energy Consumption, Expenditures, and Emissions Indicators, Selected Years, 1949–2009," http://www.eia.gov/emeu/aer/pdf/pages/sec1_13.pdf.

6. Energy Information Administration, "Primary Energy Consumption by Source, 1973–2010," http://www.eia.doe.gov/totalenergy/data/monthly/pdf/sec1_7.pdf.

7. This estimate is based on projections made by MIT researchers using the IGSM model; United States Global Change Research Program, "Scenarios of Greenhouse Gas Emissions and Atmospheric Concentrations and Review of Integrated Scenario Development and Application, Chapter 4," http://www.climatescience.gov/Library/sap/sap2-1/finalreport/sap2-1a-final-ch4.pdf.

8. If you aren't familiar with BoingBoing, it's a blog that reads a lot more like a magazine. We have several million monthly readers, and the site has been around for more than a decade. BoingBoing has a little bit of everything: technology and science, culture and art, human rights and copyright law, plus funny cat photos. Part of my job is to find cool science-related articles, videos, and photos from all over the Internet and make sure my readers know about them. The other part involves researching, reporting, and writing original features, stories, and interviews about scientific topics. We're a little bit serious, a little bit silly, and a lot geeky. That's BoingBoing in a nutshell.

1. Making Apple Pie from Scratch

1. This is according to the Thomas A. Edison Papers at Rutgers University. For more on the history of Edison lighting during this time period, I recommend checking out Paul B. Israel, Louis Carlat, David Hochfelder, Theresa M. Collins, and Brian C. Shipley, eds., *The Papers of Thomas A. Edison*, Volume 6 (Baltimore: Johns Hopkins University Press, 2007).

2. Louise Kellogg, "The Electric Light System at Appleton," Wisconsin Historical Society, December 1922, p. 189, http://content.wisconsinhistory

.org/u?/wmh,3072. In fact, the Wisconsin Historical Society is a great place to browse around and check out lots of newspaper and magazine clippings that detail the history of electricity in the state. I got most of my historical sources through the society or through the collection housed at H. J. Rogers's Appleton mansion, which is now a museum.

3. Letter of Agustus Ledyard Smith, February 3, 1883, Wisconsin Historical Society. I was lucky that this letter happened to be typed. Several other Smith letters, dating to around the same time period, were handwritten and largely incomprehensible to me. Amusingly, Smith spent a decent amount of the letter I *could* read apologizing to his sister for typing, instead of hand writing it.

4. There's an exhibit in the basement of Rogers's Appleton mansion dedicated to electricity and Rogers's other business ventures. Part of the exhibit is a box, with a flap on one side that you can open and get a whiff of what a nineteenth-century gas-lit house would have smelled like. The stench is hard to describe, but it is most emphatically *not* the rotten-egg, sulfur smell we associate with gas leaks today. That sulfur tinge is added into modern natural gas pipes to make sure it's immediately obvious when gas is being released into a house. In contrast, nineteenth-century natural gas smelled less immediately alarming but equally disturbing in the long run. To give you an analogy: if the sulfur smell is like a stink bomb being set off indoors, then nineteenth-century gas was more like something rotting at the bottom of a trash can.

5. *The Papers of Thomas A. Edison.* There are a lot of delightful stories in this book. My other favorite is even more demented. In 1882, shortly after Edison opened his central power plant, he and his team of engineers discovered that one of the junction boxes they'd buried under a New York City street corner was faulty. They discovered this because it wasn't buried very deep, and electricity was being conducted through moist soil, turning the street corner into a giant joy buzzer. Naturally, the citizens of New York responded by hanging around the corner, waiting for unsuspecting horse carts to go by, so that they could watch the horses get zapped and rear back in terror. Edison fixed the junction box, but the next day he got a visit from a used-horse salesman who wanted to install an intentionally faulty junction box under his horse pen, hoping to make his old, burned-out horses look more active than they actually were. There is no mention of whether or not Edison took the salesman up on this businesses opportunity.

6. Energy Information Administration, "The 2010 Energy Outlook," http://www.eia.gov/totalenergy/data/annual/pdf/sec17_1.pdf. This document contains data on U.S. energy use going back to 1635.

7. This analogy was worked out in personal correspondence with the help of Philip J. Marshall, Royal Society University Research Fellow, Department of Physics, Oxford University. Turning numbers into something more "real" is an invaluable skill, and Dr. Marshall deserves a shout-out for it.

8. This is all from the Energy Information Administration's 2009 Annual Energy Review, http://www.eia.gov/emeu/aer/contents.html. Complete data take a while to put together, so these reviews lag a little. The 2010 review was due out in July 2011. So, by the time you read this, newer data will be available. That said, the proportions that we're talking about here—what percentage of our energy comes from what source and what it's used to do—don't vary all that much from one year to the next. It's highly unlikely, for instance, that transportation will suddenly usurp electricity as our biggest energy expenditure.

9. "Edison K Dynamo" was the official name of this contraption. The electric engineers of the day called it a "Long-Legged Mary Ann," which is what passed for a dirty joke back in 1882.

10. Solar photovoltaics work a little differently. I'll explain that later. Yet every other source of electricity we have fits this mold. Fossil fuels, nuclear power, and geothermal are all about heating water to make steam, which turns the turbines, which move the metal through the magnetic field. Hydroelectric power and wind do this more directly, skipping the steam and going straight to turning the turbine.

11. Forrest McDonald, *Let There Be Light: The Electric Utility Industry in Wisconsin, 1881–1955* (Madison: American History Research Center, 1957), 35.

12. The replica of the world's first hydroelectric power plant is surprisingly neglected. When I visited Appleton in April 2010, I wanted to drop by the site—pay a little homage, if you will. Yet none of the people who worked at the museum in Rogers's mansion or the paper mill museum or the county historical society museum knew where it was. I finally located the address through an article posted online by the Institute of Electrical and Electronics Engineers. The replica sits today in the parking lot of a paper mill. The paint is peeling. Several windows are broken. It looks as though nobody has been inside in years.

13. A lot of these stories about how the Appleton electrical system operated in the early days come from the memories of one of the first grid controllers, a man named A. C. Langstadt. In 1922, when he was an old man, he gave a speech, which was typed up for posterity, to the Wisconsin Electrical Association, reminiscing about his years as a young grid operator. I picked up a copy from the historical archives at Rogers's mansion in Appleton.

14. Appleton got meters somewhere around 1888. The first electric meters actually operated via a chemical reaction. You had a box, with a couple of metal plates resting in a liquid chemical bath. Whenever electricity was being used in the house, the metal plates had an electric current running through them, which reacted with the liquid and caused a sort of crusty buildup on one of the plates. Every now and then, somebody would come by, scrape off the buildup, and weigh it. You were charged for electricity based on the weight. According to Langstadt, a gram of light cost $17.74. It's not clear whether he was speaking in 1922 dollars or 1882 dollars. If it's 1882, that gram of light was worth almost $400 today. If it's 1922, the value would be closer to $228. Langstadt doesn't really say how many hours of light a gram was worth. I would hope it would be a lot, but, it's worth noting, electricity was a luxury item back then—so maybe not. This system, as you might imagine, was not terribly time efficient. It was a good day's work to bill six customers using the scrape-and-weigh method.

2. One in a Quadrillion

1. Official Earth Hour FAQ, http://www.earthhour.org/mediasite/faq.aspx.

2. Paraphrasing Keith Lockitch, "The Real Meaning of Earth Hour," Ayn Rand Center for Individual Rights, www.aynrand.org/site/News2?page=NewsArticle&id=22887&news_iv_ctrl=1021.

3. As with all IPCC reports, the full paper is available online for free, at http://srren.ipcc-wg3.de/report.

4. Renewable here is defined as either wind, solar, hydroelectric, geothermal, bioenergy, or ocean energy. Each of these types represents more than one specific technology. You can read more about this in the report's executive summary, beginning on page 4, at http://srren.ipcc-wg3.de/report/srren-spm-fd4.

5. In fact, some scientists I spoke with didn't think it would be possible to stay below 440 ppm, even if we did somehow manage to agree to that target. On the other hand, we'd still benefit even if we tried and failed to hit the specific emissions goal. It's not really the exact goals that matter; it's reducing our fossil fuel use as much as possible, as fast as possible.

6. IPCC Working Group III, 2007 assessment report, p. 12, http://www .ipcc-wg3.de/publications/assessment-reports/ar4/.files-ar4/SPM .pdf.

7. From the High Plains Regional Climate Center, Climate Change on the Prairie, 2009, www.hprcc.unl.edu/publications/files/ HighPlainsClimateChangeGuide.pdf.

8. United States Global Change Research Program, regional reports on the Great Plains and the Midwest, 2009, http://www.globalchange .gov/publications/reports/scientific-assessments/us-impacts/regional-climate-change-impacts/midwest, and http://www.globalchange.gov/ publications/reports/scientific-assessments/us-impacts/regional-climate-change-impacts/great-plains.

9. FEMA mitigation case study on Merriam, Kansas, http://www.eeri.org/ mitigation/resource-library/fema-mitigation-resources-for-success/ mitigation-case-studies/city-of-merriam-johnson-county-ks-case-study.

10. This paper is the product of a partnership between a corporate consultancy, Mercer Group, and the World Bank's International Finance Corporation. See http://www.mercer.com/climatechange.

11. It's important to be clear about what experts mean when they talk about carbon emissions goals. Below 550 ppm is not a "safe zone." Climate change is already happening. People are already being affected. Money is already being lost. So 550 ppm is not a cutoff point, after which things will go bad. The reality is, the higher we go, the worse the effects are likely to be, and 550 ppm is just an arbitrary line in the sand. It's a goal that researchers think we can achieve. Yet even if we hit that target, there are still consequences. The lower the ppm, the better things are for us. The higher the ppm, the worse off we are. The McKinsey Report can be read in its entirety at http://www.mckinsey.com/mgi/ reports/pdfs/Carbon_Productivity/MGI_carbon_productivity_full_ report.pdf.

12. You can read more about IGSM at http://globalchange.mit.edu/igsm/.

13. All ppm targets are somewhat arbitrary. Because climate change is already happening and because of uncertainty about its effects, we can't really draw a line and say there's a safe zone. Since the 1880s, our global CO_2 concentrations have risen to 392 ppm and the global average temperature has gone up .8 degrees C, according to NASA's Goddard Space Center. Because temperature lags behind increases in CO_2, we know that if we stopped the CO_2 concentrations from getting any higher, the world would still keep getting hotter for a while.

14. I've chosen to focus on IGSM for a couple of reasons. First, compared to some other commonly referenced models, it assumes that we'll be wealthier and thus will be using more energy in 2030. All things considered, most of us would prefer a future in which we are wealthier. So why don't we plan for that? Second, IGSM is designed to model how various stabilization goals would produce different prices for carbon emissions and different timelines for the market adoption of emissions reductions. If the emissions cutoffs are more stringent, the price we place on emissions starts higher, and the change is likely to happen more rapidly as businesses can expect a better rate of return—and vice versa. Third, IGSM assumes a shift away from conventional oil and toward synthetics—liquid fuel made from substances such as coal. That's not a particularly appealing assumption, but it's something that the pessimistic side of me assumes is likely to happen as conventional oil supplies peak and prices rise. Finally, IGSM solutions rely more heavily on energy-use reductions than the other two models do. I don't know that's necessarily the best way to do the job, but it is a lot *cheaper* to use less—whether through efficiency or reduction of consumption—than it is to invest in additional generation of energy. To me, IGSM's assumptions seem a little more realistic when it comes to what people want and the way businesses and government usually meet those needs. There are good cases to be made for the other models and against IGSM as well—which is why scientists seldom consult only one—but, in this case, to make things a little more clear for you, I'm going to pick a pony. You can see full data from all of the 2012–2030 scenarios IGSM has run and compare them to a couple of other common models at http://www.climatescience.gov/Library/sap/sap2-1/finalreport/sap2-1a-final-ch4.pdf.

15. Most Americans drive with one person to a car, so you can assume that a car generally burns through 597 gallons of gas in a year. With 137 million cars in the United States—and 114,000 BTUs per gallon—that's 931 trillion BTUs per year. Vehicle statistics come from the Bureau of Transportation Statistics and the Federal Highway Administration, http://www.bts.gov/publications/national_transportation_statitics/html/table_04_23.html, http://www.bts.gov/publications/national_transportation_statistics/html/table_01_11.html, and http://www.fhwa.dot.gov/ohim/onh00/bar8.htm.

16. This is different from Energy Information Administration (EIA) estimates for 2010, due to variations in how the estimations were done,

and because IGSM was predicting what would happen in 2010 before it actually had happened, rather than estimating what has already happened, which is how EIA annual reports work. Yet the differences aren't that big, and this will still give you a good idea of the scale and the types of changes that you could expect by 2030.

17. You can read about the McKinsey U.S.-specific energy plan at http://www.mckinsey.com/en/Client_Service/Sustainability/ Latest_thinking/Reducing_US_greenhouse_gas_emissions.aspx.

18. From a *New York Times* article summarizing several different estimates of the war's cost. On the high end, some economists had placed the number closer to $2 trillion. On the low end, there was an estimate of $700 billion. See http://www.nytimes.com/2007/01/17/ business/17leonhardt.html.

19. Obviously, this would cost more now. If you tried to implement the McKinsey plan, starting in 2012, the cost has now risen to $55 billion a year. Stephen Pacala, the director of the Carbon Mitigation Initiative at Princeton University, calls this the "penalty of procrastination." In 2004, he and colleague Robert Socolow came up with a game to demonstrate how many energy solutions have to be combined to make a *single* climate change solution. To play the game, Pacala used a chart that showed the projected growth in annual greenhouse gas emissions during the next fifty years. Then he drew a perpendicular line, marking emissions levels for 2004. The idea of the game isn't necessarily to reduce emissions right away, but rather to simply stop emissions from increasing every year—stabilize them at 2004 levels for half a century. Players choose from a variety of energy solutions, each one a wedge that fills part of the gap between 2004 emissions levels and what those levels are likely to be in 2050 if we make no energy changes. Each wedge is worth 1 billion tons of greenhouse gas emissions. Players must keep adding more energy solutions until the gap between stabilization levels and the 2050 projections is filled.

Back in 2004, Pacala says, it took seven wedges to win the game. Not anymore. "The point is that if you delay, you've put more stuff in the atmosphere, which means the cuts to stabilization have to be steeper, in a shorter amount of time. Simply by delaying for six years, we've made the game something like 20 percent harder," he says.

20. N. C. Aizenman, "New High in Prison Numbers," *Washington Post*, February 29, 2008, http://www.washingtonpost.com/wp-dyn/content/ story/2008/02/28/ST2008022803016.html.

21. Stephen Schwartz and Deepti Choubey, "How $52 Billion on Nuclear Security Is Spent," Carnegie Endowment, January 12, 2009, http:// www.carnegieendowment.org/publications/index.cfm?fa=view&id=22602.

22. See the McKinsey and Company Report, p. 19, mckinsey.com/ clientservice/ccsi/pdf/US_ghg_final_report.pdf.

3. The Efficiency Paradox

1. This table at the U.S. Energy Information Administration website shows the total flow of energy in 2009: http://www.eia.gov/totalenergy/data/ annual/pdf/sec1_3.pdf. This includes energy that went to waste as conversion losses in the process of making electricity for buildings.

2. I'll be referencing "comfort and convenience" a lot as we go through this book. They've sort of become my shorthand for the benefits we get from using energy—and why simply telling people to "use less" isn't necessarily reasonable. It's an idea I picked up from Horace Herring, a visiting research fellow at the United Kingdom's Open University. Comfort, convenience, and cleanliness figure heavily in a paper he wrote about energy efficiency and the rebound effect titled "The Rebound Effect: Efficiency, Sufficiency, and the Meaning of Life," http://design.open .ac.uk/herring/documents/HerringReboundsufficiency.pdf.

3. This estimation comes from David MacKay's *Sustainable Energy without the Hot Air*, a book that explains, beautifully, the numbers behind a lot of the broader ideas I tackle in this book. MacKay's book is available for free online at http://www.withouthotair.com/Contents.html. MacKay estimates that average Europeans and the British use the equivalent of 125 kWh of energy per day, while the average American uses 250 kWh of energy per day. That figure includes the energy used to light buildings and power appliances, heat water, heat air, provide transportation, and manufacture products within the country. It doesn't include the energy used to produce imported goods, and it doesn't include energy that is, essentially, unharnessed. For instance, the energy from the sun that is used to grow plants isn't included. Energy captured by solar panels and turned into electricity, however, is included.

4. For example, see this study of Passive Houses that were built in Sweden in 2001, http://www.ebd.lth.se/fileadmin/energi_byggnadsdesign/ images/Publikationer/Energy-efficient_terrace_houses_in_Sweden_ Maria_W.pdf. A review of literature on Passive Houses found that the standard could reduce energy consumption by a factor of 3. See http://

www.sintef.no/upload/Energiforskning/Transes/article_life%20
cyle%20energy_ENB.pdf. The Passive House Institute in the United
States says that their houses use 60 to 70 percent less energy than the
average American home.

5. Architecture 2030 is an organization dedicated to designing more
energy efficient buildings. They have calculated the average energy
usage of different types of homes in different regions of the United
States: http://www.architecture2030.org/files/2030_Challenge_
Targets_Res_Regional.pdf. On this chart, I'm looking at what's called
the "Average Source EUI." That number takes into account not only
the energy used within a home's four walls, but also the energy consumed *producing* energy. Source EUI doesn't ignore the energy wasted
at inefficient power plants. Passive House requirements don't ignore
that, either. When someone designs a Passive House, they have to think
about the energy the house will use and the energy used at a power
plant miles away.

6. I'll come back to this later, but, in general, opting for Passive House
design tacks an extra 10 percent onto the cost of construction.

7. The Passive House Institute in the United States has been monitoring
energy use in Dallas's house, and this number comes from them. See
www.passivehouse.us.

8. The 10 percent markup assumes that you have an architect and a
builder who have experience with Passive Houses. Without that experience, the markup can be closer to 20 percent.

9. Calculated through Zillow.com, http://www.zillow.com/local-info/
IL-Urbana-home-value/r_7645/.

10. In fact, in Europe, studies have shown that Passive Houses aren't necessarily the most cost-effective way to get an energy-efficient home. Instead,
there's a faster payback for houses that meet the European "low-energy
home" standard. These houses use more energy than a Passive House,
but a lot less energy than standard homes, and you recoup the extra
expense of building them in less time than it would take for a Passive
House. See https://lirias.hubrussel.be/bitstream/123456789/2205/1/
HRP30.pdf. The trade-off, however, is that you don't reduce energy use
as much. In Belgium, where this paper comes from, a low-energy home
has to use 40 percent less energy than a standard home, while a Passive
House has to use 60 percent less. See http://ec.europa.eu/energy/
efficiency/doc/buildings/info_note.pdf. In either case, many of the
same technologies are being used, and we're still talking about changes

that work on a systemic level. It's just that in a Passive House, there are more.

11. As I mentioned, Passive Houses do need a little help with heating in the winter. Rather than messing with the "thermostat," Dallas's son learned to turn on the electric baseboard heaters instead.

12. That figure is from 2009 and is according to the Architecture 2030 Foundation, which used data from the federal Energy Information Administration. The EIA calculated how we use energy in a rather different way, which included building energy use as a part of other sectors, such as commercial, residential, and industrial. Architecture 2030 dug through that and added up the actual energy use attributable to buildings.

13. Peterson is referring to codes that were put into effect in 2004. The new 2010 codes mandate energy use levels 30 percent lower than the 2004 codes, but, as of this writing, they haven't yet been adopted and implemented.

14. Energy Information Administration 2009 Residential Energy Consumption Survey results. There are many interesting statistics in these results, and you can find them online at http://www.eia.gov/consumption/residential/index.cfm.

15. The EIA recently published a report on the impact of plug loads, which you can find at http://www.eia.gov/consumption/residential/reports/electronics.cfm.

16. Much of this explanation of why some researchers think the Jevons paradox always triumphs comes from interviews with Blake Alcott, Ph.D., a candidate at the Sustainability Research Institute, University of Leeds, and Horace Herring, a visiting research fellow in the Energy and Environment Research Unit at the United Kingdom's Open University.

17. I owe a lot to Harry Saunders, the managing director of Decision Processes Incorporated and a Senior Fellow of the Breakthrough Institute, for helping me work out this aspect of the rebound effect debate.

18. According to a congressional report, the direct rebound effect is usually between 10 and 40 percent. See CRS Report for Congress, RS20981, *Energy Efficiency and the Rebound Effect: Does Increasing Efficiency Decrease Demand?* July 30, 2001, http://www.ncseonline.org/nle/crsreports/energy/eng-80.cfm?&CFID=11262148&CFTOKEN=7028302.

19. Kenneth A. Small, *The Effect of Improved Fuel Economy on Vehicle Miles Traveled: Estimating the Rebound Effect Using U.S. State Data, 1966–2001* (Irvine: University of California, 2005).

20. Much of the argument against the full Jevons Paradox and in favor of various levels of the rebound effect comes from interviews with Steven Sorrell, a fellow and the deputy director of the Sussex Energy Group and a senior lecturer at the University of Sussex; Skip Laitner, the director of Economic and Social Analysis for the American Council for an Energy Efficient Economy; and Karen Turner, reader in the division of economics at the University of Stirling and honorary reader in the department of economics at the University of Strathclyde, Scotland.

21. Everybody I talked to agrees that there are ways around even the worst-case scenario. I'll talk a bit about that later.

4. The Emerald City

1. This is another thing that's changed since the old days. The first grids operated on direct current—all of the electrons moved in the same direction, all the time. Today, we use alternating current. Basically, the electrons go through cycles where they move first in one direction and then in another. Another way to think about it: direct current is a straight line, and alternating current is a wave.

2. At the time of this writing, the most recent report on greenhouse gasses covers emissions produced in 2009. You can read the whole thing online at http://www.eia.gov/environment/emissions/ghg_report/pdf/0573(2009).pdf.

3. I happen to really like the way the World Resources Institute puts its chart together—it does a particularly good job of breaking down the big categories of energy use into subcategories that average people can relate to. Yet the people at the institute are far from the only ones doing this kind of data visualization. The other source I'd really recommend is the Lawrence Livermore National Laboratory, which makes flowcharts with more regularity and constructs them for both emissions data and data on energy use and waste. You can find archives of both at https://flowcharts.llnl.gov/index.html.

4. See World Resources Institute, "U.S. Greenhouse Gas Emissions Flow Chart," http://www.wri.org/chart/us-greenhouse-gas-emissions-flow-chart. The EIA report the chart is based on can be found at ftp://ftp.eia.doe.gov/pub/oiaf/1605/cdrom/pdf/ggrpt/057303.pdf.

5. Yes, this chart is based on older data, but, as of 2009, the situation hadn't changed much. The EIA report for that year contains a table that

shows carbon dioxide emissions by sector for the years 1990 through 2009. Every year, electricity production produced more CO_2 than transportation did. See http://www.eia.gov/environment/emissions/ghg_report/pdf/tbl7.pdf.

6. Surprising absolutely no one, Quebec is also its own separate grid.

7. American Wind Energy Association report for the fourth quarter of 2010.

8. See U.S. Energy Information Administration, "Electric Conversions," http://www.eia.doe.gov/cneaf/electricity/page/prim2/charts.html.

9. U.S. Energy Information Administration, "Electricity Explained," http://www.eia.doe.gov/energyexplained/index.cfm?page=electricity_use.

10. Texas has the most installed wind capacity of any state. Iowa is second. California is third. Yet here's something interesting that I noticed: being number one in installed wind capacity is not the same thing as being number one in wind energy use. States with much smaller installed capacities than Texas actually get a higher percentage of their overall electricity from the wind. Texas didn't even break the top five in 2010. Neither did California, actually. It turns out that the states that get the biggest percentage of their electricity from the wind are all in the Midwest—Iowa, North Dakota, Minnesota, South Dakota, and Kansas, respectively. See U.S. Energy Information Administration, *Electric Power Monthly*, April 2011, http://www.eia.doe.gov/cneaf/electricity/epm/epm.pdf. This is another one of those cases where a number can be very big and very small at the same time—depending on your perspective. Yes, Texas has the most installed wind capacity of any other state, but those 10,000 megawatts are only a small part of Texas's total electric-generating capacity. In 2006, that was more that 109,000 megawatts. Texas is still getting most of its electricity from fossil fuels. See Window on State Government, "Electricity," http://www.window.state.tx.us/specialrpt/energy/uses/electricity.php.

11. No power plant operates at full capacity. That's simply a mechanical impossibility. The difference between the stated capacity of a power plant and the amount of electricity it actually produces is called the capacity factor. The capacity factor of wind is particularly bad. The EIA says that wind has a capacity factor of 34 percent, so you get to use 34 percent of the stated capacity on average during the course of a year. A 100-megawatt wind farm can reliably produce only 100 megawatts on an ideal day. Some days, it won't be able to produce anything. On average over the year, you can expect it to produce 34 megawatts. This

is one place where fossil fuels really have a leg up on renewable generation. Gas and coal power plants operate at capacity factors above 80
percent. Meanwhile, hydroelectric plants have a capacity factor of 52
percent, and solar photovoltaics, 25 percent. The only low-emissions
generation that can really compete are geothermal and nuclear, which
both operate at above 90 percent capacity factor.

12. The Energy Information Administration says 1.9 percent, as of the end of
2009. See U.S. Energy Information Administration, *Electric Power Annual*,
http://www.eia.doe.gov/cneaf/electricity/epa/epa_sum.html#yir and
http://www.eia.doe.gov/cneaf/electricity/epa/epates.html.

13. Other, independent sources agreed with him. That night wasn't normal, but it wasn't a unique disaster, and it was solved pretty smoothly.
Basically, there was a problem. There are always problems. The response
worked exactly like it should.

5. A Box Full of Lightning

1. This is a generalization. Even within Plains states, wind patterns vary
a lot from place to place and season to season, says Greg Polous,
Ph.D., a meteorologist and director at V-Bar, LLC, a company that
consults with energy companies about trends in wind patterns. In
general, though, wind farms from Texas to North Dakota are subject
to something called the Great Plains Low Level Jet. This phenomenon happens because the Plains are flat. There's very few geographic
features out there to impede the strong winds that blow through the
region. During the day, heat rising off the ground causes turbulence
and friction in the atmosphere above the Plains, slowing the wind
down some. But at night, that turbulence disappears, and the wind
accelerates.

The exceptions to this rule, however, can be really, really interesting.
For instance, if you build a wind farm in the Texas panhandle, you have
to deal with the Great Plains Low Level Jet. If you build the wind farm
on the Texas coastline, on the other hand, you don't. Instead, wind turbines on the coast are subject to something called the sea breeze effect,
caused by differences in temperature between the air above the water
and the air above the land. In those places, wind production actually
peaks on summer afternoons, which fits much better with trends in
how people use electricity.

Polous is a big proponent of taking advantage of these regional
differences, and siting wind farms in places where the wind patterns

match electricity consumption patterns. This is another trick that could help us add more wind power to the grid. Storage is only one possible solution.

2. The life span of individual batteries can vary greatly, but scientists who work on energy storage say this is about what you can expect from lead-acid batteries as a class, according to my interviews with Imre Gyuk, the energy storage systems program manager with the Department of Energy, and Georgianne Huff, a mechanical engineer with Sandia National Laboratories. Gyuk interviewed March 2009. Huff interviewed March 2009 and March 2010.

3. A study done in 2010 by Bentek Energy for the Independent Petroleum Association of the Mountain States (http://www.bentekenergy.com/WindCoalandGasStudy.aspx) is often cited by blatantly anti-wind power sources as definitive proof that wind power actually increases emissions and air pollution. There is, however, a lot more nuance to the argument being made in the Bentek paper. Likewise, a broader analysis of research on the subject shows that there are emissions benefits to wind—but *how much* benefit and the economic value of that benefit vary a lot by location.

First, the Bentek study focuses on specific incidents of wind variability and the impact they had on specific fossil fuel power plants in Colorado. It shows that ramping up production in *coal* power plants and then cutting power down makes them give off more emissions, which decreases the overall emissions benefits of wind power. It doesn't show that wind power has no emissions benefit. In fact, one key suggestion put forward by the paper is that states with high levels of wind generation should use natural gas power plants as backup, instead of coal. In other words, the Bentek study is about what happens at individual power plants, not what happens in the state overall. The study also considers the type of backup power and is not strictly an indictment of wind power in general. Significantly, XCEL Energy, the utility company whose region is being studied in the Bentek paper, has stated that its overall emissions went down, even if some of its individual power plants had increased emissions at certain times. See Frank Prager, "Setting the Record Straight on Wind Energy," Denverpost.com, May 28, 2010, http://www.denverpost.com/opinion/ci_15177817.

Second, other research shows that wind power generally does lead to overall reductions in greenhouse gas emissions. The primary question—which hasn't really been answered definitively—is whether the value of those emissions reductions justifies the amount of money put into wind power subsidies. *That* seems to vary greatly from place to place, and there's still a lot of disagreement on the best way to calculate those values. Either way, though, while cost-to-benefit analyses are important, they're different from the question of whether there *is* a benefit. I think this is summed up nicely by Dave Corbus, a senior engineer at the National Renewable Energy Laboratory, in a quote he gave to GreenTech Media in September 2010: "Asked if he knew of anybody who fully understands transmission and would argue that wind doesn't reduce emissions, he simply said: 'No.' After a pause, he went on. 'I think there's room for people to say it reduces emissions 60 percent versus 80 percent. There's certainly room for disagreement and uncertainty because it's such a complex system. But nobody that I know that understands the grid is going to say that it doesn't reduce emissions.'" Herman K. Trabish, "Undermining the Critics of Wind Power, September 1, 2010, Greentechmedia, http://www.greentechmedia.com/articles/read/undermining-the-critics-of-wind-power/.

Some good resources to check out include M. Milligan et al., "Wind Power Myths Debunked," *IEEE Power and Energy*, November/December 2009, www.ohiowind.org/PDFs/Wind%20Power%20Myths%20Debunked.pdf; D. Kaffine et al., "Emissions Savings from Wind Power Generation," *Inside Mines*, December 2010, http://inside.mines.edu/~dkaffine/WINDEMISSIONS.pdf; Joseph A. Cullen, *Measuring the Environmental Impacts of Wind-Generated Electricity*, University of Arizona, December 2010, http://www.u.arizona.edu/~jcullen/Documents/measuringwind.pdf; Warren Katzenstein and Jay Apt, "Air Emissions Due to Wind and Solar Power," *Environmental Science and Technology*, 2009, http://www.sustainable.gatech.edu/sustspeak/apt_papers/51%20Air%20Emissions%20Due%20To%20Wind%20And%20Solar%20Power.pdf; Lisa Göransson and Filip Johnsson, "Large-Scale Integration of Wind Power: Moderating Thermal Power Plant Cycling," *Wind Energy*, 2010; and Eleanor Denny and Mark O'Malley, "Quantifying Total Net Benefits of Grid Integrated Wind," *IEEE Transactions on Power Systems*, 2007, http://ee.ucd.ie/erc/member/2007TransNBwindDenny.pdf.

4. Interview with Seth Blumsack, an assistant professor of energy policy and economics at Penn State, December 2010.

5. That doesn't take into account other greenhouse gases, so you'll sometimes also hear people talk about ppm CO_2e, or "carbon dioxide equivalent." I've used CO_2 here, because that's what the IGSM model used

to set its climate goals, and I don't want to keep switching units around on you.

6. The measurement of 390 ppm CO_2 comes from the monthly mean of various measurements recorded by the global network of National Oceanographic and Atmospheric Administration monitoring stations in May and June 2011. See Earth System Research Laboratory, *Trends in Atmospheric Carbon Dioxide*, http://www.esrl.noaa.gov/gmd/ccgg/trends/global.html.

7. Scientists are able to tell this because of indirect measurements taken from ice cores. See Earth System Research Laboratory, *Time History of Atmospheric Carbon Dioxide from 800,000 Years Ago until January 2009*, http://www.esrl.noaa.gov/gmd/ccgg/trends/history.html.

8. The greenhouse effect is a very old idea. For a quick refresher, the greenhouse effect describes the cycle of heat transfer that keeps our planet from becoming a frigid ball of dirt, no more habitable than Mars. First, heat from the sun passes through our atmosphere. Some is absorbed by the ground and the oceans, and some of that heat gets reflected back toward space. But the gasses in our atmosphere don't let all of that reflected heat out. Instead, atmospheric gasses bounce most of the heat back down again. It's kind of like turning on a laser pointer in a hall of mirrors. Because of the greenhouse effect, Earth is able to trap enough heat to sustain life as we know it. We've known about this effect since 1824.

   Climate change is really just an exaggeration of the greenhouse effect. Carbon dioxide is better than a lot of other gasses at bouncing heat back down to Earth. The more carbon dioxide in the atmosphere, the more heat gets trapped, and the higher our global average temperature rises. We've known about the way rising carbon dioxide levels enhance the greenhouse effect since 1896. These basic ideas are very unlikely to be disproved.

   Personally, I find that I understand scientific ideas a lot better if I can follow the history of how various scientists built up evidence and came to the modern conclusions. Basically, I like to "rediscover" the science for myself. If that's true for you, too, then you might enjoy *The Discovery of Global Warming*, a book by Spencer Weart that traces the history of climate science. Weart also has a website, maintained through the American Institute of Physics, that highlights several key parts of the book and some of the background material that didn't make it into the finished manuscript. You can read it online or download the entire website as a series of PDFs at http://www.aip.org/history/climate/index.htm.

9. Stabilization level is based on the IGSM model and *Issue Brief 2: US Climate Mitigation the Context of Global Stabilization* by Richard G. Newell and Daniel S. Hall, which summarizes the stabilization levels from several other different models. This estimate of America's 2009 annual emissions comes from the Energy Information Administration, http://www.eia.gov/environment/emissions/ghg_report/.

10. The Environmental Protection Agency has a nice online calculator that helps put big abstract numbers like this into a context that makes sense with your daily life. I've used it to make the estimates here. You can try it out yourself at http://www.epa.gov/cleanenergy/energy-resources/calculator.html. Vehicle information comes from the Bureau of Transportation Statistics at http://www.bts.gov/publications/national_transportation_statistics/html/table_01_11.html.

11. In reality, not all of these plants are equal. When I say that 576 MMTCO$_2$e is equal to the annual emissions of 137 power plants, I'm talking about an averaged-out figure, which doesn't take into account the plant's size or variations in how clean one plant is compared to another.

12. National Academy of Sciences Report in Brief, *Climate Stabilization Targets*, 2010, http://www.nationalacademies.org/includes/Stabilization TargetsFinal.pdf. If you're interested in learning what scientists expect to happen as the Earth gets warmer, I also recommend checking out Mark Lynas's book *Six Degrees: Our Future on a Hotter Planet* (Washington, DC: National Geographic, 2008), which details the research on what is likely to happen at each degree of warming.

13. There are other ways to deal with the problem of variable generation, and I'll talk a bit more about that as we go along. In general, though, storage might be the simplest and cheapest way to do it. For instance, one way that you could balance generation is to have more renewable generation situated in diverse parts of the country. That way, if it was cloudy in Los Angeles or there wasn't enough wind blowing in Texas, those places could import solar and wind power from parts of the country that had plenty. However, in order to do that, you'd need to make some big changes to the rules and regulations that govern the American electricity system, and you'd need to build lots and lots of very expensive transmission lines.

14. This particular battery doesn't have much of anything to do with renewable energy. It exists because the town of Presidio is very remote and isn't well connected to the rest of the Texas grid. Over the years, the town has had a lot of problems with losing power. The battery was installed to improve reliability.

15. Willett Kempton, "Vehicle to Grid Power Implementation: From Stabilizing the Grid to Supporting Large-Scale Renewable Energy," *Journal of Power Sources*, 2005, http://www.udel.edu/V2G/KempTom-V2G-Implementation05.PDF.

16. The researcher who is in charge of this project is Willett Kempton, a professor of marine policy and electrical and computer engineering at the University of Delaware. His calculations suggest that if somewhere between a quarter and half of all of the light-duty vehicles in the United States were electric and vehicle-to-grid equipped, we could increase our reliance on wind to up to 50 percent of our total capacity. See Willet Kempton and Jasna Tomic, "Vehicle-to-Grid Power Implementation: From Stabilizing the Grid to Supporting Large-Scale Renewable Energy," *Journal of Power Sources*, December 8, 2004, http://www.udel.edu/V2G/KempTom-V2G-Implementation05.PDF. The money-making scheme I describe here is merely the first step in what Kempton sees as a much larger plan. Not everybody will be able to make a good return on investment with a vehicle-to-grid equipped car, but if enough people can, Kempton thinks it will work as an incentive, bringing in early adopters of the technology who will influence more people to start driving vehicle-to-grid cars, even if those other people don't make a profit doing it. For a good summary of what Kempton is trying to do and why some outside researchers are skeptical, I recommend reading Joann Muller's 2008 *Forbes* article "A Lightbulb Goes On," http://www.forbes.com/forbes/2008/0107/100.html.

17. That delay could be reduced. Governments, universities, and some companies own large fleets of vehicles that they use as part of doing business. If one of those fleets was completely swapped out for lithium-ion battery cars, you'd get to critical mass a lot faster. Yet it would still be expensive to buy the cars and to build the infrastructure. The fleet owner, the utility company, and the ISO would all have to be pretty motivated to make this happen.

18. This isn't totally emissions-free energy. There's natural gas involved, too. Yet it's a lot cleaner than backup provided by a fossil fuel power plant.

19. Interview with Georgianne Huff, a mechanical engineer with Sandia National Laboratory, March 2009 and July 2011.

6. Good and Good Enough

1. It is a little misleading to say "clean." No energy system is ever going to be "clean," as in "zero emissions," because there are emissions involved in the production and maintenance of the generation sources, even if you aren't actively burning anything. For instance, an International Energy Agency report from 2002 looked at the emissions associated with various energy sources in Japan. The energy source with the lowest output of grams of carbon per kilowatt-hour was hydro, at 4.81. Wind power produced 9.51 grams of carbon per kilowatt-hour (g-C/kw-h). Solar power produced 16.01 g-C/kw-h. If the solar panels were freestanding, rather than on somebody's roof, they produced even more—34.31 g-C/kw-h. Yet these emissions are so much lower than those associated with burning coal (269.89 g-C/kw-h) or natural gas (177.67 g-C/kw-h) that as a colloquialism, it's reasonable to call hydro, wind, and solar power "clean." See International Energy Agency, *Environmental and Health Impacts of Electricy Generation*, http://www.ieahydro.org/reports/ST3–020613b.pdf.

2. Backup generation is necessary, even if you don't have any renewables on the grid. To avoid blackouts, regulations require utilities to have extra capacity available, even if the wizards' predictions suggest that this capacity won't be needed. There's also another reason utilities pay demand-response customers for their services—if the demand response isn't there, then the utility has to ramp its generators up and down. We already talked about how that isn't an efficient way to run coal and nuclear power plants. "Inefficient" also means that it costs the utility more, and the alternative option—natural gas—is generally a more expensive fuel. If utility companies can rely on demand response instead, then they get to save some money.

3. Actual output: the word *giraffe* spelled three different ways and a short treatise on how much I liked my cat, Bugle Boy.

4. Some of the worst reactions to demand-based pricing have happened when utility companies installed the "smart meter" necessary to make demand pricing work long before they actually started to *offer* demand pricing. The meters were good for the utility company—they made it cheaper and easier to read meters remotely, without paying a guy to go house-to-house. Yet the customers didn't get a benefit at all, and when bills went up because of weather or other normal price hikes, those

customers assumed that the fancy new meters were overcharging them. Pacific Gas & Electric, a California-based utility company, has actually been sued by its customers over this, and even though an independent study done in 2010 found that the smart meters weren't putting a digital thumb on the scale, so to speak, there's still a lot of opposition. Contrast that with GridWise results, and you can see that *how* technology is introduced matters as much as what the technology actually does.

5. Interview with Rob Pratt, a senior research scientist at PNNL, December 2010. More information can be found in two papers that PNNL published about their GridWise results: D.J. Hammerstrom, et al., "Pacific Northwest GridWise Testbed Demonstration Projects: Part I and Part II," prepared for the U.S. Department of Energy under contract, October 2007, http://www.pnl.gov/main/publications/external/technical_reports/PNNL-17167.pdf and http://www.pnl.gov/main/publications/external/technical_reports/PNNL-17079.pdf.

6. Rob Pratt, a senior research scientist at PNNL, did a study of the CO_2 impact of this type of smart grid. If the technologies from GridWise were expanded to the entire United States, it could reduce greenhouse gas emissions 12 percent between 2010 and 2030—equivalent to the emissions produced by sixty-six typical coal-fired power plants a year. See U.S. Department of Energy, *The Smart Grid: An Estimation of the Energy and CO2 Benefits*, January 2010, http://energyenvironment.pnnl.gov/news/pdf/PNNL-19112_Revision_1_Final.pdf.

7. Some studies separate coal and lignite, which is another fossil fuel that is similar to coal but more moisture-rich. Electricity made from coal or lignite will produce about the same levels of greenhouse gas emissions, but lignite is associated with more deaths and serious illnesses than coal is. Yet the two aren't always considered separately. The Energy Information Administration describes lignite as a type of coal, for instance. Lignite makes up only 7 percent of U.S. coal use. See U.S. Energy Information Administration, "Coal Basics: Coal Takes Millions of Years to Create," http://www.eia.doe.gov/kids/energy.cfm?page=coal_home-basics.

Some studies on deaths from coal and other energy sources include Anil Markandya and Paul Wilkinson, "Electricity Generation and Health," *Lancet*, September 15, 2007, www.canwea.ca/pdf/talkwind/Electricity%20generation%20and%20health.pdf; Richard Wilson et al., "Comparative Risk Assessment of Energy Options: The Meaning of Results," *IAEA Bulletin*, March 1999, www.iaea.org/Publications/Magazines/Bulletin/Bull411/article4.pdf; http://www.ieahydro.org/

reports/ST3–020613b.pdf, and Nils Starfelt and Carl-Erik Wikdahl, *Economic Analysis of Various Options of Electricity Generation: Taking into Account Health and Environmental Effects*, http://manhaz.cyf.gov.pl/man-haz/strona_konferencja_EAE-2001/15%20-%20Polenp~1.pdf.

8. Most of the studies I was able to find on this use data taken from the European Union, rather than from the United States. Yet in terms of power plant design and facility safety, they're similar enough to extrapolate. A 2007 study, based on EU data and published in the *Lancet*, found that lignite and coal separately both produce .12 deaths per terawatt-hour from accidents. When it comes to air pollution, lignite kills almost thirty-three people per terawatt-hour, and coal kills almost twenty-five. Nothing else killed that many, not even oil and natural gas—and definitely not nuclear power, which killed .022 people per terawatt-hour from accidents and .074 people per terawatt-hour in other ways. See Markandya and Wilkinson, "Electricity Generation and Health."

9. There is a range of estimations for how many deaths are attributable to nuclear power. Ultimately, it all comes down to the three major nuclear energy disasters: Chernobyl, Three Mile Island, and Fukushima. In the wake of events such as those, it's very difficult to know exactly which cancers and other health effects, spread out over the course of fifty years, wouldn't have happened otherwise. Even where there's correlation, causation is difficult to prove. Really, though, the same thing is true about deaths caused by air pollution from coal-fired power plants; there's simply less of a public debate about those numbers.

   In both situations, scientists analyze historical data on public health and make the best estimations that they can make. Different scientists don't always agree, but more of them still come down on the side of coal being more deadly than nuclear power. For instance, if you look at the time period between 1987 and 2004, the only way the number of deaths in Europe caused by nuclear-powered electricity exceeds the number of deaths caused by coal and lignite-powered electricity is if you use the very highest estimates for deaths caused by the Chernobyl disaster. These estimations, published in the *Annals of the New York Academy of Sciences* in 2009, come out to more than 800,000 Chernobyl-related deaths. To put that in context, Greenpeace estimates that Chernobyl caused 200,000 deaths. The independent 2006 TORCH report, published in the UK, estimated 60,000 deaths. Meanwhile, in very rough numbers, coal and lignite probably caused around 384,000 deaths, on the low end, during that same time period. The big difference: nuclear deaths are centered around rare disasters. Coal and lignite deaths are centered around the effects of daily normal operation.

10. There is definitely combustible gas in some Pennsylvanian wells. But there's not yet solid evidence on how that gas ends up there. It might be caused by fracking. It might be a much more natural thing—Pennsylvania has a lot of natural gas deposits and it's completely possible for the gas to just leak into wells on its own. For more on this debate, check out this piece written by Abrahm Lustgarten of ProPublica: "Scientific Study Links Flammable Drinking Water to Fracking, http://www.propublica.org/article/scientific-study-links-flammable-drinking-water-to-fracking/single.

11. "Groundless Rumors Add to Burdens of Fukushima Evacuees," *Daily Yomiuri Online*, http://www.yomiuri.co.jp/dy/national/T110421006295.htm.

12. E. J. Bromet and J. M. Havenaar, "Psychological and Perceived Health Effects of the Chernobyl Disaster: A 20-Year Review," National Center for Biotechnology Information, http://www.ncbi.nlm.nih.gov/pubmed/18049228.

13. U.S. Energy Information Administration, "Electricity in the United States, http://www.eia.doe.gov/energyexplained/index.cfm?page=electricity_in_the_united_states.

14. This is based on total levelized system costs—a measurement that includes the costs of building a power plant, the costs associated with supplying it with fuel, the cost of operating it, and the cost of necessary transmission investment—as projected in the *EIA Annual Energy Outlook 2011*. Hydroelectric power is also pretty cheap, as is wind, but both have a lower capacity factor than gas and coal, which means that you get less for the investment. If you built a coal power plant and a wind farm, and both had a capacity of 1,000 megawatts, it would, depending on where you live, cost about the same. Yet during the course of a year, you'd reliably get an average of only 340 megawatts out of the wind farm, while the coal plant could produce an average of 850 megawatts. In order to produce the same number of megawatts with wind, you'd have to spend a lot more money building a much greater capacity. U.S. Energy Information Administration, *Levelized Cost of New Generation Resources in the Annual Energy Outlook 2011*, http://www.eia.gov/oiaf/aeo/electricity_generation.html.

15. "What Crisis? Why the Capital Should Turn Off Its Toilets," *Economist*, April 20, 2011, http://www.economist.com/node/18587187.

16. There is some debate about this. Burning natural gas does definitely produce fewer greenhouse gas emissions than burning a lump of coal, just because of the chemical makeup of these two different types of fossil fuels. The debate centers primarily around emissions associated with drilling and mining for these fuels. In particular, it's probably been underreported in the past how much natural gas (which is largely methane, a particularly powerful greenhouse gas) escapes into the atmosphere because of the fracking-and-drilling process. Research that's tried to account for those emissions has turned up various results. A report produced by journalists in January 2011 suggested that natural gas does produce fewer emissions than coal, but that the difference between the two isn't as large as we've long thought. See Abrahm Lustgarten, "Climate Benefits of Natural Gas May Be Overstated," http://www .propublica.org/article/natural-gas-and-coal-pollution-gap-in-doubt. Another study, this one done by scientists at Cornell University, found that natural gas actually produces more emissions than coal, if that natural gas is freed from shale using fracking techniques. See Robert W. Howarth, Renee Santoro, and Anthony Ingraffea, "Methane and the Greenhouse-Gas Footprint of Natural Gas from Shale Formations," http://thehill.com/images/stories/blogs/energy/howarth.pdf. This question is far from settled, but it demonstrates the complexity of the decisions we're trying to make.

17. Actual safety of operation at a nuclear plant also has to be a consideration. Safety can be good, but it will never be perfect. In the United States, we've had one major incident (Three Mile Island) in fifty years— with "major" defined as "radioactive material being released into the outside world." There have been lots of other small problems, but they were either noticed by regulators or staff before they became dangerous, or built-in safety systems stopped them from becoming dangerous. That's not a bad record, especially when you compare it to the safety records of something like airplane travel. Or, for that matter, coal. This is a pretty subjective thing, but, for any other complex system, fewer than one serious accident in fifty years is a safety record I'm willing to live with. To me, operational safety is a concern, but it isn't the deal breaker. The deal breaker is storage. To get more perspective on this, I recommend reading chapter 4 of the MIT Interdisciplinary Report *The Future of Nuclear Power*, web.mit.edu/nuclearpower.

    Of course, the key to this is that the safety precautions have to be maintained, and that takes regulation. Case in point, in 2010, the

Nuclear Regulatory Commission forced Nebraska's Fort Calhoun nuclear power plant to upgrade its flood protection systems. Just as that process was wrapping up, the area around Fort Calhoun was inundated by the 2011 Midwestern floods. As I write this, water levels haven't yet gone down, but it looks like Fort Calhoun will be okay, because the new flood protections were in place. If the NRC hadn't done its job, though, the summer of 2011 could have been a lot worse for the citizens of Nebraska. Unfortunately, there's evidence that the NRC isn't always as stringent with safety regulations as it needs to be. So my position on nuclear power needs to be modified somewhat: I'm not particularly worried about daily operations—as long as regulations are tight and well-enforced. (To read more about this, I recommend a four-part series written by Associated Press reporter Jeff Donn, which was published during the summer of 2011. The AP, unfortunately, intentionally makes it very difficult to share and link to the stories it publishes. I'm including links to the four parts of Donn's series, as they appeared on Yahoo News, but there's a good chance that by the time you read this, those links will no longer work. The best thing to do is run a search for the titles of each part of the story. "AP Impact: U.S. Nuke Regulators Weaken Safety Rules," Associated Press, http://old.news.yahoo.com/s/ap/20110620/ap_on_re_us/us_aging_nukes_part1; "AP Impact: Tritium Links Found at Many Nuke Sites," Associated Press, http://old.news.yahoo.com/s/ap/us_aging_nukes_part2; "AP Impact: Populations around US Nuke Plants Soar," Associated Press, http://old.news.yahoo.com/s/ap/20110627/ap_on_re_us/us_aging_nukes_part3; and "AP Impact: NRC and Industry Rewrite Nuke History," Associated Press, http://old.news.yahoo.com/s/ap/us_aging_nukes_part4.

18. In a book review for New Scientist magazine, Monty Python's Terry Jones once called nuclear energy "a very silly way to boil water." Terry Jones, "A Very Silly Way to Boil Water," *New Scientist*, June 18, 1987, 63, http://books.google.com/books?id=LvhAoKR-ixwC&lpg=PA63& ots=GNVDfrpsp1&dq=Terry%20jones%20new%20scientist%20nuclear&pg=PA63#v=onepage&q&f=false.

19. For a much more in-depth look at how nuclear reactions work, I recommend reading Marcus Chown's *The Matchbox That Ate a 40-Ton Truck*. It's a physics book that just about anyone will be able to understand and even enjoy. Marcus Chown, *The Matchbox That Ate a 40-Ton Truck* (New York: Faber & Faber, 2010).

20. Based on an interview with Harold McFarlane, the deputy associate laboratory director for nuclear programs and the director of the Space Systems and Technology Division of the U.S. Department of Energy's Idaho National Laboratory, June 2010.

21. This is also essentially what makes a controlled fission reaction controlled. In a nuclear bomb, there are no barriers at all, and the nuclei release all of their energy very quickly. Nuclear power plants have both fuel rods and control rods—barriers that slow the chain reaction down. So, a slowed-down reaction is a good thing, in general, but you replace the fuel rods when the reaction starts happening too slowly.

22. Don't be too quick to discount this, though. A 2010 paper in *Nature Geoscience* estimated that if underground reservoirs couldn't maintain a leakage rate of less than 1 percent per 1,000 years, then sequestration will end up merely delaying the effects of climate change, rather than halting it. See Gary Shaffer, "Long-Term Effectiveness and Consequences of Carbon Dioxide Sequestration," June 27, 2010, http://www.nature.com/ngeo/journal/v3/n7/abs/ngeo896.html.

23. Interview with Harold McFarlane, the deputy associate laboratory director for nuclear programs and the director of the Space Systems and Technology Division of the U.S. Department of Energy's Idaho National Laboratory, June 2010.

24. The French have some particularly interesting ideas about how to store spent nuclear fuel, which are worth taking a peek at. See Shaffer, "Long-Term Effectiveness and Consequences of Carbon Dioxide Sequestration."

25. This is based on interdisciplinary summaries of the technologies, produced by MIT, and on a DOE FAQ on carbon sequestration. Read the MIT paper "The Future of Coal" at http://web.mit.edu/coal/; MIT's paper "The Future of Nuclear Power" at http://web.mit.edu/nuclear-power/; and the DOE FAQ at http://www.netl.doe.gov/technologies/carbon_seq/FAQs/concerns.html.

7. The View from Merriam's Peak

1. My designation of five major metro areas encompassing eighteen counties isn't arbitrary. That's how the state of Kansas looks at demographics and economic trends. As of 2010, the metro areas were Topeka, Kansas City, Lawrence, Wichita, and Manhattan. The eighteen counties included in those metros are Jefferson, Osage, Shawnee, Wabaunsee, Johnson, Leavenworth, Miami, Wyandotte, Franklin, Linn, Douglas, Butler, Harvey, Sedgwick, Sumner, Geary, Pottawatomie, and Riley.

This comes from the *Kansas Department of Labor Economic Report for 2010*, http://www.dol.ks.gov/LMIS/economicReport/2010/Kansas_ Economic_Report_2010.pdf. County and state population data come from the 2010 census, as reported by the U.S. Census and the USDA, http://2010.census.gov/news/releases/operations/ cb11-cn63.html and http://www.ers.usda.gov/Data/Population/ PopList.asp?ST=KS&LongName=Kansas. If you're curious, Kansas is 411 miles from east to west, which lines up the center dividing line some-where around the town of Ellsworth. I mention this because Kansans are probably used to dividing the state up along Interstate 135. I used mileage instead of local convention because I think that will make more sense to people who don't live in Kansas. Regardless, the two dividing lines are pretty close together.

2. I went to high school in Salina, which at the time I thought was in the middle of nowhere. Later, in college, I found out that my Western Kansas friends had frequently driven hours *to* Salina, just to hang out at our truck stops. The grass is greener and all that.

3. This is based on the 1890 census, which was the last to draw a "Frontier Line" between settled regions of the United States and the wilderness. That census made the distinction between "settled" and "wilderness" by population density—with two or fewer persons per square mile count-ing as wilderness. As of the 2000 census, Wallace and Greely counties, both on the Kansas-Colorado border, met that criteria. It's worth point-ing out that this is not how the U.S. government classifies "frontier" regions today. There's a much more detailed methodology that takes into account both population density and the distance that people who live in those regions would have to travel to gain access to basic ser-vices. Yet several Western Kansas counties are frontier by that defini-tion as well. The comparison to the 1890 census is kind of a joke, but the issues it sheds light on are real and can be serious for the people living in these places. For Census 2000 population densities by county, see http://www.ipsr.ku.edu/ksdata/ksah/KSA43.pdf. For historical changes in population by county—where you really see the popula-tions of places such as Greely and Wallace grow, peak, and then fall— see http://www.census.gov/population/cencounts/ks190090.txt. For more on how frontier is defined today, why the frontier matters, and how low population densities affect people living in frontier regions, see http://www.frontierus.org/documents/consensus_paper.htm;

http://www.raconline.org/info_guides/frontier/frontierfaq.php; and
http://www.ers.usda.gov/Briefing/Population/.

4. Johnson County, in the east, has the highest per capita income in
   Kansas, but if you look at the top ten counties with the highest per
   capita incomes, seven of them are in Western Kansas. Likewise, the
   highest poverty rates are concentrated in the East. Only four Western
   Kansas counties have poverty rates above 15 percent. Eighteen Eastern
   Kansas counties do. There may only be two people per square mile
   in Greeley County, but they're doing pretty well for themselves. See
   http://www.ipsr.ku.edu/ksdata/ksah/income/percapinc.pdf; http://
   www.ipsr.ku.edu/ksdata/ksah/income/9pov2.pdf; and http://www
   .ipsr.ku.edu/ksdata/ksah/KSA43.pdf.

5. In 2004, 20 percent of the population in twenty-six counties in Western
   Kansas was older than sixty-five. That was true of twelve counties in Eastern
   Kansas. See Rural Policy Research Institute, *Demographic and Economic
   Profile: Kansas,* July 2006, http://www.rupri.org/Forms/Kansas.pdf.

6. Different people in different parts of the country come up with different figures for how many homes are powered by a megawatt of capacity. This estimate comes from Richard Brown, a researcher with the
   Lawrence Berkeley National Laboratory. See "How Many Houses Can
   1 MW Supply?" http://enduse.lbl.gov/info/CA_Presentation/sld011
   .htm. And remember: capacity isn't the same thing as the actual amount
   of electricity the power plant produces.

7. If you want to learn more about this, I recommend visiting Saul Griffith's
   Energy Literacy blog at www.energyliteracy.com/.

8. United Nations, "Minimum Development Goal Indicators," http://
   mdgs.un.org/unsd/mdg/SeriesDetail.aspx?srid=749&crid=.

9. In fact, in February 2011, the Environmental Protection Agency
   objected to the Holcomb plant for exactly that reason. See John Hanna,
   "EPA Questions Air-Quality Permit for Kansas Coal Plant," LJWorld
   .com, http://www2.ljworld.com/news/2011/feb/06/epa-questions-air-
   quality-permit-kansas-coal-plant/.

10. Steven Mufson, "Power Plant Rejected over Carbon Dioxide for the First
    Time," *Washington Post,* October 13, 2007, http://www.washingtonpost
    .com/wp-dyn/content/article/2007/10/18/AR2007101802452.html.

11. This may or may not be the final word. In January 2011, the Sierra
    Club asked the State Court of Appeals to prevent the smaller plant's
    construction. As of July 2011, the case was still pending. See "Sierra

Club Plans Challenge to Holcomb Permit," Associated Press, www
.wibw.com/home/headlines/Sierra_Club_Plans_Challenge_to_
Holcomb_Permit_113680394.html. Meanwhile, an investigation into
the permitting process that allowed Mark Parkinson to grant official
approval to the Holcomb plant has drawn attention to what looks like
a way-too-cozy relationship between the regulators and the regulated.
That could also end up having an effect on what Sunflower Electric
is eventually allowed to build and when. See Karen Dillon, "Kansas
Agency, Utility Worked Closely on Permit for Coal Plant," *Kansas City
Star*, June 18, 2011, accessed June 25, 2011, http://www.kansascity
.com/2011/06/18/2959875/kansas-agency-power-company-worked
.html. This link is no longer active, however. If you'd like to read the full
story, it has been reprinted online by the Midwest Democracy Project.
The MDP is not an unbiased source, but their reprint of the story
matches the saved version I have from the *Kansas City Star* site: http://
midwestdemocracyproject.org/articles/kansas-agency-power-company-
worked-closely-on-permit-for-coal-fired-power-plant/.

12. Jennifer Bradley and Bruce Katz, "A Small-Town or Metro Nation?" *New
Republic*, October 8, 2008, http://www.brookings.edu/articles/2008/
1008_smalltowns_katz.aspx.

13. It also coincides with U.S. census data showing that more than 80 percent of Americans live in urban communities, as opposed to strictly
rural. The census doesn't count any categories in-between. This is
another broad definition, but taken together, these two ways of looking
at the world give you an idea of what's actually happening. See https://
www.cia.gov/library/publications/the-world-factbook/geos/us.html.

14. Just to clarify: "Climate change" and "global warming" are two names
that describe the same phenomenon. I use "climate change"—as do
many scientists—because "global warming" has, over the years, led to
a lot of confusion as to what kind of impact we can expect. This phenomenon is causing an increase in the global average temperature, but
zoom in to the city where you live, and the effects of that global temperature increase aren't as simple as, "It will be hotter." For instance,
during the last century, as greenhouse gas concentrations in the atmosphere got higher and the global average temperature increased, the
U.S. Midwest got wetter. I think the name *climate change* describes what's
going on a lot better, from an individual perspective.

15. Those famous reports from the Intergovernmental Panel on Climate
Change are all available online, for you to read for free. And you should

read them. The scientists who write these reports are specifically trying to summarize decades' worth of technical research for an audience of people who aren't particularly technical. They don't always succeed. The IPCC reports can be very dry reading and may be confusing at times, but they're meant to be something that a layperson can read and understand, so you really should take a look at them—especially if you're confused about what evidence we have that actually supports the existence of climate change. The place to start is the *2007 4th Assessment Report*, which is broken down into four parts. I recommend actually starting on the fourth. The first part analyzes what we know about the physical science of climate change. The second is about the impact that climate change has already had and what changes it's likely to cause in the future. The third is about what we can do to mitigate and adapt to the effects of climate change. Finally, the synthesis report ties everything together and tries to help policy makers understand what climate change means. You can read the synthesis report and then follow its footnotes to find more details on specific issues in the other reports, at http://www.ipcc.ch/publications_and_data/publications_and_data_reports.shtml#1.

16. On a related allegorical note, it's also pretty unlikely that all of the mechanics in the tri-state area—or even a large majority of them—could have successfully conspired together in order to manipulate you into fixing your transmission.

17. RealClimate, a blog written by climate scientists and other scientists who study climate change, has two pages that I think are great places to start. First, their page on climate change for beginners has many helpful links and will point you toward a wealth of information about the evidence for climate change: http://www.realclimate.org/index.php/archives/2007/05/start-here/. Second, they have a Wiki that answers questions about numerous common climate myths: http://www.realclimate.org/wiki/index.php?title=RC_Wiki.

18. This sounds like hyperbole. It is not. I have literally experienced weeks when I was bundled in a coat and a scarf on Monday and wearing shorts by the weekend. A wintertime swing from 30 degrees Fahrenheit to 65 degrees Fahrenheit during the course of a couple days is not all that rare.

19. From the High Plains Regional Climate Center guide *Climate Change on the Prairie*, 2009, www.hprcc.unl.edu/publications/files/HighPlainsClimateChangeGuide.pdf.

20. It's worth noting that the people most likely to be affected the worst are the ones who are already vulnerable for other reasons: the poor, the sick, and people who live in cities who don't have as much support infrastructure to survive a natural disaster. For these folks, even relatively modest changes can have a big impact. Christopher Field, director of the department of global ecology at the Carnegie Institution for Science, uses the example of Hurricane Katrina. We don't know (and probably won't ever know for certain) whether this storm was directly attributable to climate change, but it is a good example of how a storm that was within the range of predicted possibilities can cause damage and destruction far greater than anybody expected, simply because of where and who the storm hit. Interview with Christopher Field, July 2010.

21. The poison ivy information applies to many areas all over the country and comes from interviews with Jackie Mohan, an ecologist at the University of Georgia, and Lewis Ziska, an ecologist with the Agriculture Research Service of the U.S. Department of Agriculture. It's also based on three published journal papers: L. H. Ziska, P. R. Epstein, and W. H. Schlesinger, "Rising CO(2), Climate Change, and Public Health: Exploring the Links to Plant Biology," www.ncbi.nlm.nih.gov/pubmed/19270781; L. H. Ziska et al., "Rising Atmospheric Carbon Dioxide and Potential Impacts on the Growth and Toxicity of Poison Ivy (Toxicodendron Radicans)," *Weird Science*, July–August 2007, www.jstor.org/stable/4539573; and Patricia L. Jackson Allen, "Leaves of Three, Let Them Be: If Only It Were That Easy," *Pediatric Nursing*, May 28, 2004, http://www.medscape.com/viewarticle/475190.

22. If you want to know more about how climate change is likely to affect Midwestern farms and communities in both the short term and the long term, then I recommend reading the University of Maryland Center for Integrative Environmental Research's paper "Economic Impacts of Climate Change on Kansas," July 2008, www.cier.umd.edu/climate-adaptation/Kansas%20Economic%20Impacts%20of%20Climate%20Change.pdf. The types of impact are mixed. As I mentioned with plant growth, there are some beneficial effects, but overall, we're talking about crop losses and serious financial penalties.

23. Read more about *Cryptosporidium* at the Centers for Disease Control website at http://www.cdc.gov/parasites/crypto/disease.html.

24. From a 2008 study of climate change and waterborne disease risks in the Great Lakes region. This paper also has some information on increases

in dangerous bacteria levels following heavy downpours. Jonathan Patz et al., "Climate Change and Waterborne Disease in the Great Lakes Region of the U.S.," *American Journal of Preventive Medicine*, 2008, http:// sage.wisc.edu/pubs/articles/M-Z/patz/patzetalAJPM08.pdf.

25. For more on how heavy downpours increase our risk of exposure to dangerous bacteria, see Kristie L. Ebi et al., "Climate Change and Human Health Impacts in the United States: An Update on the Results of the U.S. National Assessment," *Environmental Health Perspectives*, May 18, 2006, http://www.ncbi.nlm.nih.gov/pmc/articles/PMC1570072/; Wisconsin Initiative on Climate Change Impacts, *Human Health Working Group Report*, http://www.wicci.wisc.edu/report/Human-Health.pdf; Timothy J. Wade et al., "Did a Severe Flood in the Midwest Cause an Increase in the Incidence of Gastrointestinal Symptoms?" *American Journal of Epidemiology*, August 19, 2003, http://aje.oxfordjournals .org/content/159/4/398.full; and Michael F. Craun et al., "Waterborne Outbreaks Reported in the United States," *Journal of Water and Health*, 2006, http://courses.washington.edu/h2owaste/group1.pdf.

26. According to a 2010 report of the Iowa Climate Change Impacts Committee, http://www.iowadnr.gov/iccac/files/completereport .pdf#page=23.

27. This is another effect that isn't limited to the area around Merriam. Researchers are finding earlier springs and higher pollen counts all over the United States. From interviews with Lewis Ziska and Paul Epstein, a researcher at the Center for Health and the Global Environment at Harvard Medical School, April 2009. Also based on a paper authored by Ziska, Epstein, and William H. Schlesinger, "Rising CO2, Climate Change, and Public Health: Exploring the Links to Plant Biology," September 19, 2008, http://www.ncbi.nlm.nih.gov/pmc/articles/ PMC2649213/.

28. Based on interviews with Aruni Bhatnagar, a professor of medicine at the University of Louisville and a project leader of the University's Center of Environmental Cardiology, and Kim Knowlton, DrPH, a senior research scientist with the Natural Resources Defense Council. Both interviews, April 2009.

29. This is also from the University of Maryland paper "Economic Impacts of Climate Change on Kansas," www.cier.umd.edu/climateadaptation/ Kansas%20Economic%20Impacts%20of%20Climate%20Change.pdf.

30. To quote Ken Caldeira, an atmospheric scientist with the Carnegie Institution's Department of Global Ecology at Stanford University:

"Targets are really an argument over how much damage is okay to do. We don't say what's an acceptable level of mugging old ladies. Instead, we set the target at zero, and recognize that we might not hit that, but the target is zero. We can't say there's a safe line here." From an interview with Dr. Caldeira, June 2010.

31. That's right. Oil isn't made from dinosaurs. But an apatosaurus makes a better corporate mascot than a phytoplankton does.

32. This is important, because in terms of how it affects us, "peak oil" isn't likely to mean that humankind will suddenly run out of oil and have none at all. Instead, it's more likely to be a situation where supplies of conventional oil—the kind that is relatively cheap to collect and process—become increasingly scarce, and prices of liquid fuel rise dramatically. There will be oil. It simply won't be as affordable.

33. You can download the full report and all of the technical papers supporting it. Or, if you want a short version written in the researchers' own words, download the executive summary. UKERC, *Global Oil Depletion Report*, October 8, 2009, http://www.ukerc.ac.uk/support/Global%20 Oil%20Depletion.

34. In addition, the researchers said that you'd also have to assume oil demand is going to grow more slowly than it has in the past. So, either peak oil will happen before 2031 (in which case, we need to change the way we use energy), or we can delay peak oil until after 2031 (but in order to make that work, we'll still need to change the way we use energy). There's not a good argument here for business as usual. To you and me, "being optimistic" might simply mean "not being a naysaying sourpuss." We think of optimism as a virtue. It's a trait of people who don't give up, a better way of thinking. But *optimistic* means something else when you're talking about science. When a scientist decides that an estimate is optimistic, she's applying that label in relation to two other possibilities: pessimistic, and *realistic*. Optimism isn't the ideal here.

35. Oil does a lot more than simply move your car around. After transportation, the industrial sector is the second largest consumer of oil in the country. It's a part of many products you buy. Oil goes into the production of the food you consume. As oil costs rise, the effects will reach far beyond what you pay per gallon at the local filling station. You can read a little more about this on page 22 of the Hirsch report at http://www .netl.doe.gov/publications/others/pdf/oil_peaking_netl.pdf.

36. James Howard Kunstler is a very popular writer on peak oil. You can get some more background on the theories he's developed in several

nonfiction and fiction books at http://www.kunstler.com/index.php. Yet it's important to keep in mind that he is not the only authority on the effects of peak oil. He's a journalist, like me, and a lot of the other sources who make their living studying the economics and the science of peak oil (including Hirsch) disagree with what Kunstler sees as obvious, unavoidable outcomes. It's also important to remember that Kunstler doesn't have to be 100 percent right (or even 50 percent right) for peak oil to be devastating and life-altering. Again, real life isn't zebra-striped. There's a spectrum of possible outcomes. As the 2009 UK summary pointed out, we don't yet know enough about peak oil to say which outcomes are most likely. But—let's just drive this point home one more time—the uncertainties involved here should be a call to action, not a reason to dismiss real risks.

37. The full Hirsch report is available online at http://www.netl.doe.gov/ publications/others/pdf/oil_peaking_netl.pdf.

38. Ibid., p. 65.

8. The Take-Charge Challenge

1. If the idea of Creation Care appeals to you, I recommend that you check out a couple of resources for more information. You can find Kansas Interfaith Power and Light at http://kansasipl.org/. For a more nationwide look at the subject, though, I recommend the Evangelical Environmental Network. This Christian group has been around since 1993. It's got a podcast, a recommended reading list, and a blog that should get you started at http://creationcare.org/. Creation Care isn't only about Christianity, either. The Coalition on the Environment and Jewish Life was founded the same year and offers many of the same resources but from a Jewish perspective; you can find it at http://www .coejl.org/~coejlor/about/. Also, Green Faith, an interfaith organization, has online statements about how the concept of Creation Care applies to Christianity, Judaism, Islam, Hinduism, and Buddhism. See http://greenfaith.org/religious-teachings.

2. The Catholic Church, for instance. In May 2011, the Vatican issued a report, calling for countries to take quick action on climate change mitigation. The paper was actually written by a team of researchers— glaciologists, climate scientists, meteorologists, hydrologists, physicists, chemists, mountaineers, and lawyers—brought together by the Vatican to discuss the impact that climate change has had on mountain glaciers. Pontifical Academy of Sciences, "Fate of Mountain Glaciers in the Anthropocene," May 11, 2011. See http://www.vatican.va/roman_

curia/pontifical_academies/acdscien/2011/PAS_Glacier_110511_
final.pdf.

3. The Blue Green Alliance now operates in several states: Kansas, Indiana,
Michigan, Minnesota, New Jersey, Ohio, Pennsylvania, and Wisconsin.
You can find it at http://www.bluegreenalliance.org/. If you're an
individual who likes to tinker, some other good resources to check out
are *Home Power* magazine, which offers guides and tips for all kinds
of DIY energy-generation and energy-efficiency projects at http://
homepower.com/home/; and Lawrence Berkeley National Labs Home
Energy Saver website, which will help you calculate the value of a variety
of different home energy projects—what various changes are worth to
you, personally, in both energy saved and dollars saved: http://hes.lbl
.gov/consumer/. Finally, DIY crew, whenever you hear about an amazing new source of free or cheap energy that you can build at home, go
look it up on the Popular Mechanics website. It has done a good job
over the years of debunking the most egregious flim-flam (and there is
a lot of flim-flam) and providing straight answers on what's real, what's
not, and what could someday be real but probably isn't worth canceling
your electric service over just yet: http://www.popularmechanics.com.

4. Think about the capacity of the Holcomb plant. Based on the current plans, it will have a capacity of 895 megawatts of electricity. One
compact fluorescent lightbulb (CFL) needs about 25 watts to light up,
which means that an 895 megawatt power plant could light more than
35 million CFLs. So, what do you think would happen if there were
only 20 million CFLs that needed to be turned on? How much smaller
could the power plant be, and how many fewer tons of CO_2 would it
produce? In the real world, reducing demand for electricity is more
complicated than this, and it's based on more than simply turning off a
few lightbulbs, but the concept works the same.

5. When it comes to saving money by saving energy, a great place to
start is the Energy Star home page, http://www.energystar.gov/index
.cfm?fuseaction=find_a_product. This site provides lists of appliances,
light fixtures, and other energy-using products you might buy that are
more energy efficient than their competitors. When you need to buy
a new refrigerator, it makes sense to buy one that will also lower your
electric bill. The Lawrence Berkeley National Lab's Home Energy Saver
website, http://hes.lbl.gov/consumer/, can help you make decisions
about what kind of energy-efficiency projects to undertake and what
various changes are worth to you, personally, in both energy saved

and dollars saved. Energy Savers, http://www.energysavers.gov/, is a government website with many resources on money-saving energy-efficiency retrofits. It can also help you find a professional to give your house or building an energy-use assessment or figure out how to do one on your own. These assessments will help you spot places where you're spending money and using energy where you don't need to. The American Council for Energy Efficient Economy, http://www.aceee.org/consumer, can help on that front as well. Also, *Consumer Reports* has a large, in-depth guide to energy-saving products and ideas at http://www.consumerreports.org/cro/home-garden/resource-center/energy-saving-guide/energy-saving-guide.htm.

6. An example: all-glass office buildings. You can design an all-glass office building that uses less energy than a similar all-glass office building, but you could hit the same energy-saving goals (and probably reach even better goals) for a lower up front cost, if you simply started with a building that wasn't all glass.

7. This is normalized, to account for economic downturn and differences in weather patterns between towns in different parts of the state. The actual energy reduction was quite a bit higher—9.9 percent, according to Chris Evans Hands in a July 2011, e-mail.

8. In fact, Lahn took a turn dressing up as Captain Powerstrip, an energy efficient superhero who visited local schools. No, really.

9. The United States used 3,741,485,000 megawatt-hours per year in 2009. Five-and-half percent of that is 205,781,675 megawatt-hours per year. In 2009, Mexico used 181,500,000 megawatt-hours of electricity. U.S. Energy Information Administration, "International Energy Statistics," http://tonto.eia.doe.gov/cfapps/ipdbproject/iedindex3.cfm?tid=2&pid=2&aid=2&cid=AS, CA, CH, FR, GM, IN, JA, RS, UK, US, ww, &syid=2004&eyid=2009&unit=BKWH; and Central Intelligence Agency, *The World Factbook*, https://www.cia.gov/library/publications/the-world-factbook/geos/mx.html.

10. Why? This has to do with the rebound effect, that tendency for energy-efficient technologies to ironically prompt us to use more energy. I'll explain more about this—and why alternative energy in tandem with efficiency can make a difference—in upcoming chapters.

11. This is one of the details of climate science that *has* changed a lot in the last twenty years, as scientists pieced together a deeper understanding of how the natural life cycle of carbon dioxide works and figured

out that some of their earlier ideas were wrong. Older versions of the IPCC report said that a molecule of carbon dioxide might remain in the atmosphere for either five to two hundred or fifty to two hundred years. The 2007 report, however, took a different perspective. On page 501 of the part of the report that covers the physical science basis of climate change, the IPCC says, "Carbon dioxide cycles between the atmosphere, oceans, and land. Its removal from the atmosphere involves a range of processes with different time scales. About 50% of a CO_2 increase will be removed from the atmosphere within 30 years, and a further 30% will be removed within a few centuries. The remaining 20% may stay in the atmosphere for many thousands of years." Basically, some of the carbon dioxide that came out of the tailpipes of American cars in the year 2011 will still be lingering in the atmosphere in the year 3011. That's not all. The atmosphere will also be harboring 20 percent of the emissions produced in 2010, 2009, 2008, and every year all the way back to the Industrial Revolution.

People talk about the power of compound interest—that financial concept that allows small investments made in your late teens to add up to serious money by the time you retire. We're basically talking about the same thing here. Only, in the case of carbon emissions, the power of compound interest is working against us. See Intergovernmental Panel on Climate Change, *IPCC Fourth Assessment Report: Climate Change 2007*, www.ipcc.ch/publications_and_data/ar4/wg1/en/contents.html, and interviews with Stephen Pacala, November 2010; Ken Caldiera, an atmospheric scientist who works at the Carnegie Institution for Science's Department of Global Ecology, June 2010; William Moomaw, a professor of international environmental policy at the Fletcher School of Law and Diplomacy, Tufts University, February 2010; and Britton Stephens, a scientist with the National Center for Atmospheric Research, February 2010.

A news article from the journal *Nature* gives a nice explanation of how the science on carbon cycles has changed since the first IPCC report: "Carbon Is Forever," November 20, 2008, http://www.nature.com/climate/2008/0812/full/climate.2008.122.html.

12. We're about 1,500 square feet. The average American home in 2009 was about 2,400 square feet. See http://www.census.gov/const/C25Ann/sftotalmedavgsqft.pdf.

13. Xcel Energy bills this program as a way to get all of your electricity from wind, although that's not exactly what happens. The grid is the grid, after all. See the Xcel Energy website at http://www.xcelenergy

.com/Save_Money_&_Energy/For_Your_Home/Renewable_Energy_
Programs/Windsource_for_Residences_-_MN.

14. Madrigal presents a really nice critique of the tendency for environmentally minded Americans to want to withdraw from society, rather
than change society, in the middle chapters of his book. What he has
to say ties in nicely with some of the issues I'll be talking about in my
chapters on distributed energy generation, and I highly recommend
giving it a read. See Timothy Gutowski et al., "Environmental Life Style
Analysis (ELSA)," IEEE International Symposium on Electronics and
the Environment, May 19–20, 2008, http://web.mit.edu/ebm/www/
Publications/ELSA%20IEEE%202008.pdf.

9. The Olive Green Revolution

1. *Department of Defense Facilities and Vehicles, Energy Use, Strategies and
Goals*—May 2009 and August 2007.
2. Denmark used 800 trillion BTUs in 2010. See U.S. Energy Information
Administration, "Denmark: Country Analysis Brief," http://www.eia
.doe.gov/countries/country-data.cfm?fips=DA.
3. Again, this is a relatively small percentage that represents large amounts
of energy. Department of Defense Facilities and Vehicles: Energy Use,
Strategies and Goals, May 11, 2009, http://www.finishingcontractors
.org/uploads/media/OSD_Energy_brief_for_May_11_2009.pdf.
4. John M. Broder, "Climate Change Seen as Threat to U.S. Security,"
New York Times, August 8, 2009, http://www.nytimes.com/2009/08/09/
science/earth/09climate.html.
5. U.S. Navy, Energy, Environment, and Climate Change, "Assessment and
Prediction," http://greenfleet.dodlive.mil/climate-change/assessment-
and-prediction/.
6. *Department of Defense Energy Security Task Force Report*, http://www.dod
.gov/ddre/doc/DoD_Energy_Security_Task_Force.pdf.
7. The paint job helps at night, too, because the light that does filter in
from outside bounces around and makes the space feel brighter.
8. Although, thanks to the convenience of automated bill pay, we're actually losing that tool somewhat.
9. Working by daylight is different from working by sunlight. You know
that direct rays from the sun on your computer screen mean you won't
be able to read a word. That's sunlight and glare, and it's not pleasant. When I talk about daylight, I mean creating an environment that's
more akin to sitting under a tree in the shade. There's still plenty of

light, but it's diffused and reflected light, rather than direct. In a daylit space, you can see your computer screen and read a book comfortably.

10. The Default Option

1. It takes 6 kilograms of plant protein, on average, to produce 1 kilogram of animal protein. The animals, in turn, require you to use *more* energy to care for them during the course of their lives, slaughter and process them, and transport their meat. Yet a 2,000-calorie diet is still only a 2,000-calorie diet, no matter what you're eating. So we get a better bang for our energy buck if we eat more of the plant-based food ourselves, instead of feeding it to animals.

   Likewise, some animals are a better energy value than others. From 1 kilogram of beef—about the size of a small brisket—your body gets 1 kilocalorie of protein, but it took *40* kilocalories of fossil fuel energy to produce that meat. Beef is pretty much the worst fuel-to-food deal you can find. For a kilogram of pork, you get a kilocalorie of protein from 14 kilocalories of fossil fuels. Making that much chicken uses only 4 kilocalories of fossil fuels.

   Both the numbers for kilocalorie comparisons and the amount of plant protein that it takes to produce 1 kilogram of animal protein come from "Reducing Energy Inputs in the US Food System," a peer-reviewed research paper published in 2008 in the journal *Human Ecology*. There's a lot of interesting stuff in this paper. It's not only about the energy required to produce meat. In general, we aren't very energy efficient in the way we produce plant-based foods, either. There's room for improvement all over. In fact, the authors of the paper estimated that we could cut in half the amount of energy it takes to produce food in this country. That's a big deal, considering that they also estimated that the food system accounts for 19 percent of the total U.S. energy use. See David Pimentel et al., "Reducing Energy Inputs in the U.S. Food System," *Human Ecology*, 2008, http://phobos.ramapo.edu/~vasishth/ Energy/Pimentel-Energy+Food_Systems.pdf.

2. Based on an interview with John "Skip" Laitner, the director of Economic and Social Analysis for ACEEE, November 2010. Also based on "The Efficiency Imperative: Advancing People-Centered Solutions," a presentation that Laitner gave to Argonne National Laboratory on September 28, 2010.

3. In reality, they aren't. Instead, they're probably half glass or even less. Yet this just goes to show you that you can get the aesthetics of a

glass-facade building without taking the energy use hit that usually comes with it.

4. And, remember, "daylight" is different from "sunlight" in this context. Sunlight usually amounts to a lot of glare. Daylight is like the light you get sitting in the shade under a tree. Good daylighting design provides enough light to work by but avoids glare.

5. Western Area Power Administration, "Energy Services Bulletin," July 2008. http://ww2.wapa.gov/sites/western/es/pubs/esb/Documents/jul08.pdf. Initial estimates of power consumption have since been confirmed by Perkins and Will, the engineering company responsible for the building's system design. Internal documentation, March 2010.

6. Drawn from "Movement towards Sustainable Energy Use in U.S. Buildings," a series of slides put together by Kent Peterson, the former president of the American Society of Heating, Refrigeration, and Air-Conditioning Engineers, using data from the Energy Information Administration, the Environmental Protection Agency, and the Buildings Energy Data Book.

7. For the same amount of light output, an LED bulb will use about 7 watts, a compact fluorescent bulb will use 14 watts, and an old-fashioned incandescent will burn through 60 watts.

8. You'll hear people talk up this side benefit a lot. There is some good evidence that this is true, but the published studies show mixed results, so it's not really something you can guarantee outright. See Peter Boyce, Claudia Hunter, and Owen Howlett, "The Benefits of Daylighting through Windows," Department of Energy, September 12, 2003; Jennifer A. Veitch, and Guy R. Newsham, "Exercised Control, Lighting Choices, and Energy Use: An Office Simulation Experiment," *Journal of Environmental Psychology*, 2000; and Jennifer A. Veitch, Guy R. Newsham, Carol C. Jones, et al., "High-Quality Lighting: Energy Efficiency that Enhances Employee Well-Being," *Proceedings of CIE 2010 "Lighting Quality and Energy Efficiency,"* 2010, 197–204.

9. Interestingly, coal made up about 40 percent of the total capacity GRE owned that year. Another 37 percent of their capacity was natural-gas-powered plants. But when it came down to what sources of energy the company was actually using for production, coal made up 72.30 percent of generated electricity—and less than 2 percent of the generated electricity came from natural gas.

10. The DVR figure comes from Noah D. Horowitz, *Cable and Satellite Set Top Box Energy Savings Opportunities*, Natural Resources Defense Council,

March 2005. The refrigerator comparison is based on Energy Star program statistics, which can be found at http://downloads.energystar.gov/bi/qplist/refrigerators.pdf.

11. Environmental Protection Agency, "MSW Recycling Rates, 1960–2009," http://www.epa.gov/epawaste/facts-text.htm#chart3.

12. Energy Star, "Light Bulbs," http://www.energystar.gov/index.cfm?fuseaction=find_a_product.showProductGroup&pgw_code=LB.

13. This is a marked contrast to commercial buildings, especially office buildings, where lighting is one of the top uses of energy. Different types of buildings use energy in different ways. See American Council for an Energy-Efficient Economy, "Lighting," http://www.aceee.org/consumer/lighting.

14. This study looked at the results of Opower programs operating in eleven different utility regions, representing millions of residential customers. See Matt Davis, "Behavior and Energy Savings: Evidence from a Series of Experimental Interventions," Environmental Defense Fund, May 25, 2011, http://opower.com/company/library/verification-reports.

15. U.S. Energy Information Administration, "State Energy Data System: Table C11," http://www.eia.gov/state/seds/hf.jsp?incfile=sep_sum/plain_html/rank_use_per_cap.html; and Bureau of Economic Affairs, table 3, http://www.bea.gov/newsreleases/regional/gdp_state/2010/pdf/gsp1110.pdf.

16. In 1974, the state consumed about 5.8 quadrillion BTUs of primary energy and had a population of 21 million. In 2009, the state consumed about 8 quadrillion BTUs and had a population of 37 million. That works out to a per-capita energy use of 276 million BTUs in 1974 and 216 million BTUs in 2009. Energy use information comes from the EIA at http://www.eia.gov/state/seds/hf.jsp?incfile=sep_use/total/use_tot_CAcb.html&mstate=California. Population data come from the California Legislative Analyst's Office and from the California Department of Finance at http://www.lao.ca.gov/1995/010195_calguide/cgep2.html and http://www.dof.ca.gov/research/demographic/reports/documents/CPS_Multi-Year_3–10.pdf.

17. U.S. Energy Information Administration, "State Energy Data System: Table CT2," http://www.eia.gov/state/seds/hf.jsp?incfile=sep_use/total/use_tot_CAcb.html&mstate=California.

18. Anant Sudarshan and James Sweeney, "Deconstructing the Rosenfeld Curve," Stanford PIEE Working Paper Series, 2008, http://piee

.stanford.edu/cgi-bin/htm/Modeling/research/Deconstructing_the_
Rosenfeld_Curve.php.

19. Alan H. Sanstad, W. Michael Hanemann, and Maximillian Auffhammer,
"End-Use Energy Efficiency in a 'Post-Carbon' California Economy:
Policy Issues and Research Frontiers," in *Managing Greenhouse Emissions
in California*, University of California at Berkeley, p. 25, http://hydrogen.
its.ucdavis.edu/eec/education/EEC-classes/eeclimate/class-readings/
sanstad%20chap%206.pdf.

20. Between 2010 and 2011 I spoke multiple times with several people who
are currently studying the rebound effect and/or working with applying the research being done on this subject to public policy. Key in
shaping my take on the subject were Blake Alcott, a PhD candidate
at the Sustainability Research Institute, University of Leeds; Karen
Turner, Reader in the Division of Economics at the University of
Stirling and Honorary Reader in the Department of Economics at the
University of Strathclyde; Steve Sorrell, a senior fellow at the UK Energy
Research Centre and a senior lecturer in science and technology policy
research at the University of Sussex; John "Skip" Laitner, the director
of economic and social analysis for the American Council for an Energy
Efficient Economy; Horace Herring, a visiting research fellow at the
Energy and Environment Research Unit in the Faculty of Technology
at the UK's Open University; and Harry Saunders, an energy econo-
mist, the managing director of the consulting firm Decision Processes
Incorporated, and a Senior Fellow of the Breakthrough Institute.

21. A quick example: The economic benefits of the rebound effect don't
necessarily apply to rebound that happens in the residential sector, says
Karen Turner, reader in the division of economics at the University of
Stirling and honorary reader in the department of economics at the
University of Strathclyde. So how do you apply a single carbon price,
meant to capture economic benefits of rebound, across the board,
when some sectors don't have economic benefits from rebound? A carbon price is useful, but it's not an easy, quick-fix solution.

22. D. E. Peterson et al., "The Effects of State Cigarette Tax Increases on
Cigarette Sales: 1955 to 1988," *American Journal of Public Health*, 1992,
http://ajph.aphapublications.org/cgi/content/abstract/82/1/94.

11. Home Fires

1. Americans used 98 quadrillion BTUs in 2010, but only about 76 percent
of that energy came from the United States. The rest was imported.
Most of the energy we import comes in the form of oil. It's worth

noting, however, that we no longer get most of our oil imports from OPEC. Since the early 1990s, most of our oil has come from outside the OPEC block. In 2009, 59 percent of our oil imports came from non-OPEC countries, mostly Canada and Mexico. Of the 41 percent of our oil that we do get from OPEC, we're mainly doing business with Saudi Arabia, Venezuela, Nigeria, and Iraq. Compare U.S. Energy Information Administration, "Primary Energy Production by Source," http://www.eia.doe.gov/totalenergy/data/monthly/pdf/sec1_5.pdf, and "Today in Energy," http://eia.doe.gov/totalenergy/data/monthly/pdf/sec1_3.pdf, and "Energy Perspectives," http://www.eia.gov/totalenergy/data/annual/pdf/perspectives_2009.pdf.

2. It's not only oil that we import, either. We've had to import natural gas since the late 1960s, and our imports of it have been rising significantly since the mid-1980s. See pp. xxii and xxviii of "Energy Perspectives."

3. Although nuclear power rises up just enough above the plain that Kansans would probably try to ski on it. See "Energy Perspectives."

4. The difference between what we use and what we make comes into play here. Americans use more petroleum than they do any other kind of fuel source. For U.S. energy *production*, however, coal is number one. If you break down the fossil-fuel energy production statistics for 2010, they look like this: 22 quadrillion BTUs from coal, 22 quadrillion from natural gas, 11.7 quadrillion from crude oil, and 2.7 quadrillion from liquid natural gas. See U.S. Energy Information Administration, "Primary Energy Production by Source," http://www.eia.doe.gov/totalenergy/data/monthly/pdf/sec1_5.pdf.

5. Obviously, not all solar power is centralized, but the type that contributes to Energy Information Administration measurements is. In fact, decentralized solar photovoltaics are such a small contributor (and currently so difficult to track) that the EIA doesn't consider this at all in its calculations. When the EIA talks about solar, it's only talking about solar power installations that are hooked up to the grid and that have a capacity of 1 megawatt or more.

6. This is derived from the National Energy Technology Laboratory's estimation of total distributed generation, http://www.eia.doe.gov/cneaf/electricity/epa/epaxlfile1_2.pdf, and 2009 EIA statistics on total U.S. electric generator nameplate capacity, http://www.netl.doe.gov/smart-grid/referenceshelf/articles/10–18–2010_BUGS%20article.pdf.

7. I need to be clear that any homes-to-megawatt estimation is talking about on average (not peak usage) and that the California ISO/

Lawrence Berkeley estimate that I use—1 megawatt = 750 houses—
applies only to traditional power plants. Coal, natural gas, and nuclear
can be said to power 750 houses for 1 megawatt of capacity. Wind, solar,
and hydro would all be lower, because they have that lower capacity
factor I mentioned earlier. "How Many Houses Can 1 MW Supply?"
Enduse Forecasting and Marketing Assessment, http://enduse.lbl.gov/
info/CA_Presentation/sld011.htm.

8. For example, Tim Roughan, director of distributed resources for
National Grid, a Northeast transmission and distribution company, says
that New Yorkers today can't rely on their neighbors up the Hudson
Valley to send in electricity: "You can't get any more generation without building within the pocket. You have no choice but going down to
smaller projects that take less space."

9. Surprisingly, this paradox can work out better than you might expect.
In Europe, for instance, where wind power developers are building on
a decentralized scale, they've found ways to work around NIMBYism, by
giving communities a stake in the generation that's being built nearby.
Denmark has a lot of wind power but not much of an issue with anti-
wind NIMBYism. That's because, to build a wind turbine, a developer
legally has to give the nearby community a 20 percent financial stake.
To build a multiturbine wind farm, the developer has to offer the community at least one of the turbines. I wrote a little about this and the
research that's gone into better understanding NIMBY in a BoingBoing
article from 2009 titled "Rethinking NIMBY: Why Wind Power Could
Lead to New Ways of Defining (and Dealing with) Public Naysaying,"
http://boingboing.net/2009/11/23/rethinking-nimby.html.

10. Energy is also lost as we move electricity around the grid. Imagine that
power lines are a truck, and the electricity they carry is a big tall stack of
moving boxes. In the process of driving from one city to another, some
of the boxes will always fall off the stack. This loss is significant, but it's
really tiny compared to the conversion losses. In 2009, 1 quadrillion
BTUs were lost during the transmission and distribution of electricity. These conversion losses are different from the capacity factor—the
percentage of stated capacity that a given generator can reasonably be
expected to produce.

11. The American Council for an Energy Efficient Economy says that cogeneration power plants can reach efficiencies of 80 percent. Roughan says
those numbers are real but only in certain situations. A few days or
weeks of 80 percent efficiency is different from what the power plant

does during the course of a year. What I'm trying to show here is that at its very best, a standard power plant still can't beat a cogeneration plant operating at its most average.

12. Oak Ridge National Laboratory ran the numbers on what would happen if 20 percent of the U.S. electric capacity in 2030 came from cogeneration plants. It found an emissions reduction of 848 million metric tons, equivalent to taking 154 million cars off the road. How real-world plausible is that scenario? Not bad, actually. It's primarily policy and regulations that hamper expansion, not technical details or fundamental economics. We'll get into that shortly. "Combined Heat and Power: Effective Energy Solutions for a Sustainable Future," Oak Ridge National Laboratory, 2008.

13. It would take 1,000 kilowatts to equal 1 megawatt. Or, to put it another way, you'd need ten thousand 50-kilowatt power plants to equal the capacity of *one* of the big 500-megawatt centralized plants I talked about earlier.

14. From an interview with Paul Friley, an energy economist at Brookhaven National Laboratory, October 2010. This matches up pretty closely with EIA estimates as well. The EIA says 34 percent capacity factor for wind and 25 percent for solar photovoltaics, but the EIA also predominantly focuses on large-scale, centralized solar PV—the kind that is more likely to be capable of moving with the sun.

15. Of course, if you're talking about solar panels, no amount of panels will get you that 100 megawatts on a stormy day or in the middle of the night. For that, you'd need storage.

16. Excluding the parts of Corpus Christi that are water. This is only the square footage of the land. See http://www.census.gov/statab/ccdb/cit1010r.txt.

12. Bigger Little

1. This is both a success and not really as much of a success. It took thirteen years to get a 9 percent reduction in river pollution. In order to meet the state water quality goals, Meschke told me, pollution in the Blue Earth River system would have to be reduced by something like 40 percent. So what Meschke did in the past worked, but it worked very slowly. At that rate, it would take almost sixty years to clean up the river. To learn more about the Blue Earth River system and Meschke's program—called the Blue Earth River Basin Initiative—I recommend reading this 2007 report to the Environmental Protection Agency, http://www.threeriversrcd.org/project%20information/

GBERWI%20final%20report%20June%2007%20%201.pdf, and the 2010 Blue Earth River Watershed Progress Report at http://mrbdc.wrc.mnsu.edu/progress/pdf/4.%20Report%20-%20Blue%20Earth%20&Watonwan.pdf.

2. Department of Agriculture, 2007 Census of Agriculture, http://www.nass.usda.gov/research/2007mapgallery/album/Crops_and_Plants/Field_Crops_Harvested/slides/Acres%20of%20Corn%20Harvested%20for%20Grain%20as%20Percent%20of%20Harvested%20Cropland%20Acreage.html.

3. Ibid.

4. USDA Economic Research Service, "Fertilizer Use and Price," http://www.ers.usda.gov/Data/FertilizerUse/.

5. If you stop at the highway rest area in Adair County, Iowa, just off Interstate 80, you can see this topsoil loss turned into art. A series of descending pillars marks declining topsoil depths over time. See RDG, http://www.rdgusa.com/projects/adair-county-eastbound-rest-area. For more information on how this soil loss happened and where the lost soil goes, see Iowa Association of Naturalists, Agricultural Practices and the Environment, http://www.extension.iastate.edu/Publications/IAN104.pdf.

6. Interview with Kurt Spokas, University of Minnesota, February 2010. Spokas is one of the few USDA researchers running these real-world experiments on biochar-as-fertilizer.

7. Verdant's turbines spin much more slowly than do the blades on a traditional hydroelectric dam—thirty-two rotations per minute, compared to a thousand.

8. Out of curiosity, I asked Verdant's logistics manager, Dean Whatmoor, what the capacity factor of this system turned out to be. In the East River, which is a tidal strait and, thus, doesn't run as constantly as a normal river, the turbines have a capacity factor of 30 percent, But that has more to do with the type of water resource than with the technology itself. In a normal river, Verdant's turbines should be able to reach the 60 to 70 percent capacity factor seen in more traditional run-of-river hydroelectric systems. E-mail correspondence, October 2011.

9. Jonathan Colby says there are 4 tides in the river every 25 hours. The flood tides lasts 6 hours, the ebb tides lasts 6.5 hours. The time of slack tide—that in-between stage when the river hardly moves—changes relative to our 24-hour clock.

10. Idaho National Laboratory hydroelectric power program. There's a lot more interesting information about how hydro works and how

it has developed on the lab's website at http://hydropower.inel.gov/hydrofacts/index.shtml.

11. Based on U.S. Energy Information Administration, Annual Energy Review, table 8.2a, http://www.eia.gov/totalenergy/data/annual/pdf/sec8_8.pdf.

12. There are ways to address both of those problems, at least to a limited extent. See U.S. Department of Energy, *Hydropower: Setting a Course for Our Energy Future*, hydropower.inel.gov/techtransfer/pdfs/34916.pdf.

13. Although they are cheaper to build than a coal or nuclear power plant and *far* cheaper to run. See Idaho National Laboratory, "Hydropower: Plant Costs and Production Expenses," http://hydropower.inel.gov/hydrofacts/plant_costs.shtml.

14. Fourteen percent of hydroelectric dams are "large hydro," but 89 percent of hydroelectric capacity comes from "large hydro" dams. See Douglas Hall and Kelly S. Reeves, *A Study of United States Hydroelectric Plant Ownership*, Idaho National Laboratory, June 2006, http://hydropower.inel.gov/hydrofacts/pdfs/a_study_of_united_states_hydroelectric_plant_ownership.pdf.

15. U.S. Geological Survey, "Hydroelectric Power Water Use," http://ga.water.usgs.gov/edu/wuhy.html.

16. U.S. Energy Information Administration, "Existing Capacity by Energy Source," http://www.eia.doe.gov/cneaf/electricity/epa/epaxlfile1_2.pdf. This chart will also show you the 2009 stated capacity of all of our other electricity sources. See also U.S. Energy Information Administration, "Renewable Electric Power Sector Net Generation by Energy Source and State," http://www.eia.doe.gov/cneaf/solar.renewables/page/trends/table18.html.

17. You can read the entire report and see how small hydro would increase the hydroelectric potential for your state online at http://hydropower.inel.gov/resourceassessment/index.shtml. Check out appendix B for the state listings.

18. This is a good place to point out that not all man-made lakes have hydroelectric dams. Kansas has forty-eight state fishing lakes, created by damming creeks and small rivers, but those lakes don't generate electricity. They're only for recreation. Just because you have the right conditions to build a lake doesn't mean you have the right conditions to build a hydroelectric power plant.

19. *Hydropower Resource Assessment*, appendix B, p. 4, http://hydropower.inel.gov/resourceassessment/pdfs/appendix_b_1_final.pdf.

20. U.S. Energy Information Administration, "Kansas Electricity Profile," http://www.eia.doe.gov/cneaf/electricity/st_profiles/kansas.html.

21. There are even researchers who think that nuclear power could be done safely in a decentralized way. Many different technologies could produce nuclear power plants with capacities under 100 megawatts. The issue, as with all nuclear power, is more of a matter of public opinion and what to do with the spent fuel rods. See World Nuclear Association, "Small Nuclear Power Reactors," http://www.world-nuclear.org/info/inf33.html.

22. Energy Power Resources, "Glanford," http://www.eprl.co.uk/assets/glanford/overview.html.

23. U.S. Environmental Protection Agency, "Municipal Solid Waste," http://www.epa.gov/epawaste/nonhaz/municipal/index.htm.

24. U.S. Environmental Protection Agency, "LFG Energy Products," http://www.epa.gov/lmop/faq/lfg.html#02.

25. U.S. Environmental Protection Agency, "Landfill Gas," http://www.epa.gov/lmop/faq/landfill-gas.html.

26. U.S. Environmental Protection Agency, "National and State Lists of Landfills and Energy Projects," http://www.epa.gov/lmop/projects-candidates/index.html#map-area. Interestingly, as of March 2010, only 60 percent of those projects were at landfills required to collect their landfill gas. That suggests the incentives of landfill gas energy are already inspiring landfill owners to make environmental improvements without being forced to do it. U.S. Environmental Protection Agency, LFG Energy Projects FAQ, http://www.epa.gov/lmop/faq/lfg.html#09.

27. Another key benefit: the machinery driving these projects is well past the research phase. Sure, Verdant Power is doing something new by using wind turbine–style machines to generate electricity underwater. But the turbines themselves are still pretty similar to technology that we already know how to use well, and that we already make enough of to use relatively cheaply. Other river hydro systems are even more familiar. Using proven technology cuts costs and makes the whole system more reliable.

13. Good Citizens of the Grid

1. If you're expecting me to add something like "and some parts of the house were still uncomfortably cold," well, don't hold your breath. My Grandpa Gus got around the uneven heating of a wood stove by keeping the fire ridiculously hot. The parts of the house farthest from the stove were a little too warm. The dining room, where the stove sat, was

like summer in south Texas. Everyone wore layers for our Christmas visit and slowly stripped down to a tank top as the day wore on. Grandpa had a fine collection of polo-style collared shirts that were made out of some kind of mesh fabric.

2. The Wisconsin Historical Society has many great online resources relating to the early days of electricity. I could have spent a year of research simply gawking at stuff like this. See Wisconsin Historical Society, *The Electrical House That Jack Built,* http://content.wisconsin-history.org/cdm4/document.php?CISOROOT=/tp&CISOPTR=5041 5&CISOSHOW=50394. If the early history of energy in America has caught your attention as well, I must recommend that you read Alexis Madrigal's *Powering the Dream* (DeCapo Press, 2011)—the story of wind, solar, hydro, and other forms of renewable energy in the years before the 1970s. These technologies all go back a lot further than you might think.

3. For instance, an April 2011 Zogby poll found that solar was the most popular choice when Americans were asked which energy source they would rather get their electricity from, if they could pick. See Corry Shiermeyer, "Earth Day Poll: Solar at 27% & Nuclear 23% Are Favored Choices for Electrical Supply; 80% Routinely Recycle," IBOPE Zogby International, http://zogby.com/news/2011/04/26/earth-day-poll-solar-27-nuclear-23-are-favored-choices-electrical-supply-80-routinely-recycle/.

4. Stan Lee, or more specifically Spider-Man's uncle Ben.

5. From interviews with Ed Regan of Gainesville Regional Utility, August 2010.

6. In fact, solar energy doesn't even have to mean solar electricity. You can also use the Sun's warmth to preheat hot water, reducing the amount of natural gas or electricity that you have to feed a hot-water heater. This type of solar energy can actually be cost-effective in places where home solar electricity doesn't yet make financial sense.

7. I say "some way" because there are a lot of different ways to make money off a solar panel. You might use the electricity directly at home and lower your utility bill. You might sell the electricity you make to the grid. Or you might have a contract with a third party that maintains the solar panel, sells the electricity it makes, and pays you a stipend for the use of your roof.

8. The three locations studied were Sacramento, California; Boulder, Colorado; and Newark, New Jersey. National Renewable Energy

Laboratory, *Solar Photovoltaic Financing: Residential Sector Deployment*, March 2009, http://www.nrel.gov/docs/fy09osti/44853.pdf.

9. As of 2009, there were feed-in tariffs in Wisconsin, Oregon, Washington State, Vermont, and California. These programs are different from the one in Gainesville because they base the set rate that utility companies pay FIT participants on different criteria. Gainesville (and most European programs) bases the price on how much it costs to purchase, install, and run the generation source, as explained in this chapter. Instead, some of the other U.S. FITs pay participants based on how much money the FIT saves the utility. Others pay FIT participants an arbitrary fixed price. Neither system does as good a job at enabling solar generators to recoup their costs as the European-Gainesville method. National Renewable Energy Laboratory, *State Clean Energy Policies Analysis (SCEPA) Project: An Analysis of Renewable Energy Feed-in Tariffs in the United States*, http://www.nrel.gov/analysis/pdfs/45551.pdf.

10. This isn't true only for Gainesville. No matter where you buy your electricity from, the price you pay is already somewhat artificial. The prices are set to guarantee that whoever generated your electricity will make a profit on the investments they made in building the generators. This is true even if that electricity is coming from a large coal-fired power plant. The only thing the Gainesville FIT does differently is apply those existing rules to individuals and/or decentralized generation.

11. For people who joined the FIT program in 2011, GRU pays .32 cents per kilowatt hour for installations under 10 kw in capacity, .29 cents per kilowatt hour for installations greater than 10 kw in capacity, and .24 cents per kilowatt hour for ground-mounted installations. Meanwhile, their power purchasing contracts with traditional generation sources pay around .08 cents per kilowatt hour. If you joined the FIT in 2009, you got .32 cents per kilowatt hour. E-mail correspondence with Ed Regan, October 2011.

12. The other really common program in the United States is called "net metering." With a FIT, solar panel owners sell electricity directly to the utility. The electricity their solar panels generate goes straight to the grid and doesn't necessarily power their own houses. They operate as a centralized generator would. With net metering, the solar panels on your house power your house. When there's extra electricity that you don't need, it goes to the grid, and the utility credits you on your bill for the electricity you sold it.

13. Gainesville's FIT also had some early problems with how contracts were handed out. Originally, contracts were awarded on a first-come, first-served basis. To beat the rush, a lot of people signed up for contracts without having first really worked out the details of installing a solar system. So, when I visited Gainesville in 2010, a lot of the projects that owned FIT contracts had never been built. GRU wasn't losing money on those projects—nothing was paid unless electricity was generated. Yet because only a limited number of contracts were offered, the unbuilt projects were preventing finished projects that *could* actually generate electricity from participating in the FIT.

14. National Association of Regulatory Utility Commissioners, *Feed-in Tariffs (FIT): Frequently Asked Questions for State Utility Commissions,* http://www .naruc.org/Publications/NARUC%20Feed%20in%20Tariff%20FAQ .pdf.

15. National Renewable Energy Laboratory, *A Policymaker's Guide to Feed-in-Tariff Policy Design,* p. 16, http://www.nrel.gov/docs/fy10osti/44849 .pdf.

16. Here are a couple of things to remember: in Germany, that FIT covers all renewable energy, not only solar, and this represents not just one year's worth of renewable energy, but the 2007 effects of almost twenty years' worth of renewable energy contracts. National Renewable Energy Laboratory, *State Clean Energy Policies Analysis (SCEPA) Project,* p. 28.

17. Between 2002 and 2008, we spent more than $70 billion on subsidies for oil, gas, and coal and $12.2 billion on subsidies for renewable energy such as wind, solar, and hydroelectric power. Another $16.8 billion went to corn ethanol, which, as Linda Meschke's story illustrates, isn't the most sustainable way to create fuel. Not all fossil fuel subsidies are evil. (Frankly, I think we can drop the fossil fuels part and say, "Not all subsidies are evil," but I digress.) The Environmental Law Institute—which compiled the research and created a graphic to go with it (see "Energy Subsidies Black, Not Green," http://www.eli .org/pdf/Energy_Subsidies_Black_Not_Green.pdf)—points out a great example: the Low-Income Home Energy Assistance Program. That's calculated under subsidies to fossil fuels. It's by no means a big part of fossil fuel subsidies, but it is in there. It's also worth noting that this accounting doesn't include all spending that benefits various forms of energy. For instance, there are programs that arguably spend money as a direct result of the fossil fuel industry but that aren't technically fossil-fuel subsidies: the Oil Spill Liability Trust Fund, for instance, or

federal highway construction or, more controversially, money spent on military campaigns at least partially influenced by a desire to stabilize, defend, and generally befriend oil-producing countries. Environmental Law Institute, "Energy Subsidies Favor Fossil Fuels over Renewables," http://www.eli.org/Program_Areas/innovation_governance_energy .cfm.

INDEX

GDP and, 4
illnesses and deaths from, 94
percentage of electricity from, 95
cogeneration power plants, 180–
182
Colby, Jonathan, 200–201
Columbia Law School, 177–178
commercial buildings, energy
efficiency in, 46, 140–144,
151–158
compressed air energy storage
(CAES), 81–82
condensing dryers, 44
conductivity, defined, 9–10
conservation
defined, 124
energy efficiency vs., 142–144
motivation for, 4–8
public opinion about, 1–4
See also energy efficiency
Consolidated Edison, 178–179
corn
biofuel and, 191–192
ethanol, 187, 193, 206
Creation Care, 122–123
crop rotation. See Madelia Model
Cryptosporidium, 113
cybercrime, electric grid
vulnerability to, 93

Dallas, Bernice, 36–37, 40–43,
153–154
decentralized generation, 186–210,
211–225
"bigger-little," 206
control and, 211–214
defined, 173–175
feed-in tariffs (FIT), 219–223
Gainesville Regional Utility, 211,
215–219

landfill gas, 206–210
Madelia Model, 186–198
smart grids and, 222–225
Verdant Power hydropower, 198–
201, 202–206
demand-response customers, 89–93
Denmark, energy consumption of,
137
Department of Health and
Environment (Kansas), 106
distribution networks
cogeneration, 180–182
decentralized, defined, 173–
175 (See also decentralized
generation)
defined, 21
distribution grids, 221
economy of scale, 176–180
renewable generation,
182–185
See also electric grid
dry-cask storage, 99
Dual Frequency Identification
Sonar (DIDSON), 201

Earth Hour, 23–24, 125
Eastern Interconnect, 63, 96
economic issues
of biofuel, 193–195
carbon price, 168–172
of decentralized distribution
networks, 176–180, 208–210
economywide rebound and,
166–169
energy efficiency motivation,
124, 126–127
gasoline and peak oil
production, 117–118
utility bills, 17, 163–166
Economist, 96